Forever Practice

Forever Practice

The Architect at Work

Jim Nielson, FAIA

Copyright © 2025 by John Wiley & Sons, Inc. All rights reserved, including rights for text and data mining and training of artificial intelligence technologies or similar technologies.

Published by John Wiley & Sons, Inc., Hoboken, New Jersey.

Published simultaneously in Canada.

No part of this publication may be reproduced, stored in a retrieval system, or transmitted in any form or by any means, electronic, mechanical, photocopying, recording, scanning, or otherwise, except as permitted under Section 107 or 108 of the 1976 United States Copyright Act, without either the prior written permission of the Publisher, or authorization through payment of the appropriate per-copy fee to the Copyright Clearance Center, Inc., 222 Rosewood Drive, Danvers, MA 01923, (978) 750–8400, fax (978) 750–4470, or on the web at www.copyright.com. Requests to the Publisher for permission should be addressed to the Permissions Department, John Wiley & Sons, Inc., 111 River Street, Hoboken, NJ 07030, (201) 748–6011, fax (201) 748-6008, or online at http://www.wiley.com /go/permission.

Trademarks: Wiley and the Wiley logo are trademarks or registered trademarks of John Wiley & Sons, Inc. and/or its affiliates in the United States and other countries and may not be used without written permission. All other trademarks are the property of their respective owners. John Wiley & Sons, Inc. is not associated with any product or vendor mentioned in this book.

Limit of Liability/Disclaimer of Warranty: While the publisher and author have used their best efforts in preparing this book, they make no representations or warranties with respect to the accuracy or completeness of the contents of this book and specifically disclaim any implied warranties of merchantability or fitness for a particular purpose. No warranty may be created or extended by sales representatives or written sales materials. The advice and strategies contained herein may not be suitable for your situation. You should consult with a professional where appropriate. Further, readers should be aware that websites listed in this work may have changed or disappeared between when this work was written and when it is read. Neither the publisher nor authors shall be liable for any loss of profit or any other commercial damages, including but not limited to special, incidental, consequential, or other damages.

For general information on our other products and services or for technical support, please contact our Customer Care Department within the United States at (800) 762-2974, outside the United States at (317) 572-3993 or fax (317) 572-4002.

Wiley also publishes its books in a variety of electronic formats. Some content that appears in print may not be available in electronic formats. For more information about Wiley products, visit our web site at www.wiley.com.

Library of Congress Cataloging-in-Publication Data:

Names: Nielson, Jim, author.
Title: Forever practice : The Architect at Work
 / Jim Nielson, Utah Valley University.
Description: Hoboken, New Jersey : Wiley, 2025. | Includes bibliographical
 references and index.
Identifiers: LCCN 2024062193 | ISBN 9781394324378 (paperback) | ISBN
 9781394324392 (epdf) | ISBN 9781394324385 (epub)
Subjects: LCSH: Architectural practice. | Architecture–Vocational
 guidance.
Classification: LCC NA1995 .N495 2025 | DDC 720.23–dc23/eng/20250206
LC record available at https://lccn.loc.gov/2024062193

Cover Design: Wiley
Cover Image: Courtesy of Jim Nielson

Set in 9.5/12.5pt STIXTwoText by Lumina Datamatics

SKY10119374_062025

I wrote this book for and with the help of my architecture students; I dedicate it to each of them. I retired from practice and took up teaching architecture, figuring that was a way I could give back. As it turns out, my students have been the ones that did the giving.

I have forever been on the receiving end.

—Jim Nielson, FAIA

Five story walkups in New York. Just keep climbing.

Contents

Preface *xi*
Design! *A Foreword* *xiii*
About the Author *xv*

Part I   Forever *1*

1   **Caring About the World We Live In** *3*

2   **Always Looking for Work** *7*

viii | *Contents*

Part II   Practice *13*

3   **We Just Keep at It** *15*

4   **Our Environment** *19*

5   **The Value of Green** *25*

Part III   Profession *33*

6   **The Profession of Architecture** *35*

7   **Architectural Licensure** *41*

8   **Regulation and the Code of Conduct** *47*

9   **The Architect's Standard of Care** *53*

Part IV   Career *59*

10 **Core Responsibilities** *61*

11 **Architecture and Related Fields** *65*

12 **Blog: Architecture Career and Culture** *71*

Part V   Project *75*

13 **Project Management** *77*

Contents | ix

Part VI   Firm   *89*

14 Marketing and Business Development   *91*

15 Marketing Proposals   *97*

16 Business and Financial Management   *103*

17 Business and Human Resource Management   *113*

18 Getting It Right I   *119*

19 Getting It Right II   *125*

20 What About Risks?   *129*

Part VII   Community   *135*

21 Giving Back   *137*

Part VIII   Client   *143*

22 One of a Kind   *145*

23 Delivery Methods and the Client   *149*

Part IX   Construction   *155*

24 Getting Started   *157*

25 Put It in Writing   *161*

26 Delivery Methods and the Contractor   *165*

27 Bidder-designed Work   *169*

28 Closeout   *175*

x | *Contents*

Part X   Appendices   *181*

A   The Facilities Program   *183*

B   The Project Plan   *187*

C   The Project Schedule   *189*

D   Breaking Down the Fee, Scope, and Schedule   *193*

E   Dividing up the Work   *197*

F   Employee Owned   *205*

G   The Project Progress Report   *209*

H   The Contractor's S-curve   *211*

Index   *213*

Preface

I asked a senior designer and colleague why part of a project he was working on was bright red. He shared something he had learned from an architecture professor years previously:

> If you can't make it beautiful, make it big.

> If you can't make it big, make it red.

What struck me is that I actually thought this concept made sense in a way!

During my years in architecture school and as a licensed architect, I went from loving one building in our community that was merely tolerated by most, to adoring another, our new federal courthouse. That building, a cube in shape, has come to be known, and almost universally reviled by community members, as the Borg, of Star Trek fame.

The gift, or perhaps the burden, of being an architect is that we have learned to see things differently. At some point, perhaps, in preparing for a career in architecture, in professional school, or even in practice, some of us may have become accustomed to the idea that painting a building element red, as a design flourish, might somehow make sense.

Becoming an architect, and practicing it, requires both creativity and lengthy preparation. For many, it is a surprising and all-consuming challenge. An architecture student realizes one day that he is in over his head, yet the prospect of tunneling through may motivate. Returning to the interplanetary courthouse metaphor above, it may be that the daunting nature of architecture brings the emerging professional to understand, as the Borg Collective was prone to put it, that "Resistance is futile."

For a student, professional practice may be unexpected and unfamiliar. Since my move from practice to teaching, my aim has been to make the profession a bit less mysterious. Teaching at a nascent architecture program pursuing NAAB accreditation, I designed our first professional practice course and have been working on the course in the years since.

At some point each of my professional practice students has expressed surprise about at least one aspect of the profession. For many, puzzlement about architectural practice is a steady state. To minimize student bewilderment about their possible future, I thought first to use the AIA reference work, *The Architect's Handbook of Professional Practice*, as reading material. This book is encyclopedic and of immense value. But as the standard source of course readings, it can be a bit much.

A younger brother of mine took to occupying himself by reading from encyclopedias recreationally. My son did the same thing. But for me, as for my students, the definitive architectural reference work proved best if used mostly for looking things up.

My experience that first year inspired a different approach. I began writing brief essays about practice management concepts I wish I had been introduced to in architecture school. These conversations, which would

xii | *Preface*

ultimately become course materials, were taken not from any other volume, but from the everyday life of an architect at work. For me, architectural project and practice management became a specialty, almost the day I got out of school.

But that is not where it began. My early career before I pursued architecture spanned several years. I was a management and policy analyst in commercial and government organizations. My focus: making operations succeed. I took on challenging issues, like crafting staffing projections, formulating salaries and expense budgets for large organizations, developing complex procurements, improving credit management, dealing with public relations, communicating with organization heads, streamlining agency-wide financial management, and strengthening grants and contracts administration. I even worked on a Wall Street securitized asset transaction valued at the better part of a billion dollars. As an architect, I found I could put that experience in business and government to use. Increasingly, during my career, if there ever was a contract to write, if my firm had personnel difficulties to resolve, if financial hurdles were threatening to sink us, or if we had a furious client that was about to fire us, I was the one to address it.

In this capacity, I hired people. Unfortunately, I sometimes had to let people go. I handled most employee training. Taking over the reins of firm finances, I directed major accounting improvements, including, hiring and directing the work of a controller for our firm, changing from cash to accrual accounting, dealing with tax planning, being the first ever to gain approval for a Section 179D tax deduction for a firm from our state building authority, and vastly improving our firm's accounts payable and accounts receivable systems and performance. I created and put in place a firm succession plan (a seven-year endeavor). And I also detailed financial tools to help our project managers develop project plans and manage accordingly.

In preparing this book for publication, I have added end-of-chapter references that offer both tools for instruction and suggestions for research. Student and instructor references come from *The Architect's Handbook of Professional Practice*. Videos that instructors may wish to use in the classroom, where available, are from ACSA's *ProPEL Professional Practice Education Library*.

As far as I have been able to determine, and although I have used artistic license on occasion (modifying circumstances and changing or omitting names to ensure privacy) the interactions, events, and conversations shared as examples and case studies in this book are drawn from real events. I have taken these lessons learned and anecdotes from personal experiences as well as from conversations with colleagues and associates in the industry.

In writing this textbook, I have benefitted from the experience and input of trusted colleagues and experts within the profession of architecture and without. Although I acknowledge the critical role others have played in making this book what it is today, in the end, the work is my own; I am solely responsible for its contents.

Jim Nielson, FAIA

Design!

A Foreword

When the public thinks of architects, it is design that they cite most often. That perception is borne out by the fact that when movie makers, TV writers, or authors want a creative character audiences will recognize, it's often an architect that gets cast. Design is usually the characteristic that draws young people to undertake an education and career in architecture. Design is typically the primary focus of most architectural education programs. Without a doubt, design is the architect's superpower as they envision places that do not yet exist where people will live their lives.

But being a great designer is not the sole skill required to be a great architect. What is often overlooked in the education and public perception of architects are the business skills needed to lead a successful enterprise. As Garry Stevens writes in his classic study of the profession, *The Favored Circle*, much of the profession's minimization of the need for business skills may stem from its rise during the Renaissance in Europe. The need to focus on pleasing the patron—think Lorenzo the Magnificent in Florence—for projects, for income, for recognition, often resulted in the architect sacrificing more than they gained.

In some ways, these traditions of sacrifice over self-interest continued into the twentieth century. In the rebuilding and growth following World War II, larger and more ambitious projects were undertaken across society. These projects required larger teams, more scheduling, more financial control, more of everything to succeed. They also required architects to move from a labor-intensive profession to one that required more capital investment to enable them to do their work. The investment in a computer and BIM software, rather than a T-square and a pencil, to create construction documents illustrates the point. Thanks to industry leaders like M. Arthur Gensler FAIA, Eugene Kohn FAIA, Weld Coxe, Hugh Hochberg, and others, architects across the profession have come to understand it was not just OK but required that architects improve their business skills to maintain their position as leaders of the design and construction industry.

In this book, *Forever Practice: The Architect at Work*, Jim Nielson, FAIA undertakes the task of introducing the reader to those business skills an emerging architectural professional, as well as a more seasoned professional, needs to succeed over a long career. Jim touches on all the skills needed, from getting the work, creating a contract for services, determining appropriate fees, organizing a design team, preparing documents, dealing with contractors, closing out the project, and most importantly—getting paid. It's all there, including the tools to help execute those business tasks. Plus, he offers additional resources to explore these topics more deeply. After reading this book, you'll want to keep it near your computer as a valued reference to revisit often.

It is very important that Jim chose to introduce the reader to the "why" and the ethical standards that underpin the profession. Establishing the profession's concern for society, sustainability, resilience, and equity that guide the work architects undertake before getting to the meat of the book's business focus is a meaningful choice. As the profession focuses on making people's lives better and restoring the planet to support all living things, these concerns bring great meaning to all the work that architects do.

I hope that having read Jim's book, you are better prepared to go out and make great things happen throughout your career.

RK Stewart FAIA, Hon FRAIC, Hon JIA, Hon AIA
2007 AIA National President

About the Author

Jim Nielson, FAIA

Following college and several years in business and government, in 1991 Jim attended the University of Oregon. He graduated with an MArch degree in 1991 and found a job in Salt Lake City, Utah. Licensed in just three years, he worked at leading firms there as project manager and later principal. He would go on to become a firm owner and chief financial officer. Jim's work spanned higher education, industrial, office, retail, and multi-family projects with public and private clients. He was part of the development team for some of his projects.

During his career, Jim worked on influential sustainable projects, including university buildings rated LEED® Silver and Gold. Years before LEED was introduced, Jim managed a 100,000 SF project incorporating extensive recycled materials, xeriscaping and drip irrigation, and reduced parking with preferential spots for carpoolers. It beat the energy code by more than 50%. Some time later, Jim designed the first underfloor air and utility distribution (UFAD) system for an industrial project in the United States.

In 2021, Jim left practice to take up teaching. He has taught Professional Practice, Environmental Control Systems, and Codes and Construction Law in an emerging program at Utah Valley University currently seeking NAAB accreditation. He has also team taught the Capstone Studio each year. Jim has consulted as an architectural expert on dozens of construction defect cases. Many of the principles in this book are informed by tough lessons he has gleaned from this work. Jim serves on the **Board of Governors of Envision Utah**, an influential visioning powerhouse active in many markets locally and around the country. He has also been a member of national NCARB task forces and NAAB accrediting teams.

Jim served on the Utah architect licensing board for five years and in the State House of Representatives for four. Over the past 15 years, he has published dozens of op-ed columns to move the needle in public policy debates. As a lawmaker, he shepherded a constitutional amendment that now requires that if we are going to continue extracting nonrenewable resources from our land, a sizeable portion of the severance taxes the state levies on these extractions must be invested for future generations rather than spent as a windfall in the year they are received.

In 2015, in recognition of service to society and to the profession with national impact, Jim was elevated to the AIA College of Fellows, the highest membership distinction of the American Institute of Architects.

xvi | *About the Author*

During his career, Jim has honed his craft as a firm leader and as a writer and communicator. The art of using simple, clear explanations when telling a story is evident in what he writes, from opinion columns to internal documents. *Forever Practice: The Architect at Work* is built first upon comprehensive technical understanding of architectural practice. From that foundation Jim forges an engaging conversation, weaving a narrative that is both a superb reference work and a good read.

Irrigating in the desert. Forever lost.

Part I

Forever

Architects care deeply about our world and are forever striving to improve it. We are at our best when designing solutions to the challenges facing individuals and communities. Solving these problems requires a steady flow of work. And so, we are forever scouring our surroundings for the next meaningful project.

1

Caring About the World We Live In

On a job-hunting trip shortly before completing his architecture degree, a future architect scored an interview with the lead in-house architect for a large organization. His group wasn't hiring, but the gentleman graciously continued with a few thoughts about his city and its leading architecture firms.

At one point, the senior architect said to the job seeker rather abruptly, "Architecture is a jealous master. It can take over your life." He wondered whether the prospective architect was up to the task of balancing his life as an architect with family, community, avocations, and other passions. The field was all-consuming, he told him. If allowed to do so, architecture could easily overshadow everything else this aspiring professional cared about.

Architecture is both demanding and rewarding. Often, those that pursue it can't help but fall under its spell. Sometimes they just don't know when to quit.

He'd Keep Designing

"What would an architect do if he suddenly received a million dollars?" I think I was in architecture school when I first heard this quip.

"He'd keep designing until he had spent it all."

Ask yourself
What is it that makes architecture students pull all-nighters on studio projects? What makes architects polish a Monday design presentation all weekend long?

If they think about it, practitioners may say the reason the profession of architecture often takes over an architect's life is that almost every task an architect undertakes is so complex that in all her professional pursuits, the architect may never quite reach a point where she's got it down—where there's nothing left to figure out. Architects will generally agree that every task an architect *completes*, whether design, documentation, marketing, or mentoring, could still be improved, extended, or embellished. There is always more that could be done.

Architects tend to be possessed of a perpetual consciousness that they could improve their work further if they just kept at it a little longer. Few are those that recognize when it's time to quit.

Perhaps Architects Care Too Much

Architects may have important skills that others do not:

- An architect is often skilled at seeing solutions to problems that are not obvious
- In practice, architects learn to be unusually good at leading a team of experts

Forever Practice: The Architect at Work, First Edition. Jim Nielson, FAIA.
© 2025 John Wiley & Sons, Inc. Published 2025 by John Wiley & Sons, Inc.

- Architects generally have training and experience they can apply in designing elegant solutions
- Experienced architects may also possess the uncanny ability to understand the big picture very quickly—to recognize instantly the many factors members of their team must work through to craft a successful project

Even if some architects don't possess special skills such as these, most architects tend to have the self-confidence to convince themselves that their own personal skillsets are a cut above those of contractors, city officials, developers, facilities managers, bankers, and pretty much everyone. So, with sincere confidence in their own unique gifts, experienced architects may forge ahead as if their skills *did* stand a world apart.

Skills or no skills, because architects usually care deeply about the built environment, they often do feel a burden to put the skills they have to use in the interest of society. In a way, many architects see it as a duty to protect those around them from the dreadful impact of living, working, and playing in badly designed spaces.

For instance, consider the following case studies, based on the experiences of architects dealing with real-world challenges. As is the case throughout this book, identifying information has been removed from these accounts to ensure anonymity.

Example #1

Tom was part of the design team working on a large project near the center of a good-sized city. Tom's architecture group had teamed with an out-of-town firm for this project; Tom headed up on-site construction administration work, including shop-drawing review. The work was at the corner of two busy streets, where the city would also be doing sidewalk and utility improvements under separate contracts.

So as not to affect traffic more than necessary, the city scheduled its sidewalk and utility work at that corner concurrently with construction on the building. They engaged the contractor Tom was working with to do this separate, off-site construction, as well.

Tom and his firm weren't involved in designing utility work at the corner, but he was well aware of it. Even though his design team had no contractual responsibility to take the city's separate efforts into account in their work, he felt that coordinating with the city made sense.

The city's construction work included upgrades to the roadway, curb and gutter, walks, lights, traffic signals, and signage. When Tom saw a coordination drawing outlining the city's offsite work pinned up in the contractor's trailer one afternoon, he was dismayed. At the edge of the sidewalk, the design called for a signpost, a light pole, and a traffic signal pole: three separate elements. All of this visual clutter would interrupt the view of the pedestrian crossing the street, partially blocking visibility of the main entry to the new building Tom and his partner firm were working on.

Tom couldn't let go of his concerns. Without getting a go-ahead from his principal in charge, from the city, or from anyone else, he started working on a solution. He gathered dimensional information and made related comments in his notebook while in the contractor's trailer. Back at the office, he sketched options, picked the best solution, drew it up, and offered it to the city's civil/utilities project manager as a suggestion. His solution gathered all three verticals—traffic signal pole, light pole, and signpost—into a single element. And he showed how they could move the whole obstacle just a couple of feet to avoid blocking the line of sight to the entry from any point in the crosswalk.

Things were ultimately built just as Tom had sketched them.

Excellent work, right?

Ask yourself

What are the possible impacts of Tom's decision to become involved in the design of this off-site work by the city? Consider both positives and negatives.

Example #2

American Institute of Architects (AIA) Contract Documents typically contain a requirement that architects rarely allow to play out. AIA Document A201-2017, General Conditions, for example, includes the following provision:

> When the Contractor considers that the Work, or a portion thereof which the Owner agrees to accept separately, is substantially complete, the Contractor shall prepare and submit to the Architect a comprehensive list of items to be completed or corrected prior to final payment. (§ 9.8.2)

The document then goes on to describe responsibilities of the architect and owner to review, perhaps accept, and possibly add to the list—often called a punch list—before executing a Certificate of Substantial Completion.

This is how the AIA General Conditions of the contract divide up initial punch list responsibilities, even though some owner-contractor agreements may set things up differently.

But even with AIA conditions of the contract in place, things are rarely done that way. It turns out that tradition and the architect's own insistence almost always lead to the architect preparing the punch list—first draft and every draft.

Ask yourself

Considering example #2, how would you respond to the following questions?

- How can the architect know for sure whose responsibility it is to prepare the punch list?
- What reasons might an architect have for taking over this responsibility of a contractor?
- What are the effects of this common tactic on the part of architects?
- How does this approach affect individual project team members and the team as a whole?
- If a contractor asks an architect, "When would you like to walk the site and prepare the punch list?" Knowing it's the contractor's responsibility to prepare the list, what might an appropriate and effective response look like?

Additional Resources

The Architect's Handbook of Professional Practice[1]

| | Chapter 9 | Design Project Delivery (P. 552, ¶ 1 & 2 "Scope Creep") |

          Chapter 9   Design Project Delivery (P. 552, ¶ 1 & 2 "Scope Creep")

             10.10   Project Completion and Post-Construction

             16.4   Dispute Management and Resolution (Pp. 1031, ¶ 6 "Scope Creep," 1032, blue box text: *"Playing Outside the Contract"*)

ProPEL, ACSA Professional Practice Education Library (Videos for Classroom Use)

             https://propel.yuja.com[2]

             Failure Unit | Lesson 3 Architecture Dos and Don'ts (Time stamp 3:28 through 4:43 and 8:30 through the end of the video—"Don't Give Away...Services.")

Author's Note

A project he'd always dreamed of

Once, when my business partner showed me a Request for Proposals (RFP) that had been sent to him, he and I did a quick no-go/go check (see **Chapter 14 Marketing and Business Development**) and decided it was not for us.

A senior member of our firm, however, came looking for the RFP. He told us he had been working with potential clients to get a project like this. This project was what he was most interested in doing at this point in his career. He was confident we could get the job, and he was prepared to lead the marketing effort to do so.

He talked us into it, and our marketing succeeded.

This senior staff member dearly wanted to be successful with this project; whatever the owner asked, he just did it. When we realized he had been expanding our scope of services to include major changes to the mechanical system the owner had asked for, we asked him to get a contract change to cover the additional scope. He dutifully prepared a proposed design services amendment, but unfortunately, the contract amendment didn't end up in front of the owner until after we'd done the extra work. Things didn't go well. Perhaps it was because the owner had gotten used to asking for extras and not paying for them; perhaps it was the fact that the proposed contract amendment came as a surprise, and the client had no funding. Either way, the owner rejected the design services amendment. He then accused us of having acted in bad faith. With the project beginning construction, the client threatened to fire us.

Ultimately, we made the business decision to say goodbye to any extra compensation. And we had to work our tails off just to finish things up and get paid the rest of our original fee.

In this case, we had a team member who cared so much about the project that he willingly gave away free services without knowing if the client would pay for them. The client's anger about our desire to be paid for going above and beyond soured relationships and ensured that we *never* had another project of this type.

Notes

1 American Institute of Architects. (2013). *The Architect's Handbook of Professional Practice*, Wiley.

2 *https://propel.yuja.com* (accessed October 19, 2024). Access to the Association of Collegiate Schools of Architecture (ACSA) Professional Practice Education Library (ProPEL) requires ACSA member login. Professional architecture programs are usually ACSA members; faculty gain ACSA membership (and thereby ProPEL access) through their professional program. To obtain login credentials, faculty members validate their teaching status in a member program through the ACSA website.

2

Always Looking for Work

A recent M.Arch. graduate was applying for her third job in less than a year. She figured she was qualified and ought to have *some* job security, but times were tough. Firms seemed to be struggling, and job openings were scarce. But she was feeling good because she'd scored an interview.

In the interview, she began to feel even better. Things were looking up. The interviewer sensed that this job seeker had just the skills the firm needed. The architect conducting the interview didn't quite offer the aspiring architect a job, but he said it was quite likely they would be putting an offer together.

"That would be wonderful," said the job applicant, "I so look forward to taking a break from looking for work all the time."

A break from looking for work all the time? thought the interviewer. And more as a teaching opportunity than a criticism, he said to the job applicant, "If you want a break from looking for work constantly, you may be in the wrong profession."

An architectural project manager, for example, looks for work every day. Managing projects may be the ostensible focus, but the underlying goal is to manage things so that clients will want to hire the firm again for another project. If an organization doesn't have another project coming up, the goal is to ensure that they recommend the firm to others in their industry getting ready to build. All members of an architecture firm should share this goal.

In addition to providing services with an eye to repeat work, when there is marketing for a new project to be done, an effective project manager may be tasked with preparing a winning proposal. When an RFP comes along, the project manager and other firm members assigned to the effort are usually heavily involved managing or producing work on architectural projects. The architects and leaders that produce the best work for a firm are typically also the ones the firm relies on to do the heavy lifting on key marketing proposals.

So, during brief, yet intense stints dedicated to targeted marketing campaigns, architects, staff members, and leaders may sometimes be required to spend more time in marketing efforts aimed at new prospects than on tasks related to work on the boards. Maybe much more time.

Architects that become firm principals as their career matures will likely find that the professional priority they must place on marketing, proposals, and business development (as opposed to designing and directing projects) only becomes more pronounced; long-term success depends on it.

Most principals find themselves always looking for work—forever marketing.

Is There Such a Thing as No-effort Marketing?

When comparing notes with colleagues, architects sometimes hear marketing claims like these:

> "Our projects pretty much just walk in the door."
> "Most of our work comes through word of mouth."

Forever Practice: The Architect at Work, First Edition. Jim Nielson, FAIA.
© 2025 John Wiley & Sons, Inc. Published 2025 by John Wiley & Sons, Inc.

As experience in the business demonstrates, however, a firm that depends on work walking in the door in its early years usually finds that this pattern dwindles with the passage of time. A drop in walk-in commissions may be most precipitous when a charismatic founder retires. It's not uncommon that soon after such a founder leaves, the company's story ends with an *Out of Business* sign on the door.

A firm founder may be popular and socially well connected, but without ingrained, disciplined, and continuous marketing, the reputation and goodwill the founder builds will one day be gone. Without constant focus on landing the next job, and the one after that, a firm may soon find that there is no next job, no more revenues to finance ongoing business development, and nothing to sustain operations for the next generation of employees and leaders.

What is the impact of constantly looking for work?

One, firms that are always marketing are the most likely to survive.

Two, firms tend to reward the firm members they see bringing work in. Employees that contribute most to keeping the doors open usually receive superior compensation and increased opportunities for advancement.

It turns out everyone in an architecture firm markets. But most of the new work comes about through leaders and *key* staff members. These may include designers, project managers, and principals, all supported by a dedicated marketing team. Some are involved more than others, depending both on their capabilities and schedules and their roles in the firm.

The marketing responsibilities of key staff members often look something like this:

Designer

More than anything else, an effective designer brings in work by crafting design solutions that are so enviable, current clients will want to return, and others will dream of *being* the firm's clients.

It's hard to overstate the value of a new work of architecture that makes everyone ask, "What firm designed that?" Those preparing for an upcoming project may think: "I want one of those."

Even if the project manager gets credit for putting a successful team and proposal together, in many cases it is the designer's work, included in a proposal or interview, that is the ultimate attraction. Such design work may be expressed in evocative sketches, timeless renderings, or compelling physical models. Often, it is a bold design *tour de force* that grabs a prospective client's attention and makes the sale.

Project Manager

At the front end, though, it's often through effective project management that new inquiries come about. A good project manager manages his projects so expertly and efficiently that clients will value how they are treated and the way their resources are used. Enthusiasm for the disciplined and well-managed work of a successful project manager's firm will not end with a thank-you note; clients generally go on to share recommendations with their peers that may also be looking for an architect. Also, having appreciated the project manager's service profoundly, those same clients are likely to return with their next project.

In addition to building client trust through thoughtful, responsive management, a project manager endeavors to identify strategic marketing opportunities by asking clients regularly what else they have in the pipeline and by cultivating relationships with public entities, businesspeople, and contractors to identify and target upcoming work before it's advertised.

Over the course of what could be years for many projects, a great project manager tracks these projects, makes contact and builds trust with key players, and begins envisioning and even implementing a winning project approach, while at the same time making plans for the best architectural and consultant team, well in advance of any formal solicitation.

When solicitations do come, an effective project manager understands that the firm's chances are many times higher if the firm has laid this sort of groundwork for the solicitation ahead of time. Once the firm has green-lighted doing a proposal, a project manager may be assigned to prepare a standout submittal that will make the short list. If the project manager isn't asked to author the proposal, she should be! With assistance from one of the firm's key designers and the marketing department, the project manager is best positioned to prioritize her work so she can spend as much time as needed (perhaps even full time for a brief window) on the intense enterprise of putting everything together, followed (it is hoped) by preparations for the short-list interview. Confident in getting an interview, the project manager may even propose that interview preparations begin immediately after sending in the proposal. Such a wager means days, if not a week or more, of extra time to prepare for the hoped-for, face-to-face presentation to the client's selection team.

In all the project manager's endeavors, she is responsible for:

- Exercising leadership in preparing responses to competitive solicitations for professional services, as assigned or approved by firm ownership
- Engaging the firm's best visual interpretations and concepts the firm's premier designers can produce
- Working with clients and managing her projects well
- Identifying and preparing strategically for future solicitations

Principal

It is a truth universally acknowledged (as Jane Austen might start this story) that architecture firm leaders—principals—tend to size each other up based on two things:

1. The amount of work they have on the boards.
2. Their record of bringing in new work.

Number 2 usually carries the day. There are, of course, a few other factors, but none is as visible and crucial as new work. Yes, one principal may have heavy operational responsibilities. Others may have leadership in design, finance, marketing, or human resources. Regardless of other tasks, however, in the circle of firm principals, marketing success is noticed most. If he's not bringing more and more new work, a young firm leader may not be offered the opportunity to build or even acquire firm ownership. He may not see growth, either in compensation or influence.

It follows, then, that those in firm leadership focus much of their energy on looking for work. They generally don't rely on work walking in the door. The marketing responsibilities described for designers and project managers also apply to architecture firm leaders. As its leaders' overall marketing fortunes go, so goes the firm.

Overview: Who Markets?

As discussed above, marketing tends to be done by marketing professionals, designers, project managers, and firm principals. Together, these firm members lead out on business development, general marketing, and proposals in response to solicitations. Earlier, we touched on the connection between bringing in new work and employee pay and advancement.

Those employees known to play the largest role in marketing are often the best paid and the first ones invited to become firm leaders.

Ask yourself
Considering the general compensation levels of the following four classes of positions, why do people in these different positions make what they do?

- Principal
- Marketing Professional
- Designer
- Project Manager

Marketing Professionals

Marketing professionals may be extraordinarily effective, but they don't market on their own. A winning management plan is usually written by an engaged project manager or principal. As with the innovative work she designs and leads, this project manager or principal aims for a one-of-a-kind proposal and project approach that will include relevant and creative concepts and strategies that selection committee members will not have seen or thought of before.

In support of that effort, marketing professionals track former marketing campaigns, mine-related verbiage, and stitch everyone's input together expertly and beautifully. To achieve the innovative proposal the firm aims for, firm leaders may then begin with the framework prepared by the marketing team, build innovation by recombining ideas and concepts, and take the creative leaps that will yield ideas that are truly new. Usually, it is upon such bold, original concepts that a winning proposal is built.

Delegating Responsibility

Firm leaders often delegate responsibility in a very different way to project managers than to designers.

It may be that responsibility for marketing and running a practice consumes all of a leader's management bandwidth. Because this principal architect is preoccupied with marketing and managing her practice, she hands off *project* management to capable staff members gladly. Having identified capable managers that seem to be able to take care of projects, a firm principal doesn't tend to look back.

Design, on the other hand, is a thing that leaders often hold close to the vest. They may think, "This is what I got into architecture to do; now I have the chance. I might ask for some help realizing and executing my design ideas, but I won't give away primary design responsibility." So, whatever handoff of design responsibilities takes place may be fragmentary.

Design clearly has the power to differentiate, to make a name for a firm, and to add value. Many principals hold onto that power. If a principal holds the reins tightly, an architect that is not a principal but works as a designer may have little chance to demonstrate what she can do. Instead, the work of such a designer may be to support and develop designs created by leadership. Work of her own, if there is any, may not end up in marketing materials, and she may still not be recognized for her contributions.

In addition, true design architects are rather few. While such a designer's work might be compelling, the amount of new work her efforts bring in may still be viewed as limited. And compared to the conspicuous bottom-line impacts of the project manager's actions in the realms of budgeting, cost estimating, and personnel management (not to mention marketing impact), it can be difficult for an effective designer to demonstrate the dollar value of her contributions.

An architect teaming with a large, well-known national firm had the following conversation with a senior designer there. Pointing to his colleague, a senior project manager on the team, this designer said, "I'm a senior designer; he's a senior project manager. I don't know why he earns a lot more than I do—more than any senior designer, in fact."

In spite of this senior designer's opinion that his salary and that of his project manager colleague should have had more parity, this influential firm had come to a different conclusion.

About five years later, that same firm sent out a postcard announcing changes in leadership. The senior project manager just referred to became a member of the top cadre of owners of the established and growing firm.

And the compensation of the designer that had complained about salary disparity fell further behind.

Ask yourself
Consider the following questions, as they relate to roles and compensation levels in an architect's office:

- How could the position and responsibilities of a designer be structured to increase her impact on the success of her firm?
- Is being a marketing professional a dead-end job?
- How does a firm recruit/develop project managers?

Marketing Discussions Continue...

Having laid out a few aspects of marketing here, together with a tangential discussion about delegating responsibility, our narrative now turns to conversations in *Parts II–V about Practice, Profession, Career, and Project.*

After that, in *Part VI, Firm*, our discussion addresses marketing approaches and processes once again, this time with more focus on details, on nuts and bolts.

Additional Resources

The Architect's Handbook of Professional Practice
  6.1 Marketing Architectural Services

Author's Note

Laying the groundwork
  One of the considerations in go/no-go marketing decisions is how much a firm knows about a proposal before it comes out. Closely allied with that assessment is how strong a connection firm members have built with project decision makers. Often, the only way to win a job is through proactive promotional efforts over months and years.

  I led our firm's efforts on a university project that was canceled because the university couldn't raise the private funds needed. When that project was canceled, I researched what building was next in line for the university, hoping to leverage the relationships with the officials we'd collaborated with on the canceled project. I found that the next project promised to be a prestigious one. For almost two years, I touched base regularly with the project manager for the state and a facilities vice president at the university.

  I soon learned that the federal government would also be involved. I found the name of the contracting officer, and I added her into my calling list. She was extraordinarily helpful. As I made my calls in turn, I sometimes learned things about the project that other stakeholders on my calling list weren't yet aware of; during my periodic calls to the others on my list, I would share any news I had. The prospect of learning something useful about this priority project meant that decision makers were happy to take my calls. After hearing what I could share, they would often tell me things about the plans and schedule for the building that I was not yet aware of and could share with other stakeholders, if appropriate.

  In this process, I learned about one of the conditions of federal involvement for this project. The government was planning to require that the project be awarded to a team made up of a local and a national firm. At the time, the government was working on pre-qualifying a short list of national firms that would be eligible. Finding out who was on that list gave our local firm a bit of street cred: when we contacted these firms, we were able to tell them about an upcoming solicitation they hadn't yet heard about.

  This extended effort helped us team with the best possible partner; in the end, we got the job.

Only after a lifetime of practice. Charleston, SC.

Part II

Practice

Becoming an architect takes years. Practicing architecture continues for many more. The work can be all consuming, yet once they build up a head of steam, many architects just don't quit. For some, it is an ongoing drive to improve our built and natural environment that justifies this persistence. While an architect may get distracted by complicated and expensive technological solutions, in the end, our simple aim is mostly to cut back on energy, water, and other resources our buildings consume. A more sustainable building improves the lives of building occupants and saves green.

3

We Just Keep at It

Architecture is a slow-maturing profession. It takes time to master; to practice well requires experience and care. The path of progress in architectural practice frequently includes a substantial leadership role—as head of a design team. But the opportunity to lead a design team in crafting a significant project may not come to a newly minted architect for several years. Waiting may take more patience than some aspiring practitioners have, but the wait is worth it. The following story, shared as I remember it, was told by John Belle at a conference.

While in school in his native England and decades before his career would begin to flourish, restoration architect, John Belle of New York-based Beyer Blinder Belle, attended a RIBA (Royal Institute of British Architects) conference and somehow ended up sitting next to the famous British architect, Sir Norman Foster, over dinner. Foster made the grandfatherly gesture of asking how this young man's career was faring. Belle complained: too many repetitive details and schedules, not enough meaningful work. He said he had been working for a few years now and didn't feel like he was doing meaningful work or getting anywhere at all.

At this point, the elder statesman (who himself would wait another 40 years before being recognized internationally as a Pritzker Prize laureate) interrupted John Belle and demanded, "Young man, do you know what the definition of a bright young architect is?" Belle had no answer. Foster continued: "It is an architect that has just celebrated his 50th birthday."

It was on the weekend of his 60th birthday that Mr. Belle spoke of this encounter. That birthday celebration had given him occasion to think back on the 10 years since he turned 50. He realized Foster had been correct. Belle *was* about 50 when his career began to include prominent and meaningful work, including the landmark restoration of the Ellis Island Immigration Station, in New York Harbor. He had begun to emerge as a *bright young architect*. John Belle would continue in practice and in volunteer civic service until just a couple of years before passing away at the age of 84.[1]

By all accounts, architects often practice well into their 80s and 90s. Some go on practicing until the day they die.

Ask yourself
Why do you think many architects don't retire?

In 2008, <u>Witold Rybczynski</u>, wrote an article entitled, "The Oldest Profession: Why don't architects ever retire?" At that point, Mr. Rybczynski had been practicing, teaching, and writing (profoundly) about architecture in our modern world for more than 40 years.

The indented text that follows is an excerpt from Rybczynski's article:

> Asked why so many architects lived long lives, Philip Johnson quipped, "Of course they live long—they have a chance to act out all their aggressions." Johnson must have had a lot of acting out left to do, for his well-publicized "retirement" at 85 turned out to be only the first of many, and he continued to design and build until his death 13 years later.

Forever Practice: The Architect at Work, First Edition. Jim Nielson, FAIA.
© 2025 John Wiley & Sons, Inc. Published 2025 by John Wiley & Sons, Inc.

I.M. Pei, more judicious in all things, was 72 when he announced his retirement from the firm he had founded 28 years before. Golf, fishing, mah-jongg? Hardly. "I want to spend whatever time I have left working," he said, and he has been doing just that—in France, Germany, Qatar, China. His most recent building [at the time of the Rybczynski article quoted here], done in collaboration with his two sons' firm, Pei Partnership Architects, [was] the Embassy of the People's Republic of China in Washington, D.C.

At 91 [at the time of this article] Pei [was] the same age Frank Lloyd Wright was when he died. Wright didn't pretend to retire; he just kept drawing until the end. And what drawings! His last decade saw three great masterpieces: the Price Company Tower, the Beth Sholom Synagogue, and the Solomon R. Guggenheim Museum.

What is it with architects that they don't—or can't—retire? In part, it is the nature of their profession. Architecture is a delicate balancing act between practicality and artistry, and it takes a long time to master all the necessary technical skills as well as to learn how to successfully manipulate the thousands of details that compose even a small building. Requisite skills for the successful practitioner include dealing with clients: individuals, committees, communities, boards. The architect, proposing an as-yet-unbuilt vision of the future, must be able to persuade, and it's easier to be persuasive if you have a proven track record.

For all these reasons, architectural wunderkinds are few and far between; architects have traditionally hit their stride in late middle age. Ludwig Mies van der Rohe was 62 when he started designing the Lake Shore Drive apartments, which became the model for all subsequent steel-and-glass towers; Le Corbusier was 63 when he built the marvelous chapel at Ronchamp, setting the architectural world on its ear; Louis Kahn was 64 when the Salk Institute was built; and Frank Gehry was 68 when he produced the Bilbao Guggenheim. So once you finally get really good at it, why stop?

It's not so hard for an architect to keep going. Since building is a team endeavor, the old master is surrounded by scores of assistants. For any slowing down that occurs in later years, there are plenty of younger hands and minds to pick up the pace. The younger minds propose, but the master disposes, and the big decisions still benefit from years of practice and experience. From the client's point of view, since buildings represent large investments, it's safer, by far, to know that a seasoned practitioner is overseeing the process.

In old age, painters have the choice of retreating to their studios and picking the subject that interests them. Architects don't have that luxury; they depend on clients for their work. All architects have experienced periods when the clients stopped coming, for one reason or another—when there was no work in the office and staff had to be let go, oblivion beckoning. So when clients continue to knock at the door with large, interesting commissions, it's very hard to say no. After all, who knows for how long the knocking will continue? I met Gehry when he was 73. He said that he was turning down a lot of work and speculated that he probably would not do more than a handful of projects before retiring. That was six years—and many, many buildings—ago.[2]

(As of the time this textbook was written, Mr. Gehry was 95 years old and still going strong.)

Under the heading on his website, *Do Architects Retire?*, architect Byron Darkin shares similar insights. Below are a few of his anecdotes. I suppose they add something of a macabre twist to the conversation, but even for the architects he introduces that met an untimely demise, the fact is that most of them continued to practice well past what we usually think of as retirement age:

There's a famous adage in the world of architecture that architects never retire, they drop dead with a pencil in their hand. This was almost literally the case with my own father who passed away 10 years ago this October. As he lay ill in hospital, he was far more interested in sketching buildings and talking to me about his designs than anything else.

Architecture is most definitely a calling rather than a career. Architects are driven to shape the world around them, and my father was very typical in this regard. The career endings are even more grim for famous architects:

Le Corbusier
Famous as a pioneer of Modernist architecture, with a name that translates as "The Raven," Le Corbusier drowned at the age of 77 after going for a swim in the Mediterranean.

Antoni Gaudi
Architect of the Sagrada Familia in Barcelona which is still being worked on today, Gaudi was run over by a tram on his way to work.

Carlo Scarpa
Buried standing upright, Scarpa died after falling down a flight of concrete stairs.

Aldo Rossi
Rossi was the first Italian architect to win the Pritzker Prize; he died following a car accident in 1997.

George Meikle Kemp
The self-taught Scottish architect died after falling into a canal on the way to visit a builder on a foggy night.

The [website] author: Byron Darkin
Anecdotally it seems that I'll never retire, given the passion for creativity that runs through all architects. Worse still, it seems that if I ever become famous for my work, that I may meet a grizzly or untimely end . . . [3]

It doesn't take much googling to find more examples of architects that just go on and on. On June 23, 2021, for example, Architectural Record posted this report about Richard Meier's retirement:

> The office of Richard Meier & Partners is announcing today that the practice, begun by the award-winning architect in 1963, will now be called Meier Partners, and that its 86-year-old founder is officially retiring.[4]

Why does the pattern of practicing architecture persist into old age? "I'll keep practicing until I get it right," some may quip. "Getting it right" will be the subject of **Chapters 18 and 19, Getting it Right I and II, in Part VI Firm.**

Ask yourself
Once again, why do many architects choose not to retire?

Additional Resources

The Architect's Handbook of Professional Practice
   5.6   Ownership Transitions ("Unsuccessful Transition," P. 240)

Author's Note

Álvaro Siza and Santiago Calatrava
A couple of years before the end of the last century, my wife and I spent a day in Lisbon delighting in the works of two powerful architects of our day.

We had reasons other than touristing to be in Lisbon in the summer of 1998. On an in-between day, though, our group had scheduled a sightseeing trip to some of Lisbon's traditional sites. We had better ideas; we had noted in advance that this was the year of the Lisbon World Fair. We figured Expo '98 would be the more unforgettable experience, and as far as I know, we were right. We traveled to the waterfront by train, arriving at one of the most beautiful multimodal transit stations either of us had experienced firsthand. Muscular, organic concrete sinews marked the spaces for trains below grade; tree-like superstructures above sheltered the bus stops. As I guessed immediately, it was designed by one of my heroes, Santiago Calatrava.

In addition to a memorable transit station at its entrance, this priceless world's fair included site and architectural interventions by some of the world's best, including, for example, monumental engineering theatrics by Ove Arup. In the heart of this world's fair, we were captivated by Álvaro Siza's Portuguese National Pavilion, with its vast, airy canopy, fashioned from concrete (of all things). The genius with which that canopy was woven together with the pavilion structure itself had the feel of open stitching on fabric.

Siza was 65 when the Portuguese National Pavilion opened that year. He retired from teaching in 2003[5] but has kept practicing. His Manhattan tower, 611 West 56th Street, was completed in 2022. An addition he designed for his Serralves Museum in Porto, Portugal, was completed in November 2023, when Siza was 90.

Calatrava was younger. He was born in 1951, but with his Zürich Stadelhofen railway station and two bridges in Barcelona, he had become a "bright young architect" earlier than most. Calatrava was 47 at the time of the Lisbon Expo.

One of Calatrava's best known works may also be one of his most recent. The Oculus Transit Hub at Ground Zero in New York opened in 2016. Calatrava also designed the UAE Pavilion for EXPO 2020 in Dubai. In 2022, he completed his St. Nicholas Greek Orthodox Church, in the New York City financial district, at the age of 72.

When asked in 2020, *"What does the future hold for you?"* Calatrava said, "I will work until the last day of my life."[6]

When Siza was asked in 2009, *"Are you thinking of retiring?"* he responded, "I think I will get retired by other reasons [points to the ceiling], but I won't retire unless I am sick. To retire is to become sick."[7]

On that day in Lisbon in 1998, we admired the monumental works of these two venerable architects. As I write this book, neither shows signs of stopping.

Notes

1 John Belle told of this experience at a regional AIA conference I attended in the early 1990s. This paraphrased account comes from my recollections of a memorable personal story Mr. Belle related during his keynote address on that occasion.

2 https://slate.com/human-interest/2008/09/why-don-t-architects-ever-retire.html (accessed October 11, 2024)

3 https://www.darkinarchitects.com/news/do-architects-retire (accessed October 11, 2024)

4 https://www.architecturalrecord.com/articles/15196-richard-meier-retires-as-firm-re-organizes (accessed October 11, 2024)

5 https://www.famous-architects.org/alvaro-siza-vieira/ (accessed October 11, 2024)

6 https://www.youtube.com/watch?v=AaGiXKChquA (accessed October 11, 2024)

7 https://www.iconeye.com/back-issues/alvaro-siza (accessed October 11, 2024)

4

Our Environment

In preparing young people to go camping in the wilderness, *Scouting America* has always taught campers to *leave no trace*. After spending a night somewhere, campers should leave no evidence whatsoever that they were there. Of course, architects rarely hide their tracks when putting up a building. But when it comes to the impact of buildings on the natural world, a growing number of architects proclaim the desire that constructing and operating buildings be devoid of impact. In fact, our goal may be not just to design for zero impact, but rather to leave things improved through our design interventions.

The first and foremost aim of most architects is to minimize the resource and environmental footprint of what they do today. If that isn't an architect's aim, most of us in the field would probably agree that it should be. If we plan our buildings so that the design and construction industry consumes fewer resources today, the current work of creating our built environment will be less apt to compromise the resources and opportunities of future generations.

Unfortunately, throughout history, the building industry has been among the biggest environmental polluters.

Ask yourself
Knowing our buildings are still some of the world's biggest traffickers in natural and energy resources; realistically, how do we change that?

One might start by assessing the impact of design and construction, an enterprise that begins at the designer's drawing board.

Building scientists have developed complex algorithms for gauging the effect on the planet of building and operating a facility over its life cycle. But there exists a far simpler approximation. Granted, the analytical approach I suggest here is a blunt instrument, but if a quick estimate brings more awareness than exhaustive analysis and computer modeling we may need to spend weeks to obtain, a blunt instrument may be a wise tool for starting out.

This approximate method of assessing a building's impact on the natural world focuses on what things cost, now and in the future.

What we pay for materials or building systems, including their installation and maintenance (whether the installed components constitute wall panels, interior paneling, masonry, roof flashing, or any sort of system or material designed into a facility), is connected to the natural resources, energy, labor, transportation, and known externalities expended in fabricating and installing assemblies to create a finished work. The correlation between cost and overall resources is not precise, but it may establish an order of magnitude. And it involves simpler and far fewer calculations than more detailed analytical methods.

Ask yourself
Considering the statements above about embodied natural resources, carbon, energy, labor, transportation, and known externalities of construction, do we as architects have a responsibility to consider reducing construction costs as an important component of sustainability?

Forever Practice: The Architect at Work, First Edition. Jim Nielson, FAIA.
© 2025 John Wiley & Sons, Inc. Published 2025 by John Wiley & Sons, Inc.

If we posit that it is OK to pay a premium for a net-zero building, how big a premium can reasonably be paid back through energy savings?

The question above deserves careful consideration. If a building costs more up front, it probably begins its life with more embodied energy than does a more economical build.

For the purpose of making informed comparisons, we should begin with the assumption that a pricey and a cheaper building are the same size, have the same general functionality, and accommodate the same number of occupants. The notion that two buildings with widely differing price tags might be the same size and similarly functional is by no means an unreasonable point of departure.

By overspending to build a structure, owners and their project teams dig themselves a larger embodied-resources hole than they would if they built more economically. If the goal is, as it should be, to reduce overall resource use over the building's life cycle, facility managers dealing with an overly expensive building (weighed down with excessive embodied energy, resources, and carbon right from the beginning) start out in a hole created during construction. They may spend the life of their enterprise attempting to backfill that hole and repair the environmental damage. Saving energy and carbon overall? Starting so far behind, a building may never get to that.

Consider a conventional 25-year building filled with office or factory workers. (After 25 years, a facility will often need reconstruction or major renovation to be viable, so we'll evaluate total enterprise costs, from initial construction through the life of the building for 25 years, without considering complete rebuilding or major renovation that could be needed thereafter.)

Based on a rule of thumb I first learned 30 years ago and have seen validated throughout my practice, enterprise life cycle costs over 25 years typically break down proportionally as shown in *Figure 4.1*.

This basic cost model represents a reasonable conceptual starting point in assessing life-cycle impacts. It is important to note that in a typical building designed to meet the energy code, energy tends to represent between 20 and 50% of overall operation and maintenance expenses. To be on the conservative side, we'll set energy equal to 40% of overall O&M costs; 40% of the building's 5% O&M share over 25 years equals 2% of the total enterprise cost. (Even with a conventional building, however, it's good to remember that energy costs could be as low as half that, or only 1% of overall enterprise costs.)

Say an owner wants to achieve net zero. Thanks to a June 2024 publication by the US Department of Energy, a *National Definition of a Zero Emissions Building*,[1] understanding what that means is more straightforward today than ever before. But, as we have been considering, what happens if an owner, knowing what net zero means,

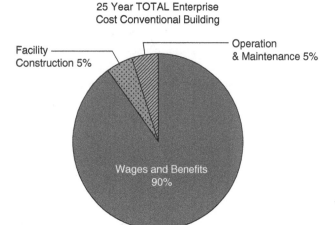

Figure 4.1 25-year TOTAL enterprise cost-conventional building.

chooses to spend twice as much as necessary on construction in an effort to achieve it? The best such projects are self-contained, including average on-site generation and storage to meet facility needs. If the project achieves net zero performance, about 2% of 25-year life-cycle costs go away. (It might be less.) But whatever the ongoing energy savings amount to in this example, the fact remains that the construction cost will have already gone up by 100% before the building is put in service.

To simplify things, this textbook uses unadjusted construction costs and energy costs as its metrics. On that basis, a quick calculation shows that the simple payback period for the net-zero energy savings of the enterprise, to offset the doubled construction costs (and associated environmental impact), is maybe 60–65 years. Say the embodied energy or carbon to cost correlation is only half as strong as the simple metric I have proposed. In that case, it would take at least 30 years to offset the embodied energy and carbon. Either of these scenarios represents a timeline that pushes the project well into the period when we *will* have to consider anticipated reconstruction costs and environmental impacts (including embodied energy for the new build). Such considerations are a factor that makes our life-cycle cost position even more tenuous.

As part of this discussion, we should also consider the fact that investors and business leaders evaluating financial pro formas for prospective business ventures and real estate deals generally look for a six- to seven-year payback. Due to concerns about changing business plans, inconsistent building performance, and changes in economic conditions, investors putting up money or C-suite inhabitants deciding to build see a payback longer than that as a risk to be avoided.

If architects are going to pursue net-zero projects, as they ought, a responsible architect should seek to accomplish this goal at no additional cost. Achievable? Yes. What *doesn't* work is throwing extra money at a project in search of sustainability.

Yes, it may make sense to pay somewhat more for increased durability and resilience in finishes (bearing masonry instead of lightweight wood framing, for example), but we should always be leery of suggestions that we double or triple construction costs to make things sustainable. Regardless of how we measure what went into a building's construction, energy savings used solely to pay off excesses in the energy, resources, and carbon built into the facility at the outset should be considered wasted.

Significant overspending in the name of sustainability is virtue signaling at its worst. It doesn't improve our environment. It makes things worse.

Ask yourself
How could we approach design and construction to create net-zero buildings at no additional cost?
How much of our energy savings over how many years can we afford to waste just to get back to where we would have been at the start if we had sipped, rather than guzzled, in our construction choices?

With respect to our overall picture of energy and resource extraction on this planet, spending way more up front is a bit like saying to a person of limited means that he must first buy an expensive car that has really good gas mileage and then make up the financial hit by reducing the amount of gasoline he buys!

Treading Lightly

If the goal is to tread lightly, in terms of both first costs and overall life-cycle costs, how should we approach that goal?

Ask yourself

- As noted in this section, when it comes to using energy and resources, one should strive to sip rather than to guzzle. It seems our ultimate goal should be not to imbibe at all. What difference do our actions in this regard make?
- Some may argue that cutting back on the use of energy and resources is an inconvenience. After all, it may feel nice to let a car warm up in the driveway on winter mornings so that it will be comfortable for the drive

to work or school. So that raises a question: what are the drawbacks of idling an internal combustion engine before driving? What externalities are associated with such a choice?

- Resilience describes buildings and spaces that can go through disasters and other changes and continue functioning with little need for rehabilitation or repair. It also describes buildings capable of persisting over generations, centuries even, rather than being destined to be discarded, torn down, and replaced. How can design teams hope to achieve architectural persistence over great lengths of time and through inevitable floods, winds, earthquakes, and unrest?

For reference and examples of many outstanding attempts to answer such questions, review the recent work based on research supported by a Latrobe Fellowship through the AIA College of Fellows: *The Architecture of Persistence.*[2]

- What is the ecological case for conservation and resilience?
- What would the economic case for conservation and resilience look like?
- Is there a business case for conservation and resilience?
- Around the year 2000, a major US city built a Net Zero, Leadership in Energy and Environmental Design (LEED®) Gold fire station. Based on their overall budget, which did not appear to include the purchase of land, in an industrial zone on the outskirts of the city, they spent roughly $450 per square foot. Based on nearby facilities and on costs at the time for the kinds of spaces included in a fire station, a fair estimate is that no-frills, durable construction of such a building could have been completed for $125-$150 per square foot. Based on this chapter, will the added costs and associated embodied energy and natural resources be offset by the facility's net-zero energy savings?
- What would be required for a net-zero building to be sustainable?
- If, based on a true life-cycle analysis, a measure doesn't reduce the overall footprint of an endeavor, is that measure of value?

For further thoughts on sustainability, spend a moment with ***Chapter 5 The Value of Green***, which draws on foundational research and case studies from the early days of LEED that are still relevant today. In reviewing this chapter, consider how architects can save energy overall without spending excessively at the outset.

Additional Resources

The Architect's Handbook of Professional Practice

4.1	Socially Responsible Design Overview
4.4	Public Service and Community Involvement
10.2	Project Teams (P. 607, ¶ 2 "Sustainable High-Performance Design")
10.5	Design Phases (P. 656, 4th Full ¶ "Sustainability," P. 659, 2nd and 3rd Full ¶ "Sustainability")
10.7	Construction Specifications (Pp. 698 beginning in the middle of page and most of 699, "Implementing Sustainable Products and Procedures")
12.2	Quality Management in Schematic Design (P. 830, ¶ 3 "Sustainability Charrettes," P. 831, ¶ 1 "Sustainability Audits")
13.1	Building Codes and Standards (Pp. 878-880, Blue box text: Backgrounder, "Energy Codes")
13.2	Planning, Urban Design, and the Regulatory Environment (Pp. 896, 897, Blue box text: Backgrounder, "Form-Based Codes," Sections, "Encouraging Sustainable Community Design" and "Implementation")
14.3	Research and Practice (Top of P. 925, "Research Consultant Model: Evidence-Based Design and Sustainability")

14.4	Evidence-Based Design (P. 945, Last two ¶s and first ¶ of P. 946, "Importance of Evidence in Sustainable Design")
15.1	Defining Project Services (P. 954 through top of P. 955, "Sustainable Design Services")
16.3	Risks and Emerging Practices (Pp. 1021-1026, "Sustainable Design")
17.5	The AIA Documents Program (Pp. 1105-1106, "Sustainable Design and Construction")
Appendix B	Glossary (P. 1137, "Sustainability" and "Sustainable Design")

Author's Note

Nonrenewable resources and future generations

A guiding principle of sustainability is that nonrenewable resources, such as minerals and high-density energy, belong to all of us in every generation, rather than just those that exploit these resources today.

Being prudent in how we use natural resources is a matter of public policy. Energy codes, for example, set energy standards for buildings, wherever they are adopted. Nationally, these codes are adopted by state legislatures, county commissions, and city councils. But responsible stewardship over energy and natural resources may extend further.

The story of Kiribati, a small island nation, provides background for a sustainable way public policy can (and should) respond to natural resource revenues (usually called *severance taxes*). In 2008, *The Economist*, a British newsmagazine reported:

> Kiribati, a Pacific island country that mined guano for fertiliser, set up the Kiribati Revenue Equalisation Reserve Fund in 1956. Today the guano is long gone, but the pile of money remains. If it manages a yield of 10% a year, the $400m fund stands to boost the islands' GDP by a sixth.[3]

In 2014, the PEW Charitable Trusts, together with the National Conference of State Legislatures (NCSL), convened a conference of western legislative fiscal leaders. As vice chair of our House Committee on Revenue and Taxation, I moderated and presented at a panel discussion on revenue from oil and gas. My subject: Utah's new policy of banking a portion of severance tax receipts for the future.[4]

I had previously sponsored and passed a constitutional amendment (subsequently approved by voters), requiring that severance taxes from nonrenewable resources be invested in a permanent fund for future generations rather than be expended in full in the year they were collected. As I had discovered in my first session on Capitol Hill, spending it all each year had been the legislature's default.

The principle at play in these public policy conversations? Revenues from nonrenewable resources belong not so much to the generation that exploits them, but rather to all generations. Using all severance tax revenues for current spending means future generations might not have a viable way to fund some of the benefits citizens enjoy today.

Being sustainable in our design efforts is akin to this public policy approach. We must do what we do today without compromising the abilities of future generations to do likewise.

Notes

1 https://www.energy.gov/eere/buildings/national-definition-zero-emissions-building (accessed October 28, 2024)

2 Fannon, David, Laboy, Michelle, and Wiederspahn, Peter. (2022). *The Architecture of Persistence: Designing for Future Use*. Routledge.

3 "Briefing: Asset Backed Insecurity," *The Economist* (January 17, 2008) (Original British spelling retained).

4 Research has not discovered a published record of conference of western fiscal leaders by The PEW Charitable Trust. The above presented here is based on the author's records and recollection as a legislative participant and session moderator.

5

The Value of Green

The term *green* gained currency in the late 1990s. At that time architects also began speaking of *sustainability*. Before that, architects often addressed concerns for the environment in our work using the language of recycled materials, low-water fixtures, or *energy efficiency measures*. The growing conversation about sustainability combined these concepts and others. Almost immediately, talk of sustainability was accompanied by claims of green design that wasn't. A new term was born: *greenwashing*.

Not long thereafter, in 1998, the U.S. Green Building Council (USGBC) created its signature green building rating tool, *Leadership in Energy and Environmental Design* (LEED®). This rating system required rigorous documentation. It had a scoring system. Obtaining credits meant justifying credits and substantiating them in the face of third-party USGBC audits. The building industry quickly learned that LEED involved substance. It could substantiate claims of reduced environmental footprints.

The first LEED-rated buildings (the pilot program, or LEED 1.0), including the 2002 Olympic Speed Skating Oval (*Figure 5.1*), were completed around the turn of the millennium.

Soon after these first certifications, USGBC released LEED 2.0 with more stringent requirements. The USGBC has since continued to raise the bar. By the mid-2000s, LEED had enough of a toehold in commercial real estate that some commercial real estate owners began to put a premium on LEED certification. They even focused marketing campaigns on LEED and its promise of more healthful spaces and savings in operating costs. Greenwashing became less of an issue, but the market as a whole still harbored concerns about the financial implications of this trend.

In 2007, researchers Lisa Fay Matthiessen and Peter Morris of Davis Langdon[1] compared costs across large west coast markets for LEED-rated and nonrated facilities with similar functions. Treating LEED certification as a proxy for sustainable buildings, the findings of the Davis Langdon study were counterintuitive to many:

> "...there is no significant difference in average cost for green buildings as compared to nongreen buildings."

Researchers found:

- Some contractors were beginning to get on board with sustainable design and construction
- Teams usually began with low-cost strategies
- Energy savings were mostly about low-hanging fruit
- Some considered sustainability as an add-on
- Still, many LEED projects came in on budget

Building green without wasting green was working because project teams began to:

- Spend less on other stuff
- Put low-hanging fruit first
- Use sustainable strategies that ***saved*** money[2]

Forever Practice: The Architect at Work, First Edition. Jim Nielson, FAIA.
© 2025 John Wiley & Sons, Inc. Published 2025 by John Wiley & Sons, Inc.

Figure 5.1 2002 Olympic speed skating oval. LEED 1.0 Certified. *Source:* Jonathan Moore - International Skating Union/International Skating Union / Getty Images.

Sustainable design need not cost more. In fact, carefully integrating design to minimize heating and cooling needs, for example, may enable downsizing or eliminating equipment that seemed necessary at first. Green design may end up costing less.

Case Study: Integrated Design and Adding Triple-pane Glazing to a House

I first heard this case study in the early 2000s in a presentation by Bill Reed, one of the founders of the sustainable movement. He told of a client building a small house that wanted to improve its energy efficiency. Bill published this same case study, which he called "Tunneling through the cost barrier," in *The Integrative Design Guide to Green Building: Redefining the Practice of Sustainability*, a book he published with the 7group in 2009.

This homeowner's initial request had been to see whether he could afford to use triple-glazed, high-performance windows. The contractor priced them and said they added $2,000 to the cost of the project. By increasing wall insulation (adding another $1,500), the project team calculated that these changes would moderate radiant temperatures at exterior walls and windows enough to allow perimeter air registers and horizontal ductwork to be eliminated, without sacrificing occupant comfort, for a savings of $3,500. In fact, these envelope improvements would reduce loads so much that the owner could also save another $4,000 by getting rid of the boiler that provided heat. Instead, they spent $1,000 to upgrade the water heater so it would cover the home's reduced heating demands. Finally, to compensate for the home's tightened envelope, they invested another $1,000 into a heat recovery ventilation (HRV) system to control humidity and provide fresh air. (*Figure 5.2* includes a graph and table summarizing the costs and savings).

In sum, this comprehensive design effort turned the extra $2,000 for the windows into a *savings* of $2,000 overall. And the resulting residence "consumes 60% less energy than the norm." Sustainable buildings need not cost more. Integrated design means they can often be built for less.

It's what Bill Reed has called, "Tunneling through the cost barrier."[3]

Case Study: Utah Department of Natural Resources Office Building

Mechanical and Electrical Equipment for Buildings (MEEB), Wiley's definitive Environmental Control Systems reference work highlights the Utah Department of Natural Resources. MEEB's illustration of building features is shown in *Figure 5.3*.

Figures 5.4 and 5.5 diagram sustainable design features of the site, including project site layouts before value engineering (VE) and after.

Case Study: Utah Department of Natural Resources Office Building | 27

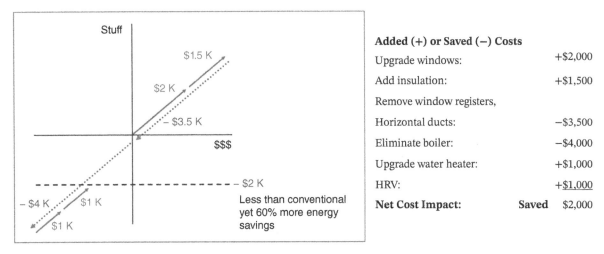

Figure 5.2 Tunneling through the cost barrier.

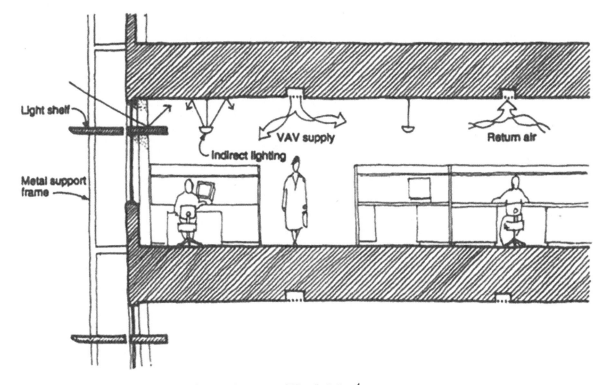

Figure 5.3 The Utah Department of Natural Resources Office Building.[4]

The Utah Department of Natural Resources case study shows VE at its best. In a meeting offsite, after the design development phase, the team agreed to:

- Provide less parking and give carpoolers preference
- Preserve a functional maintenance building
- Dedicate the savings to improvements in environmental performance

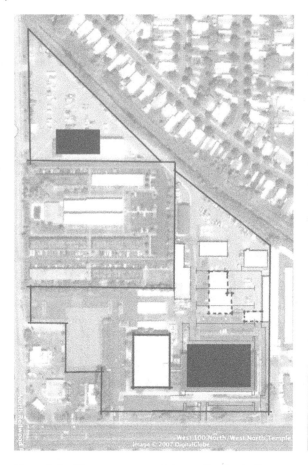 

Figure 5.4 Site as programmed. Image Overlay by the author.[5]

Figure 5.5 Site after value engineering. *Source:* Maxar / Getty Images.

Case Study: U of U Sutton Geology and Geophysics Building

Design for this building had been completed and construction was underway when the owner decided to pursue LEED® certification.

The design team built sustainable features into the base design as a matter of course:

Sustainable Sites (7 points).
- Pollution Prevention: SWPPP.
- Site Selection: Not Sensitive.
- Development Density: Urban Fabric.
- Alternative Transportation: Location, Showers, and Bike Racks.
- Parking Capacity: No New Parking.
- Site Development: Open Space.
- Heat Island Effect: White TPO Roofs.

Water Efficiency (2 points).
- Water Use Reduction: Low-flow Fixtures.

Energy and Atmosphere (2 points).
- Minimum Energy Performance: Comply with ASHRAE.
- Fundamental and Enhanced Commissioning: State Requirement.
- Fundamental and Enhanced Refrigerant Management.
- Optimize Energy Performance: Limited Glazing Bonus and Heat Exchangers.

Materials and Resources (3 points).
- Construction Waste Management: Demo of Existing.
- Regional Materials: Concrete and Brick.
- Recycled Content: Fly Ash in Concrete.

Indoor Environmental Quality (Prerequisites—0 points). Minimum Indoor Air Quality (IAQ) Performance: Comply with ASHRAE.
- Environmental Tobacco Smoke Control.

In addition, students in a cross-disciplinary sustainability course were instrumental in adding several sustainable features to the Sutton Building, including a roof garden (*Figure 5.6*).

The owner expected, and was ready to pay, a hefty price tag for the change, but costs came in lower than anticipated. LEED items added to the design (and implications/rough costs) included:

Sustainable Sites
- Construction Activity Pollution Prevention +$20,000.
- Site Development: Native/Adaptive Vegetation +$20,000.
- Storm Water Design: Post/Pre +$40,000.
- Light Pollution Reduction: Fixtures +$10,000.

Water Efficiency (Figure 5.7)
- Water-Efficient Landscaping: Drip Systems +$20,000.

Figure 5.6 Sutton building roof garden. *Source:* G. Brown Design.[6]

Figure 5.7 Sutton building-landscaping. *Source:* G. Brown Design.[7]

Energy and Atmosphere
- Optimize Energy Performance: Upgrade Glazing and Chiller +$280,000.
- Fan Wall Instead of Conventional Fan + $60,000.
- Green Power: Purchase Energy from Green Source +$10,000.

Materials and Resources
- Storage and Collection of Recyclables: Floor Plan Change.
- Construction Waste Management: Sort Waste +$10,000.

Indoor Environmental Quality
- Outdoor Air Monitoring: CO_2 Sensors +$20,000.
- Increased Ventilation +$10,000.
- Construction IAQ Management: Flush Out and Filters +$40,000.
- Low Emitting Materials: Low VOC +$30,000.
- Indoor Chemical and Pollutant Control: Mats, Filters +$40,000.
- Controllability of Systems: Additional Zones +$20,000.
- Thermal Comfort Verification: Survey/Plan +$5,000.

Is Green Better?

A high-performance building results in:
- Lower long-term operating costs
- Better quality air, lighting, and work environment
- Lower environmental impact
- Better overall design

Specifics

- Daylight improves productivity
- Construction waste management improvements reduce disposal costs
- Benefits of improving IAQ substantially exceed the cost of doing so
- More sustainable buildings have generally commanded higher rents

Too Wasteful, or Just Too Big?

A column in the British newsmagazine, *The Economist*, reported on a trend among carmakers to build "bigger, burlier cars, even when they are electric." The writer suggested that "to virtue-signal your low-carbon street cred, being featherweight rather than heavyweight should count."

"Except it doesn't," he bemoaned.[8]

Author's Note

Sustainability

I have been a LEED Accredited Professional since 2006. I have led major *LEED Silver* and *Gold* rated projects. A business partner of mine achieved *LEED Platinum* for her work on an interpretive nature center. With that project, she earned the highest number of points on record at the time. Watching LEED projects come together, I have sometimes seen them fall short in areas of energy performance or water usage—the two factors I believe are most important in making a building sustainable. In recent years, I have learned more about Passive House, which is a rating system that focuses on reducing energy use by as much as 90% by optimizing building orientation, insulation, and ventilation.

I think if we were to invent LEED today, we might—like Passive House—focus it primarily on reducing overall energy use. But a strong secondary focus should be water.

As I see it, energy and water are the things that matter most.

Notes

1 Davis Langdon, a construction consulting firm, was acquired by AECOM in 2010.

2 Matthiessen, Lisa F. and Morris, Peter. (2007). *Cost of Green Revisited: Reexamining the Feasibility and Cost Impact of Sustainable Design in the Light of Increased Market Adoption.* Davis Langdon.

3 7group and Bill Reed, (2009). *The Integrative Design Guide to Green Building: Redefining the Practice of Sustainability,* 24–28. Wiley.

4 Grondzik, Walter T. and Kwok, Alison G. (2020). "Figure 14.106" In: *Mechanical and Electrical Equipment for Buildings, Thirteenth Edition,* 654. John Wiley & Sons.

5 Site diagram by the author.

6 https://i1.wp.com/gbrowndesign.com/wp-content/uploads/2015/07/PICT0085.jpg?zoom=2&resize=300%2C200&ssl=1 (accessed October 12, 2024)

7 https://i1.wp.com/gbrowndesign.com/wp-content/uploads/2015/07/IMGP3066.jpg?zoom=2&resize=300%2C200&ssl=1 (accessed October 12, 2024)

8 Henry Tricks, "Schumpeter | The EV obesity epidemic: the supersizing trend is unsustainable, unsafe and eventually will become unprofitable," *The Economist,* 56. (August 12, 2023)

If you can't make it beautiful, make it big. Potsdamer Platz, Berlin.

Part III

Profession

Architecture is a slow-maturing but highly respected profession. The profession has taken baby steps, but it has much yet to do in welcoming women and minorities to its ranks. Licensure is coordinated nationally by the National Council of Architectural Registration Boards (NCARB) and governed by state licensing or registration boards. Obtaining a license is an exacting and often protracted endeavor.

Rules of conduct for architects include ethical and professional requirements. If a claim or legal dispute arises, an architect's professional actions are evaluated based on the architect's standard of care, a common-law benchmark addressed, variously, in contracts, state laws and rules, NCARB model code, and administrative court standards.

6

The Profession of Architecture

To be frank, almost anyone in the business that is asked for a list of favorite architects, either practicing now or in the last century, will include more men than women on the list. For example, an architect might include men such as:

Alvar Aalto	Norman Foster	Renzo Piano
Günter Behnisch	Robert Frasca	Eero Saarinen
Gunnar Birkerts	Antoni Gaudi	Álvaro Siza
Santiago Calatrava	Bjarke Ingels	Frank Lloyd Wright
Arthur Erickson	I.M. Pei	

Along with women such as:

Zaha Hadid	Sarah Susanka	Denise Scott Brown
Jeanne Gang	Billie Tsien	Maya Lin

The number of women practicing architecture *is* quite a bit smaller than men, so it might not be a surprise that male architects would predominate on a list of favorites. Even so, if the above list were considered typical, it might be worth noting that the number of women's names above as a portion of the whole (30% of those listed) is higher than the percentage of women that are licensed architects. The National Council of Architectural Registration Boards (NCARB) reported that in 2020 the United States of America had just over 120,000 licensed architects. That same year, the AIA reported that 17 percent of registered architects were women. At a Women's Leadership Summit in October 2024, AIA leadership noted that women "make up more than one-fourth—26.8 percent—of AIA's total membership." Using NCARB's most recent data, they added that the "number of female licensed architects is 27 percent."[1]

People of color have consistently been even less well represented in the profession than are women. See the first document under Additional Resources at the end of this chapter for details. Regardless of specific statistics, it would be difficult to dispute the fact that in terms of numbers, architecture has traditionally been, and often is still, dominated by men.

By old white men, one might add. See **Chapter 3 *We just Keep at It*.**

(I should note here that it is my hope that after this book has been in print for a few years, the above demographics regarding men, women, and people of color in the field will become more balanced, and this first part of *Chapter 6* will become woefully out of date.)

Participation in the field by women and marginalized populations aside, architecture is a respected profession. Over the decades, as media organizations have attempted to rank how much respect different careers garner, the field of architecture has consistently been rated as highly respected. For example, architecture was included in the June 6, 2023, Yahoo! Finance listing of the "Most Respected Professions in the World." It has long held a top ten listing in *Wikipedia*[2] as one of the most prestigious of professions.

Forever Practice: The Architect at Work, First Edition. Jim Nielson, FAIA.
© 2025 John Wiley & Sons, Inc. Published 2025 by John Wiley & Sons, Inc.

Many years ago, I read a story about a citizen-architect running for office. The candidate expressed surprise at how favorably her profession was viewed by potential voters. Such reactions would not be a surprise to any architect that has put herself forward in the past as a candidate for public office.

My own experiences in 2010 and 2012 as an architect campaigning for public office demonstrated how palpable voter respect for architects is. Prospective constituents were almost universally impressed by that career choice. They would often share stories of having once seriously considered becoming an architect or of having a friend or family member in the business. After knocking on thousands of doors over the course of months of campaigning for a primary and two general elections, I did not hear one negative comment about what I did for a living. Only respect.

A career as an architect is not only respected; it is sometimes even glamorized, a phenomenon that may play a role in attracting prospective architecture school applicants. Surely some of what people think about architecture is a result of how it is depicted on stage and on the screen. It seems that when a writer wants to depict a character that is sensitive, intelligent, talented, and insightful, *architect* is often a screenwriter's go-to career for such a character. The following is only a partial list of shows that have taken this tack, portraying a leading character as an architect, or in the case of George Costanza, as an architect-pretender (passing himself off, on occasion as Art Vandelay, a supposed architect).

Stage	*Indecent Proposal*	**Television**
The Phantom of the Opera	*Sleepless in Seattle*	*Mr. Ed*
	One Fine Day	*The Brady Bunch*
Film	*The Lake House*	*How I Met Your Mother*
Three Men and a Baby	*Mamma Mia*	*Family Ties*
Housesitter	*It's Complicated*	*Seinfeld***
	Inception	*George as architect-pretender

Yes, architecture is a respected profession, glamorized in the media, and one that a great many say they considered seriously as their life's work. The field generates interest. Perhaps positive impressions about architecture explain the fact that the supply of prospective architects sometimes exceeds demand for new professionals in practice. Occasional supply/demand imbalances may also be a reason for starting pay that often seems inconsistent with the educational preparation, licensure hurdle, and substantive work responsibilities of aspiring architects.

Consider what outsiders looking in at the profession have to say about choosing architecture as a career. Although pay information in such reports is not 100% current, the relative pay for architects hasn't really budged in comparison to many other professions.

- Under the heading, "Careers to Avoid: Lowest-Paying Professional Jobs," Investopedia lists priest, journalist, paramedic, and teacher, then adds a paragraph: "What are Some Other Low-Paying Jobs?" This clean-up section includes "accountant, graphic designer, [you guessed it] *architect*, and police officer" (emphasis added). The text continues, "Seniority will often determine salary in these roles, but all four require certification and education well beyond other jobs with similar pay."[3]
- Salary.com also weighed in with an article entitled, "9 Surprisingly Low-Paying Jobs." *Architect* was fourth from the bottom, just one step better than police officer and firefighter. "For people who can barely manage a teepee made of sticks, being able to visualize and then design the intricacies of a habitable building seems like it would pay a small fortune. But amazingly, . . ." the author laments, ". . . the national median annual salary doesn't even crack the $50,000 mark."[4] Thankfully, the field has experienced *some* growth in pay since then.

So, when we start out in the field of architecture, perhaps we should ask ourselves whether we are underpaid engineers or reasonably well-paid artists.

Ask yourself

Based on the research you are able to do, what are the average pay ranges today—

What is the average full-time starting pay with no architectural office experience and an accredited degree in architecture?

What is the pay rate?
- Nationally?
- In your state?

What are average architect salaries (at all experience levels)?
- Nationally?
- In your state?

What are the average salaries by position nationally and in your state?
- Principal
- Project Manager
- Architect I
- Architect II
- Architect III
- Job Captain (licensed architect)
- Job Captain (not licensed)

To be clear, it is possible to make a good living as an architect, but the profession is slow maturing; it takes time and patience to get there. As this book does its best to make clear, the complexity of architectural practice means we rarely see a whiz kid that moves through the ranks quickly in this field and lands at the top early in his career. Those that do move ahead early on often do so by striking out on their own. A principal in a small firm doesn't make what most principals do in large firms, but if an architect establishes a firm of her own, she will be a principal of her new firm right from the start.

However, if she chooses this path, she will probably need to have health insurance from a source other than her new firm. She will also need a Plan B for her career path in case the new enterprise doesn't work out.

Attitude

In spite of any insecurity architects might feel about whether they're paid enough, architects still present themselves powerfully to clients and to the public. One design firm joked about renaming the American Institute of Architects. They suggested the professional organization should rebrand itself as the *AWA, Architects with Attitude*. All architects would qualify for membership automatically. Competition between architects is fierce and self-promotion central to success. Architects study the limits of puffery in marketing endeavors. It doesn't take long for an architect to realize she can get away with putting *Best Architecture Firm in Texas* on her letterhead.

Architects that have applied for AIA chapter or national awards and for membership in the AIA College of Fellows understand these submittals are no place for humility. Architects must become their own best advocate.

This practiced self-interest and self-advocacy is critical to success in the profession. From the day an architect markets to the time she begins early program definition, and throughout a project life cycle from there, the architect leads a team that must believe in her. To succeed, she must build belief in the power of a design and in her leadership ability to make it real. Every project seems inevitably to come to a crossroads at some point on that journey when team members become discouraged or uncertain, when they entertain doubts about the outcome. It is at that moment that the architect's inspiration, and yes, her attitude, carries the project forward to fruition.

38 | 6 *The Profession of Architecture*

A story about Frank Lloyd Wright may shed light on what it means to be a member of *Architects with Attitude*. It may be the stuff of folklore, but it doesn't seem inconsistent with the professional demeanor of this legendary architect. The story goes like this: when Wright designed the corporate headquarters for the Johnson Wax Company, Herbert Johnson, the president of that company just might have said something along these lines:

"As we were crafting our new headquarters building, at first, Mr. Wright worked for me."
"Halfway through the project," Johnson would go on to explain, "We were equal partners."
"By the time the project was finished," Johnson is reported to have proclaimed, "I was working for him."

Ask yourself
Do you think the prior discussion about Architects with Attitude hits or misses the mark?
What are your own thoughts and expectations about the architects you will work with as graduate and then as architect? What are your expectations for your experiences in the profession?

Additional Resources

The Architect's Handbook of Professional Practice

2.1 Diversity and Practice Management (Blue box text: Backgrounder, "AIA Diversity History," Pp. 33–34)

3.3 The Career Paths of an Architect, Pp. 82–92.

5.2 Entrepreneurial Practice: Starting an Architecture Firm, Pp. 185–202.

ProPEL, ACSA Professional Practice Education Library (Videos for Classroom Use)

https://propel.yuja.com

Professionalism Unit | Lesson 1 Professionalism

Author's Note

Forms of contract: more complication

The profession of architecture is indeed complicated. Some of the jargon we use in the Architecture, Engineering & Construction industry to describe all of this complexity varies, depending on whom you ask. To cover the ins and outs of architecture and related construction work, these chapters touch on the nature of practice, sustainability, licensure, ethics, culture, project and firm management, community, project delivery methods, and standard forms for contractor communication in depth.

For clarity and consistency, wherever possible in these discussions, I use the terminology and definitions of the AIA and the contract documents it publishes. The AIA standard agreements, forms, and general conditions incorporate and reflect recommended terms and nomenclature for the component systems and parts of a successful project. They are available to the general public on the AIA website.[5]

But the AIA is not the only organization offering standard agreements, terms, and conditions. Standard documents similar in many ways to those available from the AIA are available from the organizations listed below on their websites (links in footnotes). But these documents sometimes construe things differently, increasing complexity further. I suggest that any architect being asked to consider contracts and conditions published by these other organizations go over the proposed agreements carefully in order to understand the framework of the associated forms and determine how the architect's responsibilities may differ under the suggested contracts from the requirements of their AIA counterparts. In addition to comparing the standard documents of these organizations against each other, see also the CSI Project Delivery Practice Guide, Chapter 7.3 and Appendix A for additional information about these organizations and key differences among their standard documents. The Practice Guide is available for sale on CSI's website.[6]

Organizations other than the AIA that provide standard documents are listed below, with their websites footnoted.

ConsensusDocs®[7]
Construction Management Association of America (CMAA)[8]
Design-Build Industry of America (DBIA)[9]
Engineers Joint Contract Documents Committee (EJCDC)[10]

Notes

1 https://www.prnewswire.com/news-releases/aia-womens-leadership-summit-marks-15th-anniversary-with-milestones-three-years-of-national-female-leadership-and-record-female-membership-302270275.html (accessed October 12, 2024)

2 "Wikipedia: Occupational Prestige," last modified August 23, 2024, 20:54 (UTC), https://en.wikipedia.org/wiki/Occupational_prestige#List_of_occupations_by_prestige (accessed October 12, 2024)

3 https://www.investopedia.com/articles/personal-finance/041515/careers-avoid-lowest-paying-professional-jobs.asp (accessed October 12, 2024)

4 https://www.salary.com/articles/9-surprisingly-low-paying-jobs/ (accessed October 12, 2024)

5 https://shop.aiacontracts.com/ (accessed October 12, 2024)

6 https://www.csiresources.org/learning/practice-guides/pdpg (accessed October 12, 2024)

7 www.consensusdocs.org (accessed October, 2024)

8 www.cmaanet.org (accessed October 12, 2024)

9 www.dbia.org (accessed October 12, 2024)

10 www.ejcdc.org (accessed October 12, 2024)

7

Architectural Licensure

Throughout the United States, a person not licensed to practice architecture is generally prohibited from using the title *architect* or any form of the word *architect* personally, in advertising, or in the name of a business. One calling herself an architect must be licensed to protect the health, safety, and welfare of the public.

This public responsibility means designing facilities that are havens where people will survive disasters, such as earthquakes, fires, hurricanes, tornadoes, or floods. The architect's duties include designing egress systems so people may exit a damaged or burning structure safely. It also means designing our facilities to use resources and energy wisely, not creating damaging externalities affecting the public and future generations. And protecting health, safety, and welfare includes creating indoor environments that sustain and enhance, fostering improved attitudes, well-being, and performance.

Life-safety responsibilities, such as developing lateral-force-resisting systems or optimizing a building's energy performance, are mostly designed by consultants and *coordinated* by the architect. A similar division of responsibilities applies to other critical occupant life-safety systems, including emergency power and lighting, emergency mechanical operations, fire protection and alarm systems, and smoke control, as applicable.

Some key health, safety, and welfare roles, however, are largely the province of the architect. Egress systems are a notable example. It is the architect that must ensure that there are:

- Adequate exits
- Sufficient separation between exits
- Sufficient exit widths
- Protected pathways to exits
- Protected stairway shafts for exits
- Appropriate materials (doors, glazing, wall and floor finishes, and furnishings) in egress paths
- Additional code requirements for specific circumstances.

Becoming Licensed

If an aspiring professional makes the decision today to become licensed, she embarks on a journey that, including schooling, may take a dozen years or more to complete. (It may be worth noting a recent NCARB report that on average, women get through the process one year quicker than men![1]) If the candidate has just graduated with a professional degree accredited by the National Architecture Accrediting Board (NAAB), she generally still has five to eight years ahead of her before becoming licensed. Some do become licensed in as little as two or three additional years, but that has become less and less common as exam and experience programs have changed.

In October 2024, after an extended period of research and practice analysis over several years, NCARB issued new guidance that is bound to affect licensing in years to come. In NCARB's words, the resulting document, *Competency*

Forever Practice: The Architect at Work, First Edition. Jim Nielson, FAIA.
© 2025 John Wiley & Sons, Inc. Published 2025 by John Wiley & Sons, Inc.

Standards for Architects, represents "a new framework that establishes competency-based qualification as the foundation of initial licensure as an architect."[2] This research, which seems likely to lead to substantive impacts on future licensing requirements, is currently available for download on NCARB's website at the link in this footnote.[3]

Based on discussions surrounding the release of these new standards, it is possible they may lay the foundation for increased flexibility and added available options for becoming a licensed architect. Stay tuned to this conversation. This chapter describes the current path to licensure, but the prospect for alternatives may be imminent.

Education, Experience, Examination

Becoming a licensed architect is based on three key essential components: a NAAB-accredited degree, the Architectural Experience Program® (AXP®) or experience component, and the Architect Registration Exam® (ARE®), also referred to as the licensing exam.

Licensing boards for most jurisdictions require the emerging professional to complete the following. These requirements are consistent with those needed for NCARB Certification:

1. Complete an accredited professional degree in compliance with NAAB conditions of accreditation. (Note that currently 18 of NCARB's member boards do not require an accredited degree.)
2. Complete the AXP, with experience demonstrating competence in areas of practice spanning the full range of the comprehensive practice of architecture. (Note that some member boards stipulate further experience requirements for candidates without an accredited degree.)
3. Pass the ARE, currently a six-part professional licensing exam

NCARB Record

Applicants create an NCARB record to document AXP experience (discussed below) and register for the ARE. After all requirements are met, the simplest route to licensure is usually to have NCARB transmit the candidate's record to a state's architect registration board (or state licensing board). An NCARB record ensures expeditious action on a candidate's license application. An NCARB certificate, which may be obtained after receiving licensure in the candidate's state of initial registration, facilitates reciprocal applications for licensure in additional states. Some jurisdictions also stipulate an additional exam or requirement of their own before granting licensure.

Although architect licensing requirements may seem demanding, they are intended to ensure that newly-minted licensed architects are properly prepared. These requirements are established to provide emerging professionals with an opportunity to demonstrate the level of competence necessary to perform the functions required to practice architecture independently. After having demonstrated this degree of competence and then having obtained a license, as their career progresses, young practitioners will likely find that they still have a healthy learning curve ahead.

As noted, an NCARB record is needed to document experience requirements and register for and take the licensing exam. Obtaining an NCARB certificate after initial licensure provides the most expeditious path to reciprocal licensure in additional states one day. Yes, there are sometimes ways to obtain reciprocity by transmitting a flotilla of documents oneself, but it is usually much quicker and easier to have NCARB handle it. One other potential bonus of having an NCARB record is that with such a record, an architect may use the letters NCARB as a professional suffix, as an alternative to AIA membership. Either suffix indicates that he is a licensed architect. A young architect's signature could be:

John Doe, NCARB

The next few paragraphs provide further details about the three major requirements for licensure.

NAAB-accredited Degree

Although some states provide a path to licensure without a NAAB-accredited degree but with an additional experience requirement, most require the candidate to have completed an-accredited degree. Accredited degree programs may be either a Bachelor or Master of Architecture (B.Arch. or M.Arch.). A B.Arch. program is typically a five-year program; an M.Arch. usually takes one to three years to complete, depending on the program and on the bachelor's degree a student earns beforehand.

NAAB accredits architecture degree programs based on its published criteria. Programs report on how they are meeting those criteria. Accreditation visiting teams review these reports and corroborating evidence submitted with direct observations during their visit. Teams submit their findings to NAAB. With this input, the NAAB board decides whether to grant accreditation, under what terms. After initial accreditation, this process is repeated every eight years at a minimum.

Initial accreditation requires a series of visits over six or seven years with a two-year look-back for degrees granted prior to initial accreditation.

Architectural Experience Program

Like its exam counterpart, the AXP has also been refined. In the past, if an employer supported a young professional and provided opportunities to gain experience in all the necessary categories, it took approximately three years to complete the necessary experience hours. Today, with *a very supportive firm and supervisor*, it's possible to do it in two years. As always, a candidate must get the experience that is needed in *all* the areas.

To complete the AXP in two years, a candidate spends time with her supervisor, and perhaps another senior architect and mentor, mapping out the path and monitoring it to completion. Ideally, the architect she works for understands that he has every reason to give her the necessary experience so she gain the required competency required by AXP faster. The candidate makes sure her supervisor is well aware of what categories of experience she may be lacking. She develops a plan for how to get all the experience needed; having her supervisor help with the plan fosters buy-in. A proactive and focused emerging professional is best positioned to help her employer see the value of stepping up and supporting a candidate in her efforts to gain the experience and pass the exams needed for licensure.

Ask yourself
How might employees help employers see the value of having their staff gain broad experience in preparation for becoming licensed?

Architect Registration Examination

In the last 25 years, this six-part licensing exam has been modified, streamlined, and adapted to a digital format. With tests available on-demand in this new format, pass rates have increased.

For those seeking to pass the ARE on the first try, the following suggestions may be helpful:

1. Academic skills, or book learning from architecture school, are quite easily refreshed, with the use of readily available study guides.
2. NCARB study materials have the advantage of being authored by the same people that write the exams. NCARB has full length practice exams for each division. NCARB records show that those using these practice exams score roughly 15% higher on the tests than others. NCARB ARE study aids are a no-cost option for

NCARB record holders. Depending on her approach to test preparation, an architect may find NCARB study materials to be all the preparation needed.

3. Some parts of the exams test the applicant on competency she is more likely to have gained during the first couple of years on the job than in school. So, candidates more likely to pass exams on the first try are those that have had at least two or three years of architectural employment prior to sitting for each exam.

4. A candidate should always seek his employer's support in preparing for and taking the architecture exams.

Ask yourself
How can employers best support emerging professionals in preparing for and taking the ARE and becoming licensed?

Licensure and the Workplace

Much of the work needed to satisfy the three realms of the licensing process will take place during the early years of an emerging professional's career. The experience component requires a substantial amount of work experience with a licensed architect. Although some candidates may not work while in school, many pursue work in an architect's office, juggling practical experience with architecture degree coursework.

This chapter makes repeated reference to employer support of a candidate's quest for licensure. Some candidates may question what can be done to help an employer fulfill its responsibilities to the next generation of architects. Others may wonder how to help a prospective architect find an employer willing to do that. These questions may be of particular concern to candidates that may not have come from the same background or privilege as their fellow-employee peers.

Recently, the NCARB and the National Organization of Minority Architects (NOMA) joined forces to create a *Candidate Guide* to "help aspiring architects find employers that actively support their licensure goals."[4] The guide provides valuable insights and tips for identifying firms that prioritize a candidate's professional development, offer study resources and financial support for the ARE, and provide mentorship opportunities. The footnote for the *Candidate Guide* above includes a link to this document.

A related guide is addressed to firms, helping them consider how it will benefit them if they support their employees' path to licensure aggressively. In many cases, it might be appropriate for an aspiring architect to share this link[5] with an employer.

State Licensing Board

The state licensing board referred to in this chapter governs the profession of architecture. As current or future architects, we need to know what state boards do and how they function. The following section outlines the responsibilities of a typical licensing board.

The state licensing board:

- Defines and implements licensure requirements
- Handles applications for licensure
- Assists, where possible, in providing continuing education offerings for architects
- Regulates professional practice (using authority delegated to it by the legislature)
- Oversees investigatory actions
- Participates in administrative adjudication
- Takes appropriate disciplinary action against professionals found to have violated the code of conduct for architects licensed in the state

A few minutes reviewing your state's licensing board website should be helpful in considering the questions below. Find links to all state licensing boards on NCARB's website.[6] Follow the link in the footnote just cited to find a list with the name of each state or territory, along with a link for each entity's licensing board web page.

Ask yourself
Based on this chapter, together with additional information gleaned from your licensing board's web page, why is a licensing board necessary?
A broader question: Why do we license architects?

Additional Resources

The Architect's Handbook of Professional Practice

3.2 Intern Development, Pp. 68-82 (Note that the most recent edition of this handbook refers to the experience program as the Intern Development Program (IDP). That program has been reworked and replaced by the AXP. Much of the related text on the referenced pages is applicable.)

ProPEL, ACSA Professional Practice Education Library (Videos for Classroom Use)
https://propel.yuja.com
Professionalism Unit | Lesson 5 Licensure processes in the United States

Author's Note

When I pursued licensure, experience hours didn't count unless one was employed continuously for longer than a few weeks. I had only had brief stints in an architect's office between semester breaks. At the age of 32, having just earned my Master of Architecture (a NAAB-accredited degree) from the University of Oregon, I had a strong desire to get my license quickly. In Utah, where I began practicing July 1, 1991, I was allowed to take the ARE any time after graduation. The full exam was given once a year. At that time, the exam had nine sections (yes, nine!), taken across four consecutive days. Altogether, it was almost 40 hours of testing, with the 12-hour design exam on the last day (Thursday). We brought our drawing boards to the testing center and crafted plans, sections, and elevations. As is the case with design as a topic of today's exam, this 12-hour gauntlet wasn't about design as we might think of it—it was about satisfying program requirements and meeting the code. Most people failed this last division of the ARE.

I came to understand that passing all nine parts of the exam depended not just on book learning but also on practical office experience; I waited until I had completed two years of employment before taking it. And I studied ferociously, including two all-day mock design exams of that design piece. I wanted to be sure I got it all out of the way so I could get my license as soon as I was done with the three years of experience then required.

I passed. I finished my three-year experience requirement and became licensed in July 1994.

Since the time of the nightmare paper exams, NCARB has made substantive changes to provide increased access and convenience for prospective licensees. They increased the reliability of the experience and assessment instruments. Broadened AXP categories, reduced complexity in employment settings, and a targeted and reduced experience requirement, all combine to reflect the realities of the comprehensive practice of architecture with greater fidelity. Computerizing licensing exams has allowed them to be taken at will, eliminating the stress of a once-a-year make-or-break opportunity.

Interestingly, today's convenience of at-will exam scheduling, together with the possibility of waiting for the results of one test before scheduling the next, was supposed to have helped candidates go through the licensure process faster. As it turns out, the pace at which emerging professionals ultimately obtain their licenses has instead slowed. This average length of time before licensure has gotten slightly shorter in recent years, but today the process still takes more than a dozen years.

Notes

1 For recent licensure and demographic trends, see https://www.ncarb.org/nbtn2023/demographics (accessed October 14, 2024)
2 https://www.ncarb.org/press/ncarb-releases-new-competency-standard-architects (accessed October 14, 2024)
3 https://www.ncarb.org/sites/default/files/Competency-Standard.pdf (accessed October 14, 2024)
4 https://www.ncarb.org/sites/default/files/Candidate-Guide_Building-on-Belonging.pdf (accessed October 14, 2024)
5 https://www.ncarb.org/sites/default/files/Firm-Guide_Building-on-Belonging.pdf (accessed October 14, 2024)
6 https://www.ncarb.org/become-architect/earn-license/state-licensing-boards (accessed October 14, 2024)

8

Regulation and the Code of Conduct

As discussed in **Chapter 7**, architects in the United States are licensed by individual states. States set professional requirements through laws and administrative rules. For architects, such statutes and regulations usually reference a code of conduct. This code may be based on NCARB's *Model Rules of Conduct*. For its members, compliance with the AIA *Code of Ethics and Professional Conduct* is also required.

Regulating the Profession

General regulation of the practice of architecture may cover requirements for things like incidental practice and continuing education.

Incidental Practice

Some states include detailed statutory or rule-based exceptions defining limited engineering services an architect may provide, as part of architectural practice. In such cases, similar provisions are usually in place for engineers providing incidental architectural services. Whether incidental practice is allowed and what rules govern the practice vary by state.

Some states have traditionally had regulatory language that allowed incidental practice, based solely on the allied professional being "qualified." Such language is problematic for building officials, who may not be equipped or willing to review whether a professional is qualified to provide limited services in an area outside his license.

Ask yourself
To answer and discuss the following questions, find any incidental practice provisions in the laws and/or rules governing architectural practice in your state. (In searching for legislation and regulations, remember, search engines are your friends.)

- Are your state's provisions established by legislation or by published rulemaking (regulations)?
- Discuss the pros and cons of your state's incidental practice provisions. If you think they could be improved, how would you make them better?
- If your state's laws and regulations are silent on the subject of incidental practice, what might that mean?

Forever Practice: The Architect at Work, First Edition. Jim Nielson, FAIA.
© 2025 John Wiley & Sons, Inc. Published 2025 by John Wiley & Sons, Inc.

Continuing Education Requirements

Around 2013, NCARB began an effort to simplify continuing education compliance for architects licensed in multiple states. A big part of that effort was to standardize the annual requirement at 12 hours of core coursework (HSW courses, as they are called). When NCARB adopted this policy, the number of hours required varied widely from state to state. Also, in some states, requirements were established by statute for some professions, by rule for others. Given that NCARB's recommended number of hours might change sometime in the future, one state AIA Chapter worked to modify the statute so the licensing board could establish the new requirement by rule. After a successful effort to get the required change enacted in state law, the state's licensing board then modified the requirement by rule to 12 hours, matching the national trend.

Ask yourself
Using your state's licensing board website (find it by following the link in footnote 1 at the end of this chapter), determine your state's current requirement for continuing education. Do you agree with this number of hours? Or do you think it should be higher? Lower?
Why?

Disciplinary Action

A licensing board takes action against individuals that violate the laws and rules governing the profession of architecture in that state or territory. It is often supported in such actions by investigators that serve the board.

For example, in most, if not all, states, if a complaint comes to the board's attention about someone holding himself out to be an architect, though not licensed to practice architecture, a board staff member will investigate. Under the jurisdiction of the licensing board, if they find a violation, investigators may issue a warning or a fine or refer the matter to the board for consideration.

Ask yourself
If possible, find information online about the fines the licensing board in your state may levy against violators of the laws and rules governing the profession of architecture. What is the biggest fine for a violation? Which fines are associated with which actions? What are the fine amounts in other states?

Authority to levy fines and to take action against a professional's license places substantial power in the hands of a state's architect licensing (or registration) board. Assisting in the board's enforcement responsibilities, investigators may attempt to negotiate compliance and/or levy fines directly. If, in the presence of compelling evidence, investigators find it impossible to settle a complaint privately, a state licensing board may hold a hearing to review a complaint lodged against a licensed architect. The hearing may be scheduled individually or may be part of a regular board meeting. In cases of serious allegations against a license holder, the board may be authorized to hold a hearing before an Administrative Law Judge. The outcome of such a hearing could be a memorandum of understanding or a fine. It could also be suspension, or even revocation, of the architect's license.

Ask yourself
Would you say that state licensing boards have just the right amount of power, not enough power, or too much power?

The Architect's Responsibility

Our code of conduct as architects is to practice ethically and meet the architect's standard of care.

Ethical Practice Includes (among other things):

- Protecting the health, safety, and welfare of the public, no matter what. We cannot produce designs and construction documents that disregard such responsibilities
- Rendering impartial determinations when our contract calls for us to be the initial decision maker. Even when our impartial determination may be adverse to the person that is paying us
- Exercising extraordinary care when including manufacturers and suppliers in the creation of details and specifications that become part of the contract documents
- Guarding our environment. The building doesn't belong to us, but we should do everything possible to help owners be wise stewards over our environment. This responsibility is addressed in detail in ***Chapter 4 Our Environment***

Specific Requirements for Ethical Practice

State laws, together with legally binding implementing regulations, establish the requirement for architects to practice ethically. On its website, NCARB maintains a list of licensing boards of every state and participating territory, along with their contact information and website. Board websites address legal requirements for ethical practice in their jurisdiction. See NCARB's website for a listing of licensing boards with links to their websites.[1]

The laws and rules referenced in licensing board documents and on their websites generally address the requirements for licensure, set out disciplinary procedures, and establish the requirements for stamping drawings. The website in my state of initial licensure, for example, includes a link to the state's *Architect Licensing Act Rule* that incorporates NCARB's *Model Rules of Conduct* by reference, making the standards of practice found in this document legally binding on my practice.

National Council of Architectural Registration Board

NCARB Model Rules of Conduct

State licensing laws and regulations may incorporate and thus codify the NCARB *Model Rules of Conduct* by reference. The current version of these rules is found on the NCARB website[2] and includes specific ethical practice headings as listed below.

These rules, which are requirements for license holders in many states, begin with a foreword, an introduction, and a statement of guiding principles. The document then presents the binding rules, each with sub-paragraphs, on the following subjects:

Rule 1	Competence	Rule 4	Compliance with Laws
Rule 2	Conflict of Interest	Rule 5	Signing and Sealing Documents
Rule 3	Full Disclosure	Rule 6	Further Obligations to the Profession and the Public

Ask yourself
Review the NCARB *Model Rules of Conduct, one by one. Answer the following questions:*
1. How do you think compliance with these rules might affect you in your practice as an architect?
2. How do you believe failure to comply with these rules could affect you professionally?

American Institute of Architects

AIA Code of Ethics and Professional Conduct

In addition to being required to abide by the NCARB or other rules of conduct mandated by their state, members of the AIA are bound to the institute's *Code of Ethics and Professional Conduct*. These standards elaborate on some of the provisions of the NCARB rules and seek to elevate the profession in carrying out its legal, ethical, and social obligations to our communities and the world around us. Longtime members of the AIA place significant value on the association's *Code of Ethics and Professional Conduct*. Familiarity with this code and adherence to its canons are invaluable to society and to one's career.

This AIA *Code of Ethics and Professional Conduct* includes the practice requirements outlined below. The AIA *Code of Ethics and Professional Conduct* may be downloaded at the link in this footnote.[3] The document is brief and well worth a read.

This code of ethics, applicable to members of an organization I suggest all architects be a part of, begins with a Preamble, a Statement in Compliance with Antitrust Law, and a Statement on the Professional Standard of Care. The document then presents the following canons, with associated Ethical Standards and Rules of Conduct. The specific rules are printed on the website in red.

CANON I	General Obligations	CANON IV	Obligations to the Profession
CANON II	Obligations to the Public	CANON V	Obligations to Colleagues
CANON III	Obligations to the Client	CANON VI	Obligations to the Environment

This document ends with an administrative section: *Rules of Application, Enforcement, and Amendment.*

Ask yourself:

Review the canons of the AIA Code of Ethics and Professional Conduct, one by one. Consider the same questions posed with respect to NCARB Rules of Conduct noted above.

1. How would you summarize the many responsibilities and obligations of a licensed architect?

2. After reviewing these two codes of ethics and conduct, do you see anything that surprises you?

3. Will it be a challenge to live up to such standards?

4. Consider this example of a possible conflict: architects often rely on a hardware specifier or other product representative to prepare specifications, to review details, or to provide design recommendations (at no cost). We could compare this practice to that of a commission-based financial planner, who makes his money by selling insurance policies, annuities, or only a certain family of full-load mutual funds. Since he depends on commissions from selling financial products for a living, how objective might such an advisor be when making insurance recommendations or suggesting stock and bond investments? Similarly, how objective might a product specifier be when he works for a specific manufacturer for the product he is helping you specify?

The Architect's Standard of Care

In thinking about his responsibilities as an architect, an individual may wonder what might happen if someone were to allege that there were errors and/or omissions in his instruments of services. What standard would his work be held to if that occurred, he might ask. How would they evaluate whether his work met that standard? **Chapter 9 The Architect's Standard of Care**, up next, provides an in-depth review of the *standard of care* architects are held to in providing professional services.

An architect's work is invariably custom, one of a kind, perhaps even exploratory or experimental. For much of what they do, architects can't find true precedents or look up solutions in a table. The standard of care must apply to all situations, because each of those situations is different: the standard of care is reviewed individually, based on expert testimony about the case at hand.

Before reading **Chapter 9**, it would be well to consider the following statements from a student, learning about the background and purpose of the architect's standard of care:

"I don't know what the standard of care is, so I can't be held to it."

If this student had wanted a response to this assertion, this would have been the reply:

"But you will be."

Additional Resources

The Architect's Handbook of Professional Practice

    Chapter 1   Ethics and Professional Practice

          3.1   Regulation of Professional Practice

          3.4   AIA Continuing Education System

ProPEL, ACSA Professional Practice Education Library (Videos for Classroom Use)

        https://propel.yuja.com

        Professionalism Unit | Lesson 4 Organization of the Architecture Profession

Author's Note

Licensing board and incidental practice

A few years ago, when I was serving on my state's licensing board, a group of code officials pointed out to the board that for both architects and engineers, the question of allowing incidental practice turned on whether the architect or engineer was qualified to do a portion of the other's work.

The code officials were right. Licensure provided evidence of competence in the profession for which a person was licensed. The code officials' role was to determine whether an individual stamping drawings had a license, not to evaluate whether they were qualified or competent. But what if a licensed professional was allowed to step outside of his turf? A code official had no basis for assessing the professional's qualifications. In our state, some building officials had simply stopped approving any permit request that involved incidental practice.

Our staff did research, found approaches other states had adopted, and went through the process of holding hearings and adopting modifications to the state licensing rule. At one of their regular meetings, I met with the engineer licensing board on behalf of the architect licensing board. Acting by consensus of our boards and on behalf of the members of our respective professions, we crafted a joint approach that focused permit instructions on quantitative (rather than qualitative) factors governing incidental practice that building officials could apply simply. We got rid of judgment calls by building officials. Engineering and architect boards issued parallel rules to codify the changes.

The quantitative factors in the resulting rule satisfied code officials across the state. These factors dealt with things such as the number of occupants affected, risk categories defined in the code, and the cost of the incidental work in comparison to the whole.

Notes

  1 https://www.ncarb.org/become-architect/earn-license/state-licensing-boards (accessed October 14, 2024)

  2 https://www.ncarb.org/sites/default/files/Rules_of_Conduct.pdf (accessed October 14, 2024)

  3 https://www.aia.org/sites/default/files/2024-04/aia-code-of-ethics-april-2024.pdf (accessed October 14, 2024)

9

The Architect's Standard of Care

In cases of disputes, adjudication of an architect's actions is based on adherence to professional services agreement(s) in force *and* on whether services were provided in a manner consistent with the applicable standard of care.

Compliance with the architect's standard of care is a legal requirement, whether implied or stated. As I have come to understand it, the standard of care for an architect's work is that:

> The architect's actions must be consistent with the care ordinarily exercised by a reasonably competent licensed architect providing architectural services in similar circumstances in the same general location. Similar circumstances, as cited here, may refer not only to the year of construction and site conditions but also to the project type and project delivery method, circumstances that are often directly relevant to an architect's performance on a particular project.

The standard of care is generally referenced in state Practice Acts or rules. Some states adopt the NCARB *Model Rules of Conduct*, based on common law. The AIA *Code of Ethics and Professional Conduct*, to which its members are bound, contains similar language. And the architect's standard of care is usually incorporated into owner-architect agreements as well. Most significantly, courts and arbitration panels apply the standard of care in dispute resolution proceedings involving allegations about an architect's performance. Applying this standard usually requires that attorneys representing the parties present expert opinions (in testimony and/or reports) to evaluate the architect's performance with respect to this common-law standard. A judge presiding over a jury trial provides the jury with instructions about the standard of care that they must use in evaluating an architect's performance. Some state court systems have adopted *Rules of Civil Procedure* that include standard jury instructions. These instructions explain the standard of care and how it should be applied by the jury. Sample language from such a rule is cited later in this chapter.

Ask yourself
The standard of care is established by common law and public policy. Common-law details may change somewhat over time, based on court cases.
If you become a licensed architect, how will an understanding of the architect's Standard of Care ultimately affect your work?

Forever Practice: The Architect at Work, First Edition. Jim Nielson, FAIA.
© 2025 John Wiley & Sons, Inc. Published 2025 by John Wiley & Sons, Inc.

Professional Licensing Requirements

Licensed architects practicing in any state are subject to its professional licensing requirements. The required standard of care may be addressed in state law or regulations. Some states incorporate the following, from the NCARB rules of conduct:

> *Rule 1 Competence*
> In practicing architecture, an architect's primary duty is to protect the public's health, safety, and welfare. In discharging this duty, an architect shall act with reasonable care and competence, and shall apply the knowledge and skill, which is ordinarily applied by architects of good standing, practicing in the same locality.[1]

NCARB's *Model Rules of Conduct* Document appends the following footnote to the end of the paragraph cited above: "*This rule is based on the common law 'standard of care' that has been accepted by courts in this country for over 100 years in judging the performance of architects.*"

Obligation of Professional Association Membership

Members of the AIA are also bound to a standard of care, described in its *Code of Ethics and Professional Conduct* as follows:

> In practicing architecture, Members shall demonstrate a consistent pattern of reasonable care and competence and shall apply the technical knowledge and skill which is ordinarily applied by architects of good standing practicing in the same locality.[2]

Contractual Language

The architect's contract with an owner or Design-Builder will usually also include the architect's standard of care. The language in published contract templates (such as those published by the Design-Build Industry of America [DBIA] or the AIA) is generally consistent with the established common-law standard of care. However, parties using these carefully vetted documents sometimes attempt to modify standard-of-care clauses to enhance the architect's professional performance requirements above the legal requirement. For example, I was once given a copy of a clause from a colleague's contract, in which the standard-of-care provision had been modified and enhanced by the Design-Builder. The resulting language, as finally accepted by the architect, is printed below, with additions underlined and deletions shown as strikethrough text:

> The standard of care for all design professional services performed by Design Consultant and its Design Sub-Consultants pursuant to this Agreement shall be the care and skill ordinarily used by members of the design profession _having substantial experience providing similar services on projects similar in type, magnitude and complexity to the Project. Notwithstanding the preceding sentence, if the Design-Build Agreement contains specifically identified performance standards for aspects of the Services, Design Consultant agrees that all Services shall be performed to achieve such standards._ ~~practicing under similar conditions at the same time and locality of the Project.~~[3]

To determine whether all of the added language above would be enforceable under state law would need to be tested in court. It does appear to me, however, from my work negotiating contracts in consultation with insurance agents and counsel as needed, that part of the new language is drawn from legal doctrines applying to commodities, manufacturing, production, and/or construction (i.e., *all services shall be performed to achieve [specifically identified performance] standards).* Predetermined benchmarks of this sort, from the realm of manufacturing and commodities, appear to differ from the standard of care for an architect's services that would be applied in a court of law as described in this chapter.

I should point out that the language of the DBIA clause, had it not been edited, would have been generally consistent with frequently used AIA contract templates, such as the following clause:

> The Architect shall perform its services consistent with the professional skill and care ordinarily provided by architects practicing in the same or similar locality under the same or similar circumstances.[4]

Regardless of whether a standard of care clause, edited as shown above or not, is included in any specific contract, the standard given at the beginning of this chapter will likely be what applies to the architect's performance in the event of a dispute.

Commonly used descriptions of the architect's applicable standard of care, based on professional licensing statutes and common law, share the following characteristics:

Standard of Care—General Test

As an overarching rule, the architect is expected to perform in the same manner another reasonably competent licensed architect in good standing might be expected to perform, subject to the qualifications below.

Reasonable

An architect is held to the standard of the reasonable, ordinary performance of a typical peer. Some recitations of the standard of care use the words "architects in good standing" to convey this same meaning. This part of the standard does not demand extraordinary or unusually skilled performance.

Consistent

An architect's performance is required to be consistent with the professional knowledge and technical skill that would reasonably be found in another reasonably competent architect.

Care

An architect is expected to exercise care just as would be expected of another reasonably competent architect practicing in the same circumstances.

Competence

The competence required is evaluated in comparison to what a reasonably competent professional would do under the same circumstances. Taking such circumstances into account when reviewing an architect's performance means considering factors inherent in the varying conditions an architect may encounter on a project. Conditions that typically have a substantive impact on the architect's responsibilities include, among others, the architect's assigned role under the owner's selected delivery method, the time the work is performed, its physical location, and the project type.

State Jury Instructions Regarding Standard of Care

Of all the documentation we might turn to in considering the standard of care an architect is bound to in a legal dispute, I consider the jury instructions courts apply at trial to be the most relevant. Jury Instructions regarding the common-law standard of care described in this chapter, whether prepared by a judge individually or adopted in *Rules of Civil Procedure* typically address and clarify the legal framework for the standard of care that applies to legal proceedings related to a dispute over professional services in that case. Consistent with the standard of care typically required by statute or as found in NCARB and AIA codes of conduct and ethics, and in published contract templates, these instructions will normally restate the common law standard of care, The underlying principles of such instructions also apply to a case even when there is no jury.

The following paragraph, from the *Rules of Civil Procedure* published by the state court system in my state of initial registration, provides an example of jury instructions about the architect's standard of care:

> An architect is required to use the same degree of learning, care, and skill ordinarily used by other architects under like circumstances. This is known as the "standard of care." The law does not require perfect plans/drawings/services or satisfactory results but rather requires compliance with the standard of care.
>
> The "applicable standard of care" is the standard of care existing at the time of the architect's services and in the same or similar locality as where the architect's services were performed.[5]

Ask yourself
In practice, what questions would you and your staff consider to ensure you are meeting the architect's standard of care?

Additional Resources

The Architect's Handbook of Professional Practice

Preface   About the 15th Edition of the Handbook, "The Handbook and the Standard of Care," P. xvii

- 1.1   Architects and the Law ("Legal Overview" & "Standard of Care," Pp. 168–171)
- 10.8   Bidding and Negotiation (Blue box text: "Spearin Doctrine," P. 702)
- 15.2   Services and Compensation ("Some clients expect nearly perfect. . ." 5th Bullet Point, P. 963)
- 16.1   Risk Management Strategies ("Heightened Standard of Care" and Blue box text: "The Liability Bucket," Pp. 992–993)
- 16.4   Dispute Management and Resolution ("Introduction: Prevent Disputes Before they Start," P. 1031-Entire Page)
- 17.1   Agreements with Owners ("Implied Terms and the Architect's Standard of Care," P. 1043)

17.3   Owner-Generated Agreements ("2. Understand the Risks that can be Insured" and sidebar, P. 1071, 7. Add what the Owner Left Out, P. 1081)

ProPEL, ACSA *Professional Practice Education Library* (Videos for Classroom Use)
    https://propel.yuja.com
    Failure Unit | Lesson 3 Architecture Dos and Don'ts (Time stamp 8:30 through the end of the video—"Even if there's no fee involved, you're still held to a standard of care.")

Author's Note

It's what's expected

I didn't learn about the architect's standard of care during school, during my early years on the job, or in preparation for or taking the ARE®. When I got my license, I knew that my license meant something and that there were expectations about performing competently. It's understandable, however, that a student encountering the standard of care for the first time might be perplexed. Architects are expected to meet the standard of care, but a standard that is different in each and every case may seem fuzzy; we may find it difficult to get our arms around it.

This standard is not something we can look up in a handbook. I first encountered the architect's standard of care when I was asked to help with a complex expert witness engagement. I did the pick and shovel work on what turned out to be a massive report. It was in preparing that report that I first learned to apply the standard of care to the work of the architects our attorney was representing.

Over the years, I've come to understand that, similar to standards professionals in other fields are held to, the architect's standard of care is intended to be indeterminate. This is because the architect doesn't perform services by rote. Virtually everything he does is a one-off. Project roles change; project scope changes; the core design paradigm for a project is never the same. When an architect takes on the shape-shifting endeavor we call a project, he might be blazing a trail no one has traveled. That means there is probably no way anyone would have already been able to develop specific standards for how this unique effort would have to be carried out. To do so *a priori* would be impossible. Accordingly, comparing the performance of an architect working on a unique project to another architect construed to be in precisely the same circumstances, is a construct that is usually mostly theoretical. As noted, the details of such a standard aren't found in a rule book.

Because of the non-prescriptive nature of the architect's standard of care, the legal profession relies on informed opinions and testimony of experts, with the experience and wisdom to unravel the puzzle and apply the standard of care fairly. And as a result, the newly minted architect or architecture student encountering the uncertainty of the standard of care is obliged to do the best possible job of learning from the actions of other, more experienced peers and of developing reasonable competence.

Notes

1 "Rules of Conduct," National Council of Architectural Registration Boards (NCARB), last updated July 2023, https://www.ncarb.org/sites/default/files/Rules_of_Conduct.pdf, P. 6, § 1.1. (accessed October 15, 2024)

2 "Code of Ethics and Professional Conduct," American Institute of Architects (AIA), 2017 Update, https://content.aia.org/sites/default/files/2017-08/2017%20Code%20Update.pdf, P. 1, Rule 1.101. (accessed October 15, 2024)

3 A sample of the unedited standard contract before modification can be found at "Standard Form of Agreement Between Design-Builder and Design Consultant, Document No. 540, 2010," Design-Build Institute of America (DBIA), https://store.dbia.org/wp-content/uploads/2019/08/DBIA-Contracts-540-Sample.pdf, P. 6, § 2.2.1. (accessed October 15, 2024)

4 "AIA Document B101 - 2017, Standard Form of Agreement Between Owner and Architect," American Institute of Architects (AIA), https://shop.aiacontracts.com/contract-documents/25141-owner-architect-agreement, § 2.2. (accessed October 15, 2024)

5 Model Utah Jury Instructions, Second Edition (MUJI 2d), CV501, https://legacy.utcourts.gov/muji/inc-inst.asp?site=popup&inst=741&cat=1#741 (accessed October 15, 2024)

Hangin' with the other raptors.

Part IV

Career

What is the nature of a career in architecture? What are the ins and outs? After studying architecture, would you or could you consider anything other than being a licensed architect? *Part IV* asks questions such as these, considering the career path of a graduate of an accredited professional degree program in architecture. It also links the reader to outside perspectives on the culture of architectural practice.

10

Core Responsibilities

If an architecture student continues on her present career trajectory, her most likely destination will be a profession as a licensed architect. An architect's responsibilities may seem daunting at first; the job might even seem impossible. As an attorney experienced in construction law once told me, if an architect is ever asked to defend his work as an architect in a courtroom, the natural inclination of those deciding the case will be to expect far more of her than could reasonably be expected of a mere mortal.

The instinctive reaction of judge and jury to anything going wrong with an architect's design would probably begin with these words, "The architect should have known." The architect should have been sufficiently trained, informed, and prudent to have crafted designs that didn't have such problems.

Yes, architects often face the perception that there should be no limits to what she is expected to know—that she be omniscient. If an unfortunate event occurs long after a building is occupied, observers unfamiliar with design and construction might apply 20:20 hindsight, insisting that the architect should not only have been omniscient, but even prescient, anticipating future events and crafting her designs to account for every eventuality the future might bring.

Over time, most architects adapt to society's superficial expectations of perfection. At most, our license represents competence to practice independently. We strive for reasonable competence as discussed in ***Chapter 9***, and that standard, *not* the performance of the very best, most conscientious architect that can be imagined, is what we know we will be held to in our judicial system, which seeks to consider fairly what an architect is capable of.

Ask yourself
In practice, do you believe there is a gap between expectations you and others have and your actual capabilities?
During your career, how do you expect to reconcile any gap that exists between expectations and reality?
During your architectural career, what do you expect will be your core responsibility?

What is this core responsibility an architect fulfills? The following list of duties, each presented with associated tasks, may be helpful in considering just what it is an architect does.

Planning *the work*

- Working with clients to define project scope
- Defining and organizing the scope of services
- Developing project schedules
- Allocating staff to design and produce a project
- Analyzing and obtaining entitlements
- Responding to client and consultant requirements
- Documenting design decisions
- Reviewing constructability

Forever Practice: The Architect at Work, First Edition. Jim Nielson, FAIA.
© 2025 John Wiley & Sons, Inc. Published 2025 by John Wiley & Sons, Inc.

Communicating *with stakeholders*

- Negotiating owner-architect agreements
- Making design presentations
- Developing the rationale for code compliance and design decisions
- Reviewing code and design rationale with the Authority Having Jurisdiction (AHJ) and finalizing the project narrative
- Responding to AHJ input during plan review
- Obtaining final approval
- Responding to consultant requirements
- Preparing construction drawings, specifications, and procurement documents
- Responding to bidder inquiries
- Interacting with the contractor effectively throughout construction

Designing *a facility (and developing the design process to get there)*

- Developing unique and custom approaches to owner requirements
- Turning technical challenges into creative opportunities
- Distilling and organizing architectural priorities to meet the owner's needs
- Synthesizing these priorities, together with ongoing input from the client, official requirements from the AHJ, and technical demands of consultant-designed systems to frame the project's guiding story, image, taxis, and parti
- Developing a framework for aggregating the visual and functional aspects of the project, at every scale and at every location, so that architectural choices will not only feel, but also be, consistent, contextual, and inevitable throughout

Building—*working with the contractor to turn your designs into reality*

- Focusing on constructability in design and documentation work
- Reviewing recommended delivery methods to meet owner priorities
- Facilitating the work of selecting effective and experienced contractors, including responding actively to bidder inquiries, requests for substitutions, unsolicited bidder change recommendations, and final bidder/ proposer submittals
- Partnering with the owner and contractor during construction to ensure smooth project delivery
- Working with the owner and contractor to respond effectively to owner-requested scope changes, unexpected or changed conditions, construction defects, market changes, and requests for design team information
- Providing proactive assistance to the owner and contractor to ensure efficient and effective project closeout and owner occupancy

Building, *for real (getting your hands dirty)*

Traditionally, architects were known as master builders. They were called this because they led the team of craftsmen that actually built something. They were masters that knew how to cut and lay stone on stone. An architect that truly wants to reclaim the role of master builder may expand her practice to include being a real builder. She does this by:

- Becoming an architect-developer, which includes developing pro formas, purchasing properties, securing entitlements, attracting investors, obtaining financing, designing and documenting construction to be done, hiring a contractor, and overseeing the entire process
- Considering architect-led Design-Build (D-B) work
- Possibly obtaining a contractor's license and doing both design and construction in-house

***Sustaining** the community and the environment*

- Advocating for energy- and resource-conservation-minded public policies
- Researching strategies to make the buildings the architect designs more resilient
- Designing buildings to adapt to change
- Setting persistence over generations as a goal for buildings the architect designs
- Modeling and measuring project energy use intensity and striving for continuous improvements in performance
- Designing facilities that beat the energy code consistently, by a large margin
- Striving to design sustainable, resilient, and persistent facilities for no, or only very minimal, additional cost beyond that of a standard building with the same function that meets aggressive energy targets and applicable code
- Making net-zero facilities a benchmark and aiming for net-positive, all without relying on offsets or encumbering property off-site

***Leading** a planning effort, a project, a firm*

- Building and guiding a marketing team to win a project
- Coordinating the work and priorities of stakeholders
- Conducting collaborative owner/design team meetings
- Overseeing technical work by consultants
- Guiding in-house design and production
- Using the project to develop the abilities of staff and consultants, all without compromising ultimate quality
- Performing reviews of all design-team work products
- Providing feedback to team members to support continuous improvement
- Applying appropriate quality standards in assessing contractor performance and making required outcomes clear
- Taking the lead in AHJ engagement at every step of the process, including entitlement questions, early notification of project (before plan submittal), plan review, permit issuance, inspection issues, certificate of occupancy review, and final inspection of any open issues

Ask yourself
One might consider any one of the six broad duties outlined above to be an architect's core responsibility: Planning, Communicating, Designing, Building, Sustaining, *and* Leading. *One might also have other roles in mind.*
Based on a discussion with others, which of these roles do you think might be at the core of an architect's responsibilities? Do you have any other ideas for focus areas that are most important in an architect's career?

Jack of All Trades

Some have suggested that architects are the last generalists. While architects may specialize in specific building types, an architect's expertise may still be characterized as broad, though in some ways superficial.

Regardless of so-called specialization, architects rely heavily on other professionals to implement and coordinate the many moving parts in a building. These are the consultants whose general efforts the architect directs and coordinates. An effective architect also listens to them. (Remember the comment above about *superficial* knowledge.) An architect may, on occasion, surmise that a consultant is going in the wrong direction, but he may not always have the technical experience and knowledge to be certain. Paying attention to consultant and team member interactions like this builds experience and confidence that will be needed in similar situations an architect will encounter on future projects.

64 | *10 Core Responsibilities*

And it is always possible that consultant observations, though inscrutable to a reasonably competent architect, are right on target. For example, after taking measurements to document occupant complaints, an acoustical consultant made a statement so opaque that he was mocked for it by some that did not understand acoustics. The following paraphrases what the acoustical engineer said:

The reason occupants are hearing their neighbors excessively is that it is too quiet.

Ask yourself
Considering the acoustical engineer's comment, what he might have meant, and how could it have been misconstrued?

Additional Resources

The Architect's Handbook of Professional Practice
> Chapter 3   Career Development

ProPEL, ACSA Professional Practice Education Library (Videos for Classroom Use)
> *https://propel.yuja.com*
> Professionalism Unit | Lesson 2 Who is the Architect?

Author's Note

I don't know

I took a recent graduate with me for our first meeting with a new client. Having completed a similar project successfully for one of the client's competitors, I was the reason we had gotten the job. But I had practice management priorities, including ongoing marketing, so our very capable addition to the firm was going to get the chance to run it. "I've never done a project like this," she offered right at the beginning of our meeting with the client. As the meeting continued, and during our site walk with the owner, she added a few more similar comments portraying her unfamiliarity with the project type. Driving back to the office afterwards, I suggested she adopt an air of quiet competence rather than signaling her lack of preparation audibly and directly, thereby giving the client doubts about her ability to do the job.

Architects must be quick studies, always learning about new and potential clients, projects, and construction methods. We may not have to understand acoustics, precast wall panels, or the manufacturing lines that will go into a factory, but we must be able to deal with these aspects of the built environment, and others, holistically and intelligently. In communicating with our clients and consultants that actually do understand some of the more esoteric aspects of building systems, we must convey confidence that we get it (generally) and will bring expertise from others to the table, to flesh out our designs. In the end, the client must trust that we will satisfy every owner and regulatory requirement.

This experience with our firm's new employee reminded me of my own sink-or-swim moment when I was asked to manage two big box retail projects in the early months of my career. (These warehouse stores were only about 50,000 SF, but they seemed big to me at the time.) The retail tenant representative, assuming I knew far more than I did, kept dropping terms I didn't know. Usually, I gave no hint of my ignorance at the time; I would go back and look it up or ask someone in the office. For example, when I started out, I had no idea that product display shelves were called *fixtures*; I figured that one out from the context. But here's one that stumped me. Speaking of ways they could have saved money, the tenant representative said, "Of course we could have *tilted* it."

I think those were his exact words. Seems obvious to me now, but I had to ask. What he meant was that instead of the concrete block walls we had planned, the tenant could have proposed *tilt-up* walls!

To some reasonable extent, I suppose, in this business, we may need to fake it until we make it.

11

Architecture and Related Fields

During an architect's career, relationships with contractors, colleagues, and clients might conjure up memories of high school. One of the life skills many of us learn in school is the ability to relate to just about anyone. This skill may come in handy on the job one day:

For instance, a high school boyfriend and girlfriend separately expressed exasperation with the actions of the other to a mutual friend. Neither wanted to break up, but they weren't talking, so each was worried. Their friend listened and considered the situation dispassionately, spoke privately with each of them, and helped them chart a path to reconciliation.

Owner-architect, owner-contractor, and architect-contractor relationships are often similarly troublesome; project structure may put the architect (like the mutual friend of the star-crossed lovers just mentioned) in the role not only of confidant but also of intermediary. Mediating differences on the job among project team members may leave an architect wishing she had studied counseling.

Owner-contractor

In one case, an owner and contractor almost came to blows.

The contractor selected by fixed-fee bidding had a reputation for being both dishonest *and* incompetent. On this project, the owner became so exasperated at one point that he stopped cooperating with the contractor. He wouldn't even answer the contractor's calls. Mostly, though, neither owner nor contractor was even making an attempt to communicate.

By contract, the architect had to work with both the owner and contractor. She had to find a way to keep communication channels open. Trusting the architect's fair-minded efforts, the owner and contractor soon began talking with her individually, trying to get messages through to the other. Each hoped to keep the project going but despaired as to whether a claim could be avoided.

Circumstances such as these are not uncommon in the business. Again, it is at times like these that an architect might think back to her days as a student and feel she would have been better off if she had studied psychology.

The architect in our story may not have known right away what to do with the confidences from the contractor and owner when they wouldn't even talk to each other. But an architect usually holds a position of trust. Earnest efforts on the part of the architect in this case helped the owner see a modicum of goodwill in the contractor's actions. The architect's efforts also helped put the contractor in a position to complete the work respectably. And no one ended up filing a claim.

Forever Practice: The Architect at Work, First Edition. Jim Nielson, FAIA.
© 2025 John Wiley & Sons, Inc. Published 2025 by John Wiley & Sons, Inc.

Developer-architect

Friction on construction projects is often inevitable. Perhaps it is because there is so much money at stake.

An architect worked on a large affordable housing development for a private client. While in the thick of things with this project, the architect left the firm that was working on the project with this developer.

> "We know you're no longer with your former firm, but are you in any way affected by the financial outcomes of the project we worked on together when you were with that firm?"

That was the question the architect that had changed firms heard on the phone one day from the developer of this affordable housing development.

> "No," the architect said. The former client then went on to badmouth this architect's former firm and associates, telling him they (the developers) were preparing to cancel their contract with that former firm.

The next day this same architect had occasion to be visiting the office of his former firm and business partner about a project the two were still working on together. During their conversation, his former partner told him how unreasonably that affordable housing client had been acting and how the architecture firm was preparing to take legal action against the client in order to get paid and to preserve the firm's intellectual property in the event the client bailed.

Our architect's former firm was getting ready for a fight. So was the affordable housing developer.

An affordable housing client and an architecture firm were furious with each other. Both confided in someone that had previously worked on the client's project before leaving the architecture firm. Two feuding parties had confided in an architect that both had worked with. This architect wished he had had experience as a diplomat.

Risk Management by Striking up a Conversation

If an architect possesses or develops the ability to keep communication channels open with the parties involved in a project, regardless of circumstances, that ability may not solve every problem, but it can reduce a firm's exposure. Talking openly about issues and concerns might just be a better risk management strategy than any insurance product an agent might propose.

In addition to the position of trust architects often occupy in an AEC combat zone, sometimes it is our contract itself that can land us in the middle of psychological warfare. In AIA standard agreements, for example, the architect is generally assigned the role of *initial decision maker*. In such a case, should a dispute arise between owner and contractor, the architect is the first party required to render judgment on the merits of the disagreement.

The first thoughts of an architect called upon to do this may be that her contract is with the owner, and the owner has the power to make the architect's life miserable—maybe withhold payment or even terminate the owner-architect agreement. But no, the architect must not consider that. She is required to render impartial judgment, regardless of the fact that she was hired by and is being paid by one of the parties in conflict.

The professional obligation to decide fairly, without consideration of one's own interests, applies not only to formal claims but also to routine evaluations of proposed contractor change orders and pay applications. The requirement for such objectivity is heightened when reviewing D-B change orders and pay applications, where the architect's fees may be part of what the architect reviews. Applying dispassionate professionalism is one of the most demanding and intriguing aspects of a career in architecture. The architect is, by virtue of her profession, expected to be above the fray.

This is a lot to ask of someone that really might rather be designing.

Dispassionate Professionalism and Design-Build

As mentioned, being part of a contractor-led D-B team may heighten the demands on an architect to act professionally. It varies by market and changes from time to time, but contractor-led D-B is frequently the most common form of D-B delivery. In this delivery system, the architect works for the contractor, not the owner. But the architect is still required (by code of ethics and typically also by contract) to be professional. Contract demands may include observing and reporting construction defects. That means reporting on and keeping a list of what the architect's boss does wrong. (Not surprisingly, some bosses have a problem with that.)

Architects may not have the mediation skill needed to thread the needle in such cases, but they have broad enough education and professional backgrounds to realize there's a needle that needs threading.

An architect's training and experience will often serve him well, both in putting together complex projects with systems that only architectural consultants understand *and* in reconciling warring parties.

Ask yourself
As discussed in the foregoing sections, and in light of the delicate roles sometimes expected of architects, what things can an architect do to foster the professionalism that will be required? How can she best respond in these difficult situations?

Design

Design is the most visible and obvious face of architecture, but it is usually not what architects spend the most time doing. Design deserves its own heading, however. Consider the reverence our profession extends to the concept of collaborative design. This special regard may be based on apocryphal sources. Consider the architect's core responsibilities, discussed in ***Chapter 10***, together with the statement below. My definition of design below is drawn from the review of design and its component pieces, as presented in ***Chapter 10***:

> *Designing means developing a framework for aggregating the visual and functional aspects of the project, at every scale and at every location, so that architectural choices will not only feel, but also be, consistent, contextual, and inevitable throughout.*

The consistency and inevitability described above do not become part of a building parti via committee. There must be one voice holding the line on design, enforcing the thought process consistently, and carrying the concept through religiously (with real reverence, mind you), from beginning to end. In my experience teaming on large projects with broadly talented designers from our nation's coasts and places in between, the very best design does not come about by applying a distributed process. Rather, it comes through the continuous and thorough guiding hand, the discipline and tutelage, of one brilliant, talented lead designer. This designer is, first and foremost, an artist. The power of such a designer is rare and difficult to fathom; we might think of her as a poet, a magician, or maybe even a prophet.

This designer-magician works in one of two ways. Functioning individually, she imprints each detail, each assembly, and each project she touches, reinforcing her art at every gesture and each repeat with her unified design vision. Alternatively, she shares design responsibilities with a close-knit staff of designers, but in this interactive mode, she reviews and corrects the work of her subordinates constantly to ensure that the result expresses one unified vision. Either way, design consistency, context, and inevitability all flow from the steady hand of one lead source of inspiration.

Ask yourself
Could you debate the statement in the last paragraph above about the concept of collaborative design? Would collaborating with a colleague in your preparations for such a debate be helpful?

Design vs. Management

Four or five newly anointed junior firm leaders sat around a table and shared dreams for the future of their firm. Voicing their personal priorities as future leaders, all but one said they wanted to become the design leader for the firm. In the coming years, some would ultimately leave the firm, but none of the would-be design principals ever backed down from the quest to head up design. The one that didn't speak about being the firm's design leader encountered no competition in his quest to lead out in project and practice management.

On the subject of design and management in a firm, think back to or have another look at the story in **Chapter 2 Always Looking for Work**, when a senior designer described feeling underpaid and underappreciated in comparison to a senior project manager. Regardless of whatever opinions we may have of which sort of work ought to be considered most valuable, compensation is generally based on which positions are in greater demand. Firms offer higher pay for positions they see as most crucial to firm success.

The AIA College of Fellows application process offers a contraindication. What object, or category, of application does the AIA put in first position among those an applicant might choose when applying for fellowship?

Design, of course.

Practice management and community service come later. At least on paper.

Ask yourself
What is the role of design in the comprehensive practice of architecture? When focusing on design, is it possible to overdo it?
Why do you think the College of Fellows lists design first among objects (categories) for applications?

Allied Careers

After graduating with an accredited architecture degree, being an architect is not your only option. Graduates may end up in related fields, with roles such as:

- Envelope consultant
- Roofing consultant
- Specifications writer
- Architectural hardware specifier
- Product representative
- Land developer/investor
- Developer of self-initiated projects
- Owner/operator of your own building
- Facilities director
- Preconstruction services manager for a general contractor
- Facilities programmer
- Public or corporate architect

Ask yourself
What is a facilities program?
How do you go about programming a building? More on that to come **in Chapter 13 Project Management.**

Care and Feeding

One final note. When thinking about career paths, it's good to be aware that the traditional practice of architecture, along with several allied career tracks (such as being a product representative), involves building relationships with a large pool of prospective clients, many of whom may require a generous amount of care and feeding. Building such relationships can have a marked impact on an architect's lifestyle and on the opportunity for a healthy diet.

Ask yourself
What are the pros and cons of a career as an architect and in the allied career paths listed?
What lessons about career choices do the vignettes shared in this chapter suggest?
What career paths other than those listed in this chapter might you consider?

Additional Resources

The Architect's Handbook of Professional Practice
   3.3   The Career Paths of an Architect

Author's Note

Widely respected, modestly compensated
We've all seen a movie with an architect that lives in a New York penthouse apartment, a lake house, or maybe a cottage on Martha's Vineyard. Since most architects never earn that kind of money, let's assume these celluloid architects inherited a fortune from a rich uncle. We may not be as well-paid as some professions, but there are few careers we can embark on where we will be more highly respected.

And if you hang in there, in the end, the pay's not so bad either.

12

Blog: Architecture Career and Culture

For more about a career as an architect, consider the following excerpts from posts by Evelyn Lee, an architect, software company executive, and National AIA President for 2025. You'll appreciate her insights. Look up the link for each post (in footnotes) to continue your study.

Young Architect Guide: 5 Things I Wish I Knew When I Graduated with My Architecture Degree

Congratulations, new graduates; buckle up and get ready for the ride!
  Remember the road ahead will be pretty bumpy.

1. Build your community
2. Chart your own path
3. Treat your job like your business
4. Build your brand
5. It's a journey, not a destination[1]

The Culture of Architecture Needs an Overhaul, Part I: The Necessity of Cultural Change

Architecture culture makes headlines for all the wrong reasons, and architects are recognizing the need for cultural change at an industry level.
  "Rather than looking back, it is important to take this moment in time to redesign culture as we move forward."[2]

The Culture of Architecture Needs an Overhaul, Part II: Historical Background, Today's Context and Future Steps

The great resignation, the shesession, labor shortages, burnout, and more have made culture conversations much more topical, but they aren't new.
  "The best way forward is to chart a new path and understand that organizational culture within a business is a strategic advantage to attracting and retaining talent."[3]

Ask yourself
What is the shesession *referred to above?*

Forever Practice: The Architect at Work, First Edition. Jim Nielson, FAIA.
© 2025 John Wiley & Sons, Inc. Published 2025 by John Wiley & Sons, Inc.

The Culture of Architecture Needs an Overhaul, Part III: Creating a Values-based Teaching and Learning Culture

We can't settle for complaining about the bad parts of our culture. We need to be intentional about how culture is developed in our firms.

"Organizational culture is a set of norms and values widely shared and strongly held throughout the organization."[4]

Additional Resources

The Architect's Handbook of Professional Practice

2.1 Diversity and Practice Management

3.2 Intern Development

3.5 Participating in Professional Organizations (Blue box text: Backgrounder, "Intern Development Program Coordinator Program," Pp. 111, 112)

5.4 Firm Growth and Development: How to Build a Creative Culture

Chapter 8 Human Resources

14.3 Research and Practice

Author's Note

Culture—a good thing?

The following are a few of many indicators of short-sighted attitudes and cultural biases among some of today's architects (and architecture firms) in need of changing.

Now.

- No matter whether I'm being paid to do it or not, it's the right thing to do
- I'm going to keep working on this until I solve it. I'll work all night if necessary!
- You can't represent the firm on a jobsite; you haven't paid your dues yet
- If we draw the building the way the owner wants and bids come in high, it's our fault
- Making more than a five to ten percent profit isn't fair to the owner
- If we make a mistake, we should immediately offer to pay the owner's cost to fix it
- From day one, do all of your drawing on the computer
- Don't show the client sketches or anything preliminary. Only show finished renderings.
- Going down a career path that doesn't involve getting licensed is a waste of one's education
- Only modern (or traditional, or craftsman, or art deco, or prairie) style design is acceptable here
- We shouldn't wait for our contract. The owner has a schedule to meet
- We should get fee bids from prospective consultants for every project
- We don't have the bandwidth to do accrual accounting. Let's stick with cash
- No price is too high for a net-zero building
- Even if it costs more, we should recommend renovating the existing building rather than building a new one (or the reverse: build new rather than renovating, regardless of the cost!)
- We don't go to their offices; the consultants work for us and must come to us
- The owner has no architectural or artistic training and therefore has no business dictating design decisions

Go ahead. Add to the list!

Notes

1 *https://architizer.com/blog/inspiration/stories/advice-for-recent-architecture-graduates/* (accessed October 10, 2024)
2 https://architizer.com/blog/inspiration/industry/the-culture-of-architecture-needs-an-overhaul-part-1/ (accessed October 10, 2024)
3 https://architizer.com/blog/inspiration/industry/the-culture-of-architecture-needs-an-overhaul-part-ii/ (accessed October 10, 2024)
4 https://architizer.com/blog/inspiration/industry/the-culture-of-architecture-needs-an-overhaul-part-iii/ (accessed October 10, 2024)

Keep hammering?

Part V

Project

Part V includes a single extended chapter about project management, a foundational and critical ingredient of a successful architecture firm. This chapter may warrant double the attention and study time of any other in the book. In addition to running projects, project managers manage marketing and pre-design work. Project managers have a host of architectural, organizational, financial, and administrative responsibilities, including preparing project plans and running their projects in accordance with those plans. ***Part V*** sheds light on project management approaches and includes reference to appendices that contain additional information and examples of useful tools for further study.

13

Project Management

As discussed in ***Part IV Career***, a practitioner's success might depend on more than architectural education and experience. To flourish in the business, the architect might also need to draw on education or experience in counseling, psychology, diplomacy, or maybe even poetry. Although all these pursuits could come in handy, if an architect gravitates toward the area in greatest demand within the profession, she just might find herself thinking she should have pursued an MBA. In practice, architects rarely bring in outside management specialists to run projects (or firms). Leading an architectural project requires an understanding, not just of the management and financial aspects of a project, but also of what it takes to oversee the preparation of work products that define and communicate architectural design properly.

Although we sometimes encounter a successful architectural project manager that is not a licensed professional, this circumstance is rather rare. The dual role of managing the business of an architectural project—while at the same time shepherding timeless design elements through the process unscathed—tends to favor experienced, licensed architects that also possess or develop skills as project managers.

Other chapters of this text, together with most of an architect's professional education, prepare the project manager to succeed in advocating for and sustaining the passion that underpins a project's design and guiding philosophy. However, managing the business side of architectural projects well may be the factor that ultimately determines whether a firm and its projects succeed or fail.

Project management begins with communication.

Communication is one of the key parts of the architect's job description described in ***Chapter 10 Core Responsibilities***. Alongside the project manager's many other duties, communication is where this chapter starts.

Communication

Communication about a project's design must first be compelling. If an architect cannot explain why something is designed the way it is, she will have a difficult time convincing the client or the contractor that it matters. Whether the design originated from the project manager or came from a design colleague, there must be a reason for it. The project manager must absolutely be capable of articulating that reason.

Drilling down from advocating for a design approach to the nuts and bolts of running a project, a competent project manager must also ensure that written communication addresses key activities and decisions, including a record of who made the call and who, as Lin-Manuel Miranda put it, *was in the room when it happened*. This complete, concise documentation about project decisions and happenings must become part of the written record. If something important is said verbally, in a meeting or conversation, the project manager *must* follow it up with published meeting notes or a confirming email. The manager always encourages others that participated in such a discussion to respond if their own records or recollections differ from what the project manager has recorded.

Forever Practice: The Architect at Work, First Edition. Jim Nielson, FAIA.
© 2025 John Wiley & Sons, Inc. Published 2025 by John Wiley & Sons, Inc.

78 | *13 Project Management*

Participants may not respond, but their choice not to correct the record lends credence to the written document that has thus been circulated for comment.

Why is written documentation critical? First, to keep things on track you will need to refer to the growing written record throughout the course of a project. Second, and often more significant, is the fact that buried in every project, and in many communications, is the risk of a claim. A party to a project, believing he has been damaged by another party's actions (or lack thereof), may demand a remedy. Asserting damages may begin with a contentious conversation and result in a demand letter. Such a dispute may lead to mediation, arbitration, or a lawsuit. Any or all of these actions, including settlement discussions along the way, may follow—either clustered together or in sequence.

Those considering themselves sufficiently wronged to file a claim might include the project owner, the contractor, one of the architect's consultants, or even a member of the public. Depending on the nature of the claim and the course taken, attorneys and subject experts may spend hundreds, even thousands, of hours building a case, either to defend or seek damages from the architect. Such efforts might cost the parties (and perhaps their insurance companies) tens or even hundreds of thousands of dollars.

How will the expensive attorneys and experts working on the case spend much of their time? They will pore over written records pertaining to the allegations of errors, omissions, or even fraudulent acts of the architect and others against whom a claim is lodged.

For firsthand accounts about the architect's actions, they will look to documents the project manager and others took care to create during the course of the project. A guiding principle and critical takeaway for project managers is this: write things down; write the important things down—the decisions made, record who made the decisions, and who provided input. For meetings or conversations where more than one party is present, besides recording matters discussed, assignments, decisions, and action items, make it clear who was in charge of things, who was present, and who was not. For emails, ensure that identification of parties on distribution lists extends beyond arcane email addresses. (What were the names of those addressed in an email? What was their role or position on the project team?)

When preparing key documentation as described here, assume the person digging through these records to defend you and your firm knows nothing about the project. That means the project name and date goes on everything. And as you create reports, records, and emails—anything in writing—assume that every one of the things you write will be used in court—or if not in court, in settlements or other actions precedent to adjudication.

No pressure!

Every communication, written or otherwise, must be professional. ***Never*** say or write anything like this:

> "He's just a complainer; we're not even going to think about what he is suggesting."

Or

> "What the engineer is suggesting is too expensive. We are going to find a way around it."

Also, don't allow emotion to steer your recordkeeping efforts: no name-calling; no snide remarks.

Ask yourself
In addition to being helpful in a claim or lawsuit, in what other ways can a thorough written record be helpful? What sorts of things would be important to note in documentation such as:

- Follow-up on preliminary communications with a code official
- Records of owner decisions in an earlier phase
- Requests and instructions to consultants

Entitlements

It's not just the written documents the project manager creates that make a big difference. It's also the documents written and adopted by public officials, including laws, rules, master plans, and zoning ordinances. For example, when exploring options for a given parcel, the project manager must take the time to read and understand the applicable zoning ordinance, *including* all the ordinances and documents incorporated by reference. The community planning staff may read these documents differently than an outsider, so a meeting with the planners to weigh the legalese you have made your way through is often needed. The goal is to gain a clear understanding of what *is* permitted. This understanding is a crucial first step if the project team then wants to think about seeking changes.

From written zoning ordinances, the project manager would also do well to take a step back to the community master plan, including not just the map, but also the associated narrative. If she comes to understand these documents well enough to know their intentions clearly, she will often be able to uncover opportunities to accomplish what the project team hopes to do with a piece of property. This matters because, before beginning the lengthy process of communicating proposed changes for approval, the team needs to acknowledge the intentions planners and public servants went to great lengths to communicate. Generally, the re-zoning petitions most likely to succeed (at least for mere mortals that may not be sports team owners, or influential community benefactors) are those in which the re-zone has a connection to planning concepts already staked out in the community master plan.

The project manager's role in the entitlement process is to find opportunities within public documents, develop a strategy to make use of those opportunities, work with community planners, and support the effort of incorporating necessary changes through to planning commission and city council approval. The project manager also often becomes the voice of the firm in making presentations before these approving bodies.

This is not the time for design or construction documents. The project manager must oversee a process that will result in deliverables that meet but do not exceed community planning department requirements. Providing more information than public employees and officials require may cause just as many or more problems than would providing too little.

Ask yourself
What are entitlements and why do they matter?
How do you think it could cause problems to provide more information in a public hearing than is required?

Facilities Program

A project begins with a facilities program and/or owner's statement of requirements. These documents may be made up of a brief list of spaces and square footage needs. A statement of owner requirements or program might also be an extended document containing detailed technical requirements, adjacency needs of different spaces, initial FF&E listings/potential configurations, preliminary code analysis, initial cost estimates, and even suggested starting points for architectural and engineering design. For a midsize building, such a document could easily be hundreds of pages long. See ***Appendix A The Facilities Program*** for a mock-up of what goes into a detailed facilities program that is used to guide the architect's efforts.

In AIA contracts, preparing a program is not included as part of the architect's standard scope of services. The owner is the one responsible for providing a facilities program. Owners often task the architect with creating and drafting a program as an additional service. For complex programming work, such as is often required by public entities, a separate solicitation may be conducted for facilities programming. This occurs several months before the agency puts out a solicitation for design work.

80 | *13 Project Management*

Sometimes a public entity retains an option to hire the programming firm directly for the subsequent design commission. For open design solicitations after the programming work is complete, the facilities program becomes a reference document for submitters to use in responding to the solicitation. Treat a facilities program as a road map communicating an entity's needs; it gives the architect for the building detailed requirements for what they are to design. Because it provides clear scope definition, it may also be used as an exhibit to the architect's contract.

Ask yourself
Find and review documents related to one or more facilities programs.
This document is not intended to teach future architects how to develop expertise in facilities programming, but if you were a project manager tasked with leading a team in putting such a program together, how do you imagine you would go about leading a team in preparing such a document?

Project

Entitlements and facilities programming are important and challenging endeavors a project manager may lead. These may be standalone efforts, or they may amount to predesign efforts, followed by work on a project following the scope of services included in standard AIA contract documents.

If one compares an architecture office to a business that fabricates flash memory chips, guides wilderness tours, or makes and sells shoes, the architecture firm is unique in that even a small architectural office typically engages in scores of separate and distinct business activities (projects), each of which is unique and is usually managed and accounted for separately. When an organization is built on separate, individual projects, as architecture firms tend to be, it is as if each project were its own company and the firm were a conglomerate, overseeing subsidiaries, or multiple quasi-independent businesses.

A multinational conglomerate such as 3M may be made up of many companies, some of which are quite different. (For example, manufacturing adhesive tape surely presents different management and production challenges than making personal protective equipment.) Nevertheless, while this $35 billion company might be composed of 50 or even 100 separate enterprises, a mid-sized architecture firm (with just $15 million in annual billings) could easily do work on that many separate projects in a given year.

In an architecture firm, each project is separate. They are generally tallied together in summary financial statements, but in the end, each project stands alone. It earns or loses money independently of the rest of the firm.

It is the project manager's job to plan and administer expenses and revenues for a project over its lifespan. It is her job to track actual expenses incurred and revenues earned. It is also her job to make plans to correct things if the project goes off the rails. (Or *when* the project goes off the rails!)

It is the project manager's responsibility to schedule the work, secure sufficient staff resources, assign tasks to staff members, and track work completed. The project manager adjusts and reallocates staff assignments in response to schedule status, staff progress, and scope revisions.

It is the project manager's duty to oversee quality assurance and quality control for each project and back-check the results.

It is the project manager's role to work with authorities having jurisdiction to plan for and obtain permits.

It is also often the project manager's role to negotiate contracts—with input from insurers, attorneys, and firm principals as needed. She manages client expectations and reports regularly to firm ownership.

The project manager customizes project management tools and approaches for each project to suit delivery method, project scope, and firm management priorities.

To this end, regular techniques and processes evolve, under the direction of experienced project managers, to support changing approaches to architectural practice in each individual project and in the firm as a whole.

A project manager coordinates the work of project consultants or oversees the coordination work by members of her team.

A project manager holds regular team and consultant meetings to receive updates, make adjustments, communicate progress, review revised requirements, and assess the impact of changing project parameters. She directs action in response to this input.

A project manager documents all project communication and circulates documentation to team members.

A project manager serves as the leader of the project team, ensuring success.

Ask yourself
Based on your research and work experience, how does the project manager accomplish all these things?

Project Management Plan

Part of the answer is the project management plan. Such a plan often begins with financial calculations to ensure that a proposed fee and scope of work are in balance. A spreadsheet may simplify and standardize these calculations so different projects may be compared. *Tables 13.1–13.3*, combined, show a possible way to set up a project budget, based on rule-of-thumb calculations with data that may be preliminary. A spreadsheet can calculate other values if desired. (Note that salary numbers mocked up in these tables are placeholders and are likely much different from compensation realities in any practice. These numbers must be updated to reflect the firm's actual overhead and pay rates.) See also ***Appendix B The Project Plan*** for a Project Plan overview, including illustrative charts and tables for visualization and presentation internally.

Project Accounting

A worksheet for putting together and reviewing project budgets, schedules, and staffing, begins with summary financial information. *Table 13.1 Project Accounting* shows an example. This table begins with a simple calculation of the project fee, then deducts direct and indirect expenses. The bottom-line purpose of this tool is to estimate available *Salary Dollars* for a given *Fee*. Information from *Table 13.1* feeds into *Table 13.2 Top-down Staffing Budget* and is also compared with summary information from *Table 13.3 Bottom-up Level-of-effort Budget*.

In these worksheets, cells requiring direct input of figures negotiated, anticipated, or derived for this case by the project manager are highlighted in gray. Data entered in these tables include fee, expenses, overhead, and profit. Available *Salary Dollars* are calculated and shown on line 43 of the table. These numbers make it possible to estimate the total direct salary funds supported by the fee (expected or negotiated).

The example shown in this chapter shows a firm's overhead rate as 175% (or $1.75 in overhead for every dollar of direct salary). If a firm's overhead rate has not been calculated, this value is a reasonable starting point for a mid-sized or larger firm). The example also includes a consulting architect. For projects without a consulting architect, that part of the table (line 17) is left blank. It is worth noting that the ratio of Salary Dollars to Fee will be larger for a project without a consulting architect doing part of the work; however, the architect of record would have to provide its own services in such a case plus the work of the consulting architect. Without the consulting architect on board, the additional *Salary Dollars* available and added salary expense might cancel each other out.

82 | *13 Project Management*

Table 13.1 **Project Acounting**—This table shows a method of calculating available salary dollars, based on fee, expenses, profit, and overhead, using standard accounting practices.

Table 13.1 Project Budget Worksheet
Project Accounting

Line#				
1	Project Name:		Minor League	
2	Project Number:		2025.25.173	
3	Principal in Charge:		Spar Tslover FAIA	
4	Project Manager:		Evert Yirin AIA	
5	Date Created/Updated:		Oct 20, 2025	
6	Construction Budget:		$23,000,000	
7	Fee (Fee % X Construction Budget):		$1,713,500	
8	Fee Percentage:			7.45%
				% of Construction Budget
	Direct Costs:			
	Direct Costs: Other Than Consultants			
9	Travel		$3,500	
10	Printing		$1,500	
11	Renderings		$12,500	
12	Postage		$6,300	
13	Meals & Entertainment		$2,000	
14	Miscellaneous		$1,000	
15	Total Other Direct Costs		$26,800	
16				1.77%
	Consultants:			*% of Basic Svcs Fee*
	Consulting Architect	Consultant Name:	Negotiated Fee	
17	Consulting Architect:	Stadium Architect	$224,750	
18				14.83%
	Consulting Engineers: Basic Services			*% of Basic Svcs Fee*
19	Structural Engineer:	Structural	$191,223	
20	Mechanical Engineer:	Mechanical	$180,145	
21	Electrical Engineer:	Electrical	$156,728	
22	TOTAL Consultant Fees: Basic Services		$528,096	(Target ≤35%)
23				34.86%
				% of Basic Svcx Fee
24	**Basic Services Fee: not incl Suppl Svcs**		$1,515,000	
25				88.42%
	Other Consultants: Supplemental Services			*% of Total Fee*
26	Civil Engineer:	Civil	$38,000	
27	Landscape Architect:	Landscape	$18,250	
28	Cost Estimator:	Cost	$22,500	
29	Other (list): Food Services	Food	$24,500	
30	Other (list): Broadcast/Sound	Broadcast	$45,000	
31	Other (list): Playing Field	Pitch	$27,000	
32	Other (list): Code Consultant	Code	$10,750	
33	Other (list): Interior Design	Interior	$12,500	
34	TOTAL Consultant Fees: Supplemental Services		$198,500	
35				11.58%
				% of Total Fee
36	**Total Direct Costs:**		$978,146	
37	**Net Operating Revenue (Fee Less Direct Costs):**		$735,354	
38	***Profit: (Applied to Total Fee):***		*$171,350*	
39				10.0%
	Personnel Budget			*% of Total Fee*
40	**(Net Operating Revenue Less Profit):**		$564,004	
41	***Overhead (Applied to Personnel Budget):***		*$358,912*	
42				175.0%
	Salary Dollars			*% of Total Fee*
43	**(Personnel Budget Less Overhead):**		$205,092	

Top-down Staffing Budget

Table 13.2 Top-down Staffing Budget is the second part of an effective budget worksheet. This table drills down to provide estimates of full-time employee (FTE) staffing levels the fee will support over the course of the project. The project manager must first estimate which portions of the work (or at least how much of it overall) will be done by staff at which pay rates and how that will change from phase to phase. The example in this table includes an estimate of this changing mix of personnel by phase.[1] Combining pay rates with the estimate of who does what yields weighted average pay rates for each phase. These weighted averages are calculated from data entered or calculated to this point.

The importance of calculating aggregated and weighted average salaries by phase is demonstrated in *Table 13.2*. For example, the weighted average hourly pay rate during the construction documents phase is lower than it is during earlier phases of the project. This lower average is due to the fact that during the construction documents phase, production staff generally do a greater portion of the total work done than in earlier phases.

The project manager must enter the percentage of the total fee assigned to each phase of the work by contract (or as planned). She also enters the expected start date for the work and the planned duration of each phase (in weeks). Finally, she links to the *Salary Dollars* amount from the bottom of *Table 13.1* or enters that value manually.

The table calculates the direct salary dollars, hours, and workdays, and average FTE staffing level that the fee supports and may therefore be budgeted for each phase. The FTE numbers take into account both the percentage of total fee for each phase and the duration of each of those same phases. (See **Appendix C The Project Schedule** for more information about project schedules.)

Based on all the factors considered to this point, Line 17 of *Table 13.2* shows the total hours budgeted for the work overall. This number answers the key question, "Considering our fee, expenses, overhead, and profit target, together with the people we propose to assign to the effort (and when), how many hours of work by our in-house team will this fee support?"

To determine if the fee and the level-of-effort (number of billable hours) it will support are adequate, the project manager compares line 17 from *Table 13.2 Top-down Staffing Budget* to the number of hours the project manager expects the work will take. *Table 13.3 Bottom-up Level-of-effort Budget* provides a template for estimating that overall level-of-effort.

Bottom-up Level-of-effort Budget

As a cross check, on a parallel path, the project manager studies the scope of work required for the project and comes up with a list of the tasks that will make up the required scope. An itemized list showing and reckoning hours for each task and sheet individually may be helpful. The project manager estimates the level-of-effort (or hours needed) for each task, including an estimate for what it will take to produce all drawings and specifications (or portions thereof) for which the Architect of Record is responsible. *Table 13.3* shows an example of a summary task list, which adds up the hours for the scope categories listed.

Estimates used here for the level-of-effort, or hours needed, to complete each task are informed by the project manager's experience, by input of other managers and firm leaders, and by any firm standards, if available. For example, hours required to finish a sheet from start to finish, including associated design, vary based on the type and size of the sheet and on firm documentation standards. Some firms establish overall average timeframes and apply these averages to a simple sheet list. Averages adopted by architecture firms for this planning purpose may vary from as low as 24 hours each for 24 × 36-inch sheets to an average of over 100 hours for very large sheets.

After reviewing this bottom-up level-of-effort listing carefully, the project manager compares the *Total Hours Needed* (shown on line 23 on that sheet) with the *Total Hours Budgeted* (on *Table 13.2 Top-down Staffing Budget*, line 17). In this example, the bottom-line number in the scope/level-of-effort table is 2,796 hours, or just less than one and a half person-years. Since this tally of *Total Hours Needed* estimated is lower than the *Total Hours*

13 Project Management

Table 13.2 Top-down Staffing Budget considers the mix of personnel at different phases, percentage of work by phase, project schedule, and *Salary Dollars* from **Table 13.1** to calculate FTE by phase and *Total Hours Budgeted*.

Table 13.2 Project Budget Worksheet
Top-down Staffing Budget
Weighted Average Pay Rate by Phase

Customize weighted average for each project, considering the mix of personnel that will complete the work of each phase:

Line#	Compensation Category	Avg Pay	Predesign	Schematic Design	Design Development	Construction Documents	Construction Administration
1	Senior Management	$90.00	65%	55%	40%	20%	10%
2	Project Management	$75.00	20%	25%	30%	25%	25%
3	Production	$65.00	10%	15%	25%	45%	60%
4	Support (Clerical)	$50.00	5%	5%	5%	10%	5%
5	Total		100%	100%	100%	100%	100%
6	Weighted Average Pay Rate by Phase:		$82.50	$80.50	$77.25	$71.00	$69.25

Percentage of Work by Phase

Insert percentage of contract sum payable for each phase, totaling 100%

7	Percentage per phase		3%	11%	21%	45%	20%

Design and Construction Administration Schedule by Phase
Enter Start date and number of weeks for each phase

8	Start Date	10/20/25					
9	Duration of Phase (Weeks)		2	4	6	12	56
10	Scheduled Phase Start Date		10/20/25	11/3/25	12/1/25	1/12/26	4/6/26
11	Scheduled Phase Finish Date		11/3/25	12/1/25	1/12/26	4/6/26	5/3/27

Salary Dollars

This value may be linked to or entered from line 42 of **Table 13.1 Project Accounting**

12	$205,092						

Personnel Budget by Phase

These fields should be set up to calculate automatically

13	Salary Dollars Budgeted by Phase		$6,153	$22,560	$43,069	$92,291	$41,018
14	Hours Budgeted by Phase		74.6	280.2	557.5	1,299.9	592.3
15	Workdays Budgeted by Phase		9.3	35.0	69.7	162.5	74.0
16	Constant Staffing Level (FTE) by Phase		0.9	1.8	2.3	2.7	0.3

17	**Total Hours Budgeted**	**2,805**

Table 13.3 **Bottom-up Level-of-effort Budget** tallies the tasks and level-of-effort required to do the project. The project manager then compares this estimate to the Total Hours Budgeted from *Table 13.2.*

Table 13.3 Project Budget Worksheet
Bottom-up Level-of-effort Budget

Line#	Task/Deliverable	(List)	(Qty)		(Task)		(hrs/ea)				Hours
1	**Site Drawings**										**100**
	Derive from Sheet List or Cartoon Set										
2	**Architectural Drawings**										**1,250**
	Derive from Sheet List or Cartoon Set										
3	**Specifications**										**216**
4	Systems Descriptions (SD)									24	
5	Outline Specifications (DD)									60	
6	Full Specifications & Proj. Manual (CD)									108	
7	Revise/Reissue Specs. by Addendum									24	
8	**Meetings/Client Care**										**160**
9	Design Meetings		24	mtgs	@	2	hrs./=	48			
10	Consultant Meetings		24	mtgs	@	4	hrs./=	96			
11	Other Meetings		8	mtgs	@	2	hrs./=	16			
12	**Consultant Coordination**		12	consultants	@	20	hrs./=	----			**240**
13	**Contractor Bid Inquiries**		30	questions	@	2	hrs./=	----			**60**
14	**Construction Administration**										**610**
15	Site Visits		56	mtgs	@	2	hrs./=	112			
16	Reports		56	reports	@	2	hrs./=	112			
17	Submittals		75	subm.	@	2	hrs./=	150			
18	RFIs		200	RFIs	@	0.5	hrs./=	100			
19	ASIs		8	ASIs	@	12	hrs./=	96			
20	Change Orders		2	CORs	@	20	hrs./=	40			
21	**Project Management**		80	wks	@	2	hrs./=	----			**160**
22	**Other** _____			_____	@		hrs./=	----			**-**
23	**Total Hours Needed**										**2,796**

Budgeted (2,805 hours, as shown on *Table 13.2* and relying on information from *Table 13.1* as well), the project manager incorporates the budget, schedule, and staffing management provisions of these tables into the project plan for approval and then manages the project accordingly.

See ***Part X Appendices*** for more descriptions and examples of project management products and tools, a few of which have already been mentioned or discussed. These tools and examples include:

- ***Appendix A The Facilities Program***, as mentioned in this chapter's earlier discussion of facilities programming
- ***Appendix B The Project Plan***, as discussed in the introduction to the Project Management Plan

- ***Appendix C The Project Schedule*** as already mentioned briefly. This appendix includes information about project schedules, their preparation and function, together with three examples of different ways to prepare and present project schedules.
- ***Appendix D Breaking Down the Fee, Scope, and Schedule*** divides up a scope of services into logical tasks, including the anticipated level of effort, associated fee, and schedule for each of these tasks. When the project manager develops and presents a proposal in this format, and the owner asks to reduce the fee (as most owners do), the script recommended to the architect in beginning fee negotiations goes something like this, "As you can see, we've figured out how much work we will need to do on each of these tasks needed to meet your requirements. From that careful assessment, we know what the level of effort and fee is for our work on each of the tasks you've asked for. Which tasks would you like us to remove from the project in order to bring down the fee?"

    It should then be clear to the owner that if she doesn't want to remove any scope of services from the project, the architect will not be able to cut anything out of his fee. If (as is usually the case) the owner continues to want everything she asked for initially, this worksheet will likely help her see the direct connection between scope and fee. In many cases, an owner will then agree to the fee as proposed.

    The table in this appendix is mocked up showing predesign work on a historic preservation project, including selective interior demolition, with options for interior buildout. Basic architectural services are presented as standard percentages, based on the owner's budget. Scoping and predesign services that come first in the proposal are each presented with their scope, tasks, fees, and schedules connected as described above. This framework may be modified to reflect tasks, level-of-effort, and fee for a project or part of a project, of any type or complexity.
- ***Appendix E Dividing the Work***, a simple, yet detailed quantitative tool that can be used when a project has a design or other consulting architect to determine who does what. This table is divided into categories based on the level of detail supplied in past NCARB practice analyses and experience programs.[2]

    The worksheet includes more than 100 tasks, weighted by level of effort, broken down and categorized into the major phases of work that make up the comprehensive practice of architecture. If one is able to present a proposal for dividing the work up and splitting the fee with this level of detail, a negotiating partner will have difficulty countering. "No, but I think our firm deserves more fee," he might say. As with ***Appendix D***, one may counter, OK, which tasks could we talk about you doing more of? Applying this objective approach may result in favorable teaming negotiations, even when dealing with a team member that is larger and more sophisticated than the one making the proposal.

In reviewing the project management tools in this chapter and the appendices, remember that these tools are also often used in preparing marketing materials and proposals. See ***Part 6 Firm***.

Ask yourself
Why project plans? If I need to build a project plan, how do I go about it?

Additional Resources

The Architect's Handbook of Professional Practice
    Chapter 10   Design Project Management

ProPEL, ACSA Professional Practice Education Library (Videos for Instructor Use)
        https://propel.yuja.com
        Negotiation Unit | Lessons 1-6

Author's Note

Project Management Professional (PMP)

I know people and have worked with people that have gotten their PMP certification. It's a great (but not inexpensive) way to learn the nuts and bolts of running projects of any kind. Understanding project planning, resource allocation, scheduling, and tracking is tremendously valuable, and it may help in getting a job as a project manager, but it isn't a guarantee that you'll keep that job. The nuts and bolts are just the beginning. Managing an architectural project effectively requires working with highly educated, talented individuals, all of whom may believe they are capable of running things. As a project manager, you must cajole accomplished (and often wealthy) project team members into following your lead. A PMP certificate will never confer the soft skills required to work effectively with a team of highly skilled professionals and business people or help them want to work with you. It also may not give an architectural project manager the tools for dealing with a client that is always insisting that she knows more than you do about designing buildings or is set on getting the architect do more than the scope agreed to by contract—all without added fees.

These so-called *soft* skills are immensely valuable and worth acquiring, whether through experience, education, or certifications. To help in acquiring all of the skills needed to be a successful project manager, pay close attention to available professional development offerings. One organization, for example, offers a project management boot camp that is invaluable, not only for project managers, administrative employees, and firm leaders, but also for just about anyone in a position of responsibility in a firm. If you want to be involved in crafting successful projects, you have to understand project management.

Notes

1 A schedule of fictional and seemingly egalitarian average pay rates, by employment category, is mocked up in the top-down staffing budget (*Table 13.2*) to simplify understanding. However, such information is usually hidden or derived, in some protected fashion, from a separate, secure file. As noted, the pay ranges shown in the table are not meant to represent compensation levels for any architecture firm. Authorized personnel must supply the firm's actual compensation information and must determine to what extent and how best to disclose that information to enable effective project management.

2 https://www.ncarb.org/sites/default/files/2013PA_BoxSet_AllReports.pdf (accessed October 15, 2024) I use NCARB's documents and programs from 2012 and shortly thereafter. Note that in October 2024, NCARB released a new *Competency Standard for Architects* (https://www.ncarb.org/sites/default/files/Competency-Standard.pdf, accessed October 15, 2024), a volume that will guide future testing and experience components for licensure. Like its predecessor [link above], this new volume is related to NCARB's most recent practice analysis. The *Competency Standard for Architects* lists 16 competencies, each with two or more subcategories. This most recent publication could readily be used for building a table to divide up scope and fee when teaming (similar to ***Appendix E***). Some portions of the new standard might also be useful for breaking down fee, scope, and schedule in a fee proposal for a client (similar to ***Appendix D***).

One of many. How to stand out?

Part VI

Firm

Managing an architectural practice requires skill in marketing, business, finance, human resources management, quality assurance and quality control, along with an understanding of the business and professional risks firms and professionals must deal with. Chapters in *Part VI* cover these topics in depth and, building upon the project management tools referenced in *Part V Project*, reference additional tools for managing a practice.

14

Marketing and Business Development

Firm management begins and ends with marketing and business development.

Beginning

The first thing an architectural practice needs is projects to work on. Marketing and business development are what a firm does to land those projects.

End

If the time comes when marketing and business development at a design firm cease to be a priority, the work of the firm is sure to end soon thereafter.

Our discussion of marketing began in ***Chapter 2 Always Looking for Work***, which introduced general marketing principles. This chapter continues the discussion in more detail.

Marketing comes in many forms. One architecture firm's ad on the big screen, juxtaposed with the usual pre-movie fare, stuck out—in a good way. Images and message were memorable and sticky.

Sticky? If marketing is *sticky*, it stays with those targeted. This may be ancient history, but I'd say Apple set the standard for stickiness in its 1984 Super Bowl ad for the Macintosh. Just about anyone that saw it remembers it now and can recall what it was advertising—the Apple Macintosh, which hit the market a few days later.

Grant Leboff popularized the concept of *stickiness* in the book *Sticky Marketing: Why Everything in Marketing Has Changed and What to Do about It*. This book might be a useful resource for jumpstarting an emerging professional's marketing efforts. Mr. Leboff's website, *the Sticky Marketing Club*,[1] might also be a good starting point.

Besides coming up with *sticky* marketing lines, a major challenge facing architects is that potential clients are few and far between. Targeting a message just to potential leads is a challenge. Potential leads tend to be government and industry leaders with upcoming facility needs—people that will be in need of an architect sometime soon.

Building a list of contacts and former clients, sending out direct mail with company news ("Meet our new president!"), sponsoring public radio shows, even ads like what used to show up on the screen before a movie started—all these things might be helpful, but in my experience, the best way to find leads that will turn into business for the firm is to be a joiner. A joiner becomes a member of the chamber, a service or social club, the historic landmark commission, even an antique car group. A joiner gets appointed to the planning commission, is elected to public office, or becomes active in a local historic preservation group. Such opportunities continue,

Forever Practice: The Architect at Work, First Edition. Jim Nielson, FAIA.
© 2025 John Wiley & Sons, Inc. Published 2025 by John Wiley & Sons, Inc.

14 *Marketing and Business Development*

with connections through an alumni association, through sports booster activities, and through neighborhood outdoor recreation groups. Further opportunities may emerge as a firm leverages and optimizes its website.

Marketing for a 46,000-SF tenant improvement and expansion project began with a brief conversation between an architect and a tech company founder at a reception. That was almost five years before the project became real. During that first conversation, this tech CEO wasn't sure if he would even stay in the area, but he did mention that if he and his company *did* stick around, he had some facilities needs to address. He did stick around, and the architect stayed in touch regularly over the ensuing months and years, sending him an interesting article he'd come across, taking him to lunch, and getting his name and firm in front of this industry leader in every way he could. The goal: make sure this potential client would think of this architect when the time came that he needed architectural services. The journey took twists and turns, but ultimately it turned into a great project for a solid client.

Signing up to be a member of all the right organizations and going to receptions and social functions can be immensely effective. Another way many firms obtain work is through responding to requests for proposals (RFPs). Take careful thought, though, before you take up the process of responding to your first RFP. Knowing how to evaluate, propose, and negotiate scopes of services and proposed design fees is of particular value. Since our marketing efforts focus on specific projects, the figures and tables included in **Part 5 Project** and its associated *Appendices* are immensely useful. See particularly:

- **Appendix D Breaking Down the Fee, Scope, and Schedule** correlates staffing, hours, and a fee breakdown to a list of specific scope groupings. This can be a useful tool for presenting a proposal in response to an RFP with a clear scope requirement. Linking scope and fee at the outset, as shown in **Appendix D**, may make it easier to negotiate a contract with a favorable fee.
- **Appendix E Dividing up the Work**, another tool referenced in **Chapter 13**, may be helpful when teaming with another architect. It is a method of dividing the work, estimating levels of effort, and developing an exhibit showing who does what (and how much of it). This document, once negotiated and shared with the owner, will help her understand why there are two architecture firms on a project and what the division of labor is.
- For standard architectural projects, with consultants and work phases, a *Project Worksheet* such as the one described in *Tables 13.1–13.3* provides a possible framework for figuring the architect's and consultants' fees and scopes. Using these three tables in combination helps determine whether proposed fee is consistent with the requested scope.
- Finally, **Appendix C The Project Schedule** presents three sample schedule documents graphically. These graphics demonstrate different methods of presenting a proposed project schedule to meet the expectations and satisfy the needs of different target audiences.

Ask yourself
Review the figures cited. How are they used? How could they be of value?
Do you think you could put together a project worksheet similar to the one shared in the book? In order to become familiar with such a tool, work cooperatively with a fellow student or colleague on a sample project to assemble such a worksheet and fill in the information needed.

To identify leads, some firms use advance notice services, such as those found in the Integrated Marketing Systems offered by the Dodge Construction Network. These services research and report on future RFPs well before they are advertised. If you have good connections and are paying attention, you might know about some of the RFPs on the network's long-lead list ahead of time, but an advance notice service will help you catch more of them. The advantage of knowing early is that you can meet with the key players and work on building or strengthening relationships with them. After the RFP goes out, the individuals you most need to connect with are usually precluded from talking with anyone chasing the job.

Ask yourself
Once the RFP/RFQ is issued, why do you think the public agencies would prohibit you from contacting key individuals involved with the procurement?

Requests for Proposals/Qualifications

For many firms, responding to requests for proposals, such as those published by lead services, is the source of most of their work.

An RFP may be the same as a request for qualifications (RFQs), but the phrases may also mean different things. An RFP could simply be a request for a fee proposal, sometimes including a request for information on a firm's qualifications for the work. Often, what an agency calls an RFP should probably be called an RFQ, since it asks for qualifications, but not a proposed fee.

If the request requires a fee proposal, it is often referred to as requesting a bid or a fee bid. Such solicitations often feign interest in a firm's qualifications, asking for a narrative about experience, a proposed schedule, and perhaps even uncompensated design ideas. It is usually not helpful to spend much time on these parts of the request. Almost without exception, as experienced architects and marketing professionals will confirm, if *any part* of the proposal is about fee, it's *all* about fee.

When she was a young project manager, an architect worked on a feasibility study for a city facility, maintained contact with the division director after finishing the study, and, when it was advertised, convinced her firm to go after the new facility that would be the follow-up to the previous study. The principal in charge helped put the proposal together. The project manager thought they had a strong team, an aggressive schedule, and an airtight management plan.

Together with all its other requirements, the RFP also required a fee proposal. The PM worked with her boss to make it as competitive as they could.

This firm did not get the job.

The architect that had pulled the RFP response together placed a phone call to the city's director of public works, the decisionmaker for the project. Through their work on the study, the two had become well acquainted. She wanted a debriefing, which is a good thing to ask for in any case, even when the firm *is* awarded the job. (Feedback, good or bad is *always* helpful.)

"Your bid was too high," the director told her.

That was all.

As ought to have been obvious from the RPF, this selection was not about qualifications. It should not have been a surprise, then, that the selection was just a fee bid. It is often challenging for a full-service, top-tier firm to win selections based on fee alone. In such cases, it may not even be wise to try.

Go/No-Go Decision

In fact, it is **usually** not wise to pursue such work. A firm shouldn't pursue every solicitation; a proposal might cost as much as $5,000–$10,000 to prepare. No, a firm should focus on the prospects it has a good shot at winning.

Ask yourself
How does a firm decide which solicitations to respond to? A common approach is to use Go/No-Go questions an architect can find online.[2] Putting scores to the answers for these questions can turn these marketing decisions into simple math. The online source footnoted earlier in this paragraph suggests 13 key questions. Allowing a possible

ten points for each question, the highest possible score is 130 points. Putting these questions into a table, a Go/No-Go questionnaire might look like the one shown in Table 14.1:

Table 14.1 Go/No-Go Questionnaire—Assuming the ones filling out the form are honest with themselves and don't exaggerate the firm's qualifications, if the score is three quarters of the maximum or better (in the case of this simple table, at least 98 out of a possible 130 points), moving ahead with a response to the proposal request is a solid *go*. If not, an experienced architect will know not to bother wasting time preparing a proposal.

Go/No-Go	Score
Answer each question on a scale of 1–10, ranging from	
1: *Not at all in our firm's favor* to	
10: *Could not be more favorable for our firm.*	
Are we the incumbent? If not, is there one?...	_____
Is the customer happy with the incumbent?..	_____
If not, was the RFP released to fix the issue?..	_____
Do we have a strong relationship with the customer?......................................	_____
Does the RFP play into one of our strengths?..	_____
Is the RFP geared towards a competitor?...	_____
Is the project funded? Does their budget align with our fee?..........................	_____
Are they planning to buy or is this information gathering?.............................	_____
Will winning the project require heavy investment from us (time or money)?....	_____
Will winning this project further our goals as a company?..............................	_____
Is the customer likely to be a strong account or an example case study in the future?....	_____
Would winning this give us an advantage over a competitor?.........................	_____
Are company politics affecting our decision to bid?..	_____
TOTAL	
Add it up. If the score is **98** or greater, it's a **Go**; **97 or less**? **No-Go**.	_____

The Selection Process

If the selection process, whatever name it goes by, considers qualifications only, a full-service firm's odds may increase. This approach is usually referred to as Qualifications-based Selection and is often used by public entities. Such a solicitation generally includes:

- Specific selection criteria each firm must address in its submittal
- A number of points or scoring weights assigned to each criterion
- Creation of a review panel to review submissions
    These selection committees usually include agency officials and procurement officers. It may also include a contractor or another architect that didn't submit a proposal.
- A panel decision on a short list of firms (often three or four) to be interviewed
- Interviews with the short-listed firms

- Final selection by the review panel

  Selection may seem to be largely or wholly determined based on the interview, but it will often be based on a combination of scores on both the submittal and the interview. It is not uncommon for selection committee members to make decisions by instinct and then establish their scores to justify their choice

- Fee negotiation

  Many public entities publish fee ranges before the solicitation; others don't; either way, taxpayer-funded entities must usually negotiate within the range of available funding. And with qualifications-based selection, if the client is unable to negotiate an acceptable fee with the firm judged to be most qualified, the agency will simply move to the next-most-qualified submitter and negotiate. (As you can imagine, this rarely happens. Most architects won't give up a job they have just won.)

Selection criteria often include headings such as the following:

- Strength of Team
- Relevant Experience
- Performance Record
- Management Plan (often called Project Approach)
- Design Schedule

Ask yourself
What might these selection criteria mean? What kinds of things might a typical selection committee look for?

Additional Resources

The Architect's Handbook of Professional Practice

6.4 Networking and Business Development

6.5 Qualifications, Proposals, and Interviews

Author's Note

Sharpen your pencils

Early in my career, I was asked to be the project manager for a small-town fire station, a job our founding principal had accepted as a favor. The fire department already had their contractor on board, they knew what they wanted, and they thought they knew what structural system they would use. Our architecture firm was little more than a code review and drafting service. Even though we only drew it once and our fee included no construction administration services, we barely broke even.

A couple of years after we sent those drawings in for permit, I was in the area and decided to take a detour from the freeway. I drove down an old highway in search of that fire station. I discovered that although we had taken pains to design the building with the innovative masonry system the contractor had suggested, that had all been changed in the field. This fire department, like so many other small town agencies, clearly did not have any money. Where I had expected to see tidy masonry, I saw instead a disappointing wood-framed barn, covered entirely in uneven vinyl siding.

This adventure may have killed any enthusiasm I ever had for designing fire stations.

Years later, our firm received a solicitation to submit qualifications, once again, for a fire station. Since this one was in a more urban area, we thought perhaps that they had *some* money. And besides, it looked to be a qualifications-based selection, rather than the fee bid we usually encountered with fire stations. So, I attended a pre-proposal conference. The only thing I remember from that meeting is that the fire marshal conducting the meeting asked each of the firms in attendance to submit a fee proposal alongside our qualifications. "And remember to *sharpen your pencils* when you put that number together," he said rather enthusiastically.

As was always the case during my career, our firm was not interested in fee bidding. When I got back to the office, I shared what I had learned with my partners. This fire station was a no-go.

Notes

1 https://www.stickymarketing.com/ (accessed October 16, 2024)
2 https://www.utleystrategies.com/blog/go-no-go-decision (accessed October 16, 2024)

15

Marketing Proposals

In preparing a marketing proposal, a project manager should consider what the firm is selling. What is the most marketable thing the firm does? ***Chapter 10 Core Responsibilities*** suggests six possibilities. But remember, a proposal is marketing. The key question is what will sell.

Ask yourself
What should a firm highlight in its marketing materials?

If you think design will carry the day, as it so often does, showing it off is job one. Use whatever demonstrates what the firm can do—beautiful sketches, stunning photographs, even two-page spreads, if possible. As projects finish up, hire the best photographer you can afford. In the case of the Fulton Library at Utah Valley University (UVU), the design architect brought in a prominent New York City architectural photographer. The architect of record hired a leading in-state photographer. Examples of their work are shown side by side in Figures 15.1 and 15.2.

In some marketing submittals, design may not be the thing to highlight. Perhaps a team member knows the client well enough to understand that for this owner, the main concern is business-like execution of contracted duties. The most important thing for another client might be how fast the architect can do it or how well organized he is. Maybe (perhaps most of the time) the team has no idea what will sway the selection committee, so they include a little of everything.

Careful! More often than not, a scattershot proposal that addresses every possible interest of the selection committee will fail to capture the committee's imagination. A boring proposal is not apt to win the commission a firm is hoping for.

It's better to focus on what the team *believes* is most important. Find a pithy message, or through-line, and let it permeate the proposal, from beginning to end. This message could be as simple as *We work for you*, or maybe *Coast-to-Coast Know-How; Local Presence.* How about *Sustainability that Works*? Develop this theme from start to finish, as if you were writing a novel. A pertinent, easy-to-remember theme, coupled with corresponding action, will make a meaningful and sticky impression on selection committee members.

Sometimes a firm has prepared and come to understand more about the project than is found in the solicitation. Principals may know every decision maker. They might think they have the inside track, that the project is theirs to lose. They play prevent defense.

But prevent defense, here as in a sports arena, is often a good way *not* to win.

As the selection committee game is played, the winner is usually the one that takes a risk and does something bold—something intriguing, unexpected, and surprising (in a good way). Imagine that a solicitation includes a facilities program for the project, and a team hoping to win the commission sees a big flaw in the program document.

Forever Practice: The Architect at Work, First Edition. Jim Nielson, FAIA.
© 2025 John Wiley & Sons, Inc. Published 2025 by John Wiley & Sons, Inc.

Figure 15.1 UVU Fulton Library. *Source:* CRSA.[1]   **Figure 15.2** UVU Fulton Library. *Source:* Alspector Architecture.[2]

"Have you ever considered creating two small buildings side by side instead of the big one you described in the program?" the lead-off speaker might begin. "Think about it, 50% more of your staff from every part of your org. chart would have a desk within 20 feet of a window."

This could be the opening salvo of a winning proposal.

Or the owner might say,

"Nope. Too expensive. End of interview."

Preparing a proposal and going into an interview, an architect never really knows what issue the selection will turn on. But if she takes a risk, her firm just might be the one that determines what that deciding issue will be. The team that ventures something extraordinary is usually the one that benefits.

To put it another way, taking the bold approach may indeed be a gamble, but frequently with selection committees, the gambler wins.

As questions are asked during an interview, we respond directly to the questions as presented, but like an experienced politician, we amplify our responses, answering the questions we prepared for, the questions we think a panel member should have asked.

Consider these examples:

Example #1

Let's say the RFPs asks the team to present its experience designing academic research laboratory buildings. If the team has only done two or three labs on university campuses but has a wealth of experience with research labs for other client types, the team should include *all* this experience in its response, beginning with collegiate work. As the response introduces other lab buildings for government and private research firms, it should begin its project descriptions with the assertion (which is true) that these university laboratory buildings are virtually indistinguishable, in their equipment and infrastructure, from those the team has designed for other clients.

The writer or presenter might even say that the team's track record designing many research facilities for private industry, *in addition* to university research laboratories, will turn this university lab building not only into the very best settings for researchers and faculty members but will also yield the most compelling environment for the research conducted there and the entrepreneurship that begins there. Working in a research facility inspired by the most forward-looking academic *and* private research endeavors of today, the architect tells them, will jumpstart the ability of researchers and faculty to advance their field of inquiry in the laboratories of tomorrow.

(The presenter should practice saying that sort of thing a few times in front of colleagues to ensure she says it in a way that conveys a knowledgeable, memorable, positive, and supportive impression.)

Example #2

Perhaps the solicitation asks a firm to list at least two LEED®-rated commercial or institutional buildings it has designed and certified at a level of gold or platinum. Even though highly sustainable, resilient design projects might have been bread and butter projects for this firm, fewer clients today agree to pay for certification. So the firm might not have a single LEED-certified building in its portfolio. Instead, the firm might cite the fact that it has a major Net-Zero civic building, as well as a large project that just received Passive House certification.

The firm's marketing story could go on to chart the implications of these achievements, in terms of energy use and sustainability, in comparison to LEED. A proposal can help the client see (gently) that these different ways of looking at building performance can be even more rigorous than LEED. A proposal writer could complete the firm's response to this query by noting that to support their interest in LEED certification for the new building, the design team has included a LEED-accredited Professional on the team with extensive experience obtaining LEED-gold certifications and even one platinum.

(If the team does not have such a LEED-accredited Professional handy, the team brings on a sustainability consultant to fill the bill.)

Even though each of these examples provides a response that is somewhat different from what the owner said she was looking for, the responses tell *the team's* story. They tell it in a way that clearly meets and exceeds the owner's real requirements. If this were an exam with a fair-minded professor, the team would get full credit, maybe extra credit!

Interview

A few suggestions and goals for a marketing interview:

- Everyone attending the interview for the design team should have a speaking role. Exception: it may be appropriate for a marketing staff member not to participate in the dialog but to handle boards and easels or set up and run a digital presentation.
- Presenters should be themselves and speak from the heart, not from a script. Speaking extemporaneously, a presenter may skip over something she had intended to say, but the presentation will be far more real (and helpful) this way.
- Consider asking the selection committee open-ended questions. Risky, yes, because presenters don't know where their answers will lead the conversation. And it isn't possible to rehearse what one doesn't know is coming. One effective approach: presenters convey to the selection committees that the design team usually considers the interview to be the first project meeting with the client, so they need to begin the process of finding out the client's hopes and dreams for the project.
- A prudent team presents beautiful images of prior work but tries not to give away free design work related to the project for which they are interviewing

Of course, rules like these are made to be broken, so sometimes a dynamic preview of a concept—a little taste— is in order. Here are a few things a team might put forward to turn an interview into a blockbuster:

- A large and beautifully detailed physical model, unveiled at just the right moment, showing one possible design approach
- A quasi-animation made up of a series of slides showing how architectural, mechanical, and electrical systems adapt to create flexibility for changing building requirements in the future
- A computerized walkthrough or flythrough of a design concept

15 Marketing Proposals

- A beautifully hand-drawn aerial view of a public space the way it could be one day
- A detailed architectural sketch or rendering of a possible design approach, showing the building on its site
- Detailed research into an uncommon building type, allowing presenters to ask the client pertinent questions, even if they have never done a single project of this type (It could be that no one in the United States will have done such a facility in recent memory.)

Ask yourself
Considering a different type of interview, what does design look like in design-build (D-B) competitions, where the D-B team fronts the entire design?
Can you find and review a successful D-B proposal and consider what went into winning this commission?

Management Plan (Project Approach)

Finally, a few thoughts about the management plan, often called the project approach. This document is the heart of any proposal or interview for design services and should be based on a real project management plan, developed by the project manager for this project, not repurposed from an old marketing proposal. The selection panel will be able to tell the difference, particularly if you don't change the name of the client it was prepared for. Every. Single. Time. Trust me; if you recycle content, you'll mess this up.

The management plan should discuss schedules, deliverables, team members, consultants, who does what, meetings and key milestones, internal design team communications, owner review processes, decision making models, design approach, documentation, specifications, project delivery options, and how all these things will evolve and fit together—as specifically tailored for this client and for this project.

A specific plan, written for this specific project, will trump any amount of carefully crafted boilerplate, beautiful generalities, and polished language.

"We will make a wonderful space for you and your employees!"

The above sentence doesn't do anything. Instead, a well-prepared team presents specifics, a detailed plan showing in detail how the design team will work with the client. The management plan should include statements such as the following, with clear details and specific dates:

- To keep on track, we'll need X decision on Y date
- We'll get end-of-phase documents to you two weeks ahead of that milestone and brief you when we deliver it so you will have enough review time to give us informed direction

Ask yourself
What do you believe would be the best way to become more familiar with the process of creating a proposal and interviewing for a project?

Additional Resources

The Architect's Handbook of Professional Practice

6.5   Qualifications, Proposals, and Interviews (Pp. 381–395)

Author's Note

Nothing to fear

Important interviews usually include several decision-makers. Even when I was the principal in charge of the effort, I listened to input from my partners. One of the things I always wanted to do in an interview was ask the client open-ended questions, listen to their responses, and in the process, build rapport. Usually, my partners pushed back, but despite their hesitancy I looked for ways to turn interviews into two-way conversations. Unpredictable? Yes. Risky? Of course. A chance to set our team apart from the rest? Absolutely!

One year we decided to go after a planning project for a community redevelopment agency out of state. By this time, I think I had worn my partners down a bit, so they were silent about my plans for a conversational approach. The town is well known for Cowboy Poetry, so I started things out by reciting a familiar cowboy poem and sharing my thoughts about what cultural treasures their community enjoyed. They had prepared written questions that we answered, but we also asked them questions and had a genuine conversation.

We got the job. We went on to win three more planning and feasibility study projects in the community thereafter.

My advice to anyone that loves social interactions and is light on her feet when it comes to asking and responding to questions? You have nothing to fear, little to lose, and much to gain by asking your interviewers questions and putting real give and take into your presentation.

Notes

1 https://www.crsa.com/project/uvu-fulton-library (accessed October 16, 2024)
2 http://www.alspectorarchitecture.com/Frames/Assets/Images/Projects/UVSC/14.jpg (accessed October 16, 2024)

16

Business and Financial Management

The first two chapters in *Part VI* focused on marketing, which is the *sine qua non* of running a successful firm. This chapter addresses general business management, planning, and financial management. Yes, a firm will go out of business when there is no new work. But lack of a business plan or financial system to steer it may also lead to the same fate.

Form of Company

Small architecture firms are usually sole proprietorships. One person owns the firm. If there are a few owners, the firm may be a partnership or possibly a limited liability company partnership. A larger group of shareholders may form an S Corporation. All of these legal forms are pass-through entities; firm earnings or shortfalls become Schedule C profits or losses on personal income tax returns, in proportion to an individual's ownership share.

Tax Planning

In pass-through entities, income is taxed once—as personal income. Since business and personal income are the same, accounting is simpler, and there is no double taxation, as there may be in a typical C corporation, which firms with many shareholders adopt. These organizations pay corporate taxes on company income. If income is distributed to shareholders, those receiving dividends are taxed on that income again. Leaders of C corporations may seek to reduce double taxation by converting income to compensation (pay and bonuses). An employee pays tax on such compensation, but the corporation does not. Due to the complexity and variability of an architecture firm's project-based accounting, knowing just how much income to expect, how much to convert to compensation, and whether to retain earnings and pay corporate taxes on what is retained, requires careful attention by in-house financial personnel and detailed consultations with tax accountants.

Succession Planning

Company structure may affect the owner transition or succession plan for ownership transition between generations of firm leaders. A succession plan may address stock or other forms of company ownership, key-person insurance, and buyouts (either by the firm or by members of the emerging leadership team). Successful transitions are usually based on formulas agreed to in advance. Adopting such a plan requires extended discussions. It may require ratification by all firm members, especially if leaders aim to create an employee-owned organization.

Forever Practice: The Architect at Work, First Edition. Jim Nielson, FAIA.
© 2025 John Wiley & Sons, Inc. Published 2025 by John Wiley & Sons, Inc.

104 | *16 Business and Financial Management*

A succession plan may take many forms, may involve specialty consulting, and may require years to develop and adopt. Transitions work best when plans are adopted well ahead of the first founding partner's retirement. *Appendix F Employee Owned* includes a plan framework that broadens ownership participation and reduces financial burdens on future leaders.

Ask yourself
What issues do you think succession planning ought to address? What would your succession plan look like?

General Business Planning

Planning for the future includes setting and tracking goals, including those related to monthly and annual financial performance. Firms establish plans for how they want to train and develop staff and even how large they want to be. They plan for quality assurance and quality control. Also, they set goals about what types of projects they want to continue doing and markets they want to break into. A marketing plan emerges as a subset of a firm's overall business plan.

Firm leaders often find that strategic business planning happens best in a setting away from day-to-day firm activities. An experienced third-party moderator can be extremely helpful in this effort. After agreeing on a global vision and business objectives, individual members of the team may be assigned to flesh out detailed implementation plans, goals, strategies, and metrics for general leadership review and approval. The business planning challenge architects often face is finding the bandwidth for strategic planning, while still maintaining focus on the demanding projects currently on the boards.

But it's imperative to find a way. Developing consensus on where a firm is heading, with metrics that allow straightforward follow-up assessments, lets leaders know what direction their efforts are trending, how the journey is going, and when course corrections are needed.

Goals

As noted, goals and associated metrics help a firm recognize its progress or lack thereof. Consensus goals may focus our attention and help with decision-making. "No, we're not interested in doing assisted living centers. That's not part of our experience or our business plan." "Yes, we would like to incorporate architectural and building science research into our practice." But if the firm's implementation approach is too rigid, the plan may lead the firm to narrow its focus and look past potential opportunities.

The risk of missed opportunities can be substantial. For example, a firm might understandably, leave fire stations, an often difficult project type, out of their strategic plan. However, I know of one firm that managed to turn a fire station into a one-of-a-kind opportunity. This firm designed the LEED® Gold-rated and first-ever net-zero fire station in the United States, receiving national awards and broad recognition for excellence in design.

Building Ownership

Although a firm's physical facility may not be part of an ownership transition plan explicitly, a chance for future firm leaders to become part owners of a new or existing building the firm builds or purchases provides one way emerging firm leaders may be able to begin building the financial capacity they will need to become owners.

Participating in such an endeavor carries significant inherent risks, however, the leverage of a commercial real estate mortgage, together with the predictability of a steady tenant (the firm), might help willing future firm leaders build the resources they will need to support the firm's long-term financial stability. If such a venture turns out as hoped, an opportunity to participate may be more financially rewarding for emerging leaders than any possible salary boost or any other long-term investment they might make. The forward-looking choice may be to invite them to consider becoming owners.

When considering purchasing or building new, rather than leasing, all firm leaders should understand the challenges involved and take actions accordingly. Investing in real property involves substantial risks and may require expertise in areas of investment, finance, construction, real estate, and development that firm leaders may not possess. Firm leaders considering such an investment would be well advised to seek assistance as needed from experienced professionals in fields such as these before moving forward.

Accounting

The aim of accounting is to make sure we collect what is owed to the firm, pay what the firm owes to others, and track and inform people of the financial status of projects and of the firm. The accounting department, general staff, project managers, and firm principals all have a role here, typically holding responsibilities such as those outlined below:

Accounting Department Responsibilities

Make sure we collect the money we are owed:
- Client invoices (Accounts Receivable)
- R&D tax incentives
- 179D Energy Efficient commercial buildings federal tax deductions
- Refunds on overpayments or purchases returned for credit

Monitor cash flow; depending on the urgency of the need, recommend that the firm:
- Draw down cash accounts
- Pause accounts payable briefly
- Obtain short-term loans from firm owners
- Hold back firm owner pay temporarily
- Establish/access line of credit

Make sure everyone and everything gets paid:
- Payroll
- Rent
- Consultants
- Vendors

Keep leaders and staff informed of firm and project financial status:
- Project reports
- Project Progress Reports
- Ad Hoc information as needed

Measure & report on firm financial performance:
- Project reports
- Summary billed, received, A/R, cost, and gross profit reports

16 *Business and Financial Management*

- Detailed expenses by project, phase, task, and employee
- Budget to actual analysis
- Billed, spent, profit (loss) reports
- Firm financial performance—measure and report on the firm's bottom line
- Summary firm financial position (Balance Sheet)

Maintain accounting systems, provide reports and training:
- Payroll
- Expenses
- Project reports
- Firm financial performance reports

Firm Employee Accounting Responsibilities

Understand contract scope, including reimbursable expense provisions
Understand project plan and budget
Submit expenses or prepayments for approval:
- One week before end of billing cycle
- Include receipts
- Include explanatory notes
- Indicate the period expenses or prepayments relate to, if applicable
- Indicate which expenses are reimbursable to a client and which are not

Maintain and submit personal timecards for approval:
- Within one week after end of pay period

Attend accounting systems training:
- Payroll
- Expenses
- Project reports (fundamentals)

Project Manager Accounting Responsibilities

Follow up on open accounts receivable as required
Coordinate with accountant to file preconstruction services lien notice (private clients)
Develop project plan for approval
Develop project budget by task or phase
Track project financial progress
Review and approve in-house team timecards
Assist in developing firm budgets as requested by principals
Determine monthly architect billing amount
Establish associated monthly allowable consultant billing (for budget purposes)
Review and approve consultant invoices timely (one week, typically)
Determine and approve team reimbursable expenses
Assist the firm in obtaining available tax incentives as appropriate:
- R&D tax incentives
- 179D Energy Efficient Commercial Buildings federal tax deductions

Attend accounting systems training:

- Payroll
- Expenses
- Project reports

Principal/Owner Accounting Responsibilities

Assist with accounts receivable as required

Review cash flow accounting and, when necessary, participate in solutions recommended by the accounting department, such as:

- Authorizing drawing down cash accounts
- Pausing accounts payable briefly
- Funding short-term personal loans to the firm, if needed
- Choosing not to take a paycheck temporarily
- Establishing/authorizing access to a firm line of credit

Oversee the filing of preconstruction services lien notices for private clients, firmwide

Approve project plans

Approve project budgets

Develop overall firm budgets and firm billing projections

Oversee work to claim available tax incentives as appropriate:

- R&D Tax incentives
- 179D Energy Efficient Commercial Buildings Federal Tax Deductions

Attend accounting systems training:

- Payroll
- Expenses
- Project reports
- Firm financial performance reports

Basic Building Blocks

At its core, the key role of accounting is both to:

- Know what money comes in the door and what goes out
- Ensure that the amounts coming in the doors and going out are correct

The two basic systems that follow and check these flows of money are the Accounts Payable System and the Accounts Receivable System. The first has to do with what a firm pays. The second concerns itself with payments the firm receives.

The following paragraphs provide introductory detail about how these systems work and steps a firm may take to optimize these important accounting functions.

Accounts Payable (A/P)

Architects pay out money to consultants, vendors (materials and office supplies), landlords, and service providers (3D printing, office maintenance), when payment for such expenses is due. The intent of such a system is to make payment, following payment terms, as agreed. This typically means remitting payment on or before the due date, but not much before. Companies benefit from the use of funds in their bank accounts that are due but not yet payable.

108 | *16 Business and Financial Management*

One aspect of architectural A/P system that should be noted is the concept of *pay when paid*. Since amounts payable to consultants (consulting engineers and specialists), in the aggregate, may easily represent 40%, or more, of a firm's total fees, this means the total of these expenses will usually be the firm's largest single budget line item—larger than payroll. These consultant costs are mostly pass-throughs from the owner. The problem is this: a firm sends an invoice for services (40% of which represents consultant fees). At the same time, consultants issue invoices requesting payment from the architect. As a matter of course, consultants turn on their internal accounts receivable clocks, expecting payment within 30 days. But of course, despite the architect's best efforts, the client often doesn't pay the architect's invoice for 45 or even 60 days.

As large as these amounts are, with no payment forthcoming from the client, the architect is usually unable (or unwilling) to front the money to pay consultant invoices within 30 days. So, the architect negotiates a *pay when paid* provision into the Architect-Consultant Agreement. This is standard in AIA contracts. Although the consultant may ask to change that to *net-30* payment terms, the architecture firm cannot advance funds it does not have.

Insist on *pay when paid*. An architect is not a bank and should not pretend to be one.

The following bullet points describe commonly recommended good and fair practices for accounts payable that an architecture firm might consider implementing:

- The A/P System recognizes and logs each invoice when it is received. Note that, including payroll, payables may make up 90% of receipts or more.
- Invoices are distributed to project managers or firm leaders, as appropriate, for approval and to obtain necessary information not given on the invoice. Such information might include project number, project phase and completion percentage, business purpose, and any special handling requests (for example, a request that accounting tell the project manager when payment is sent out so she can let the payee know). If a consultant has not done all the work it is billing for, it is also the project manager's job to give both the consultant and the accounting department an opinion as to what portion of the fee should have been invoiced. The consultant may then revise and resubmit the invoice, or the architect may reduce payment on the invoice in hand. Prior to the next billing cycle, the consultant should adjust its internal records to reflect the amount shown on any short-paid invoice.
- For incoming invoices, system tracking should include a notation: *out for approval*, together with the payment due date
- Even if a firm uses cash accounting, the accounting department reports on accounts payable due to be paid within 30 and 60 days following the report. Short of adopting accrual accounting, such information, together with Accounts Receivable aging discussed in the next part of this chapter, will help an organization with cash-based accounting do a better job of understanding its real financial position in the near term, taking anticipated and pending receipts and payables into account.

Accounts Receivable (A/R)

Accounts receivable systems track money a firm has earned; the systems then facilitate efforts to get those funds in the door. Earnings are generally established when a firm sends out an invoice for services performed. To the A/R system, funds are usually due and payable the day the firm sends an invoice. However, based on a firm's accounting method (accrual vs. cash), these earnings may not be booked as income until payment arrives.

Standard AIA contracts require payment within 30 days. After that, payment is overdue. An A/R system tracks and ages invoices from the day they are issued. One of the most important of any reports prepared by a firm's accounting department takes all outstanding invoices and sorts them into categories with headings listing the number of days since an invoice was sent: 0–30, 31–60, 61–90, and often one or two last categories for anything over 90 or 120 days. How a firm thinks about invoices that fall into those last groups depends on how aggressive (and how optimistic) the firm is!

Regardless of a firm's best efforts or optimism, financial managers have a name for receivables that are more than three or four months old. These unpaid invoices are called *bad debt*. Frequently, the money is uncollectible.

The goal is to keep payments current and to keep a +30 invoice (one that has gone unpaid only recently and is between 30 and 60 days out) from becoming more than 60 days overdue. The follow-up goal is to keep an invoice that is 60 or 75 days old from becoming uncollectible.

Assuming net-30 billing terms (depending on what a firm's clients agreed to), the following chart outlines commonly recommended accounts receivable actions many architecture firms perform, or at least aspire to perform, to reduce the likelihood of having invoices go unpaid. The chart shows timing, responsibility, and actions:

- 7 Days **Project Manager**: Confirm billing amount and billing instructions with client
- 0 Days **Accountant**: Send Invoice
- 15 Days **Accountant**: (For a new client): Received invoice? Correct address? Questions?
- 31 Days **Project Manager**: Phone call. "We noticed that your account is past due. When can we expect payment?"
- 45 Days **Principal in Charge**: Phone call. "Payment is now more than two weeks overdue. I've asked the project manager to hold off for now. Consider this notice that we will stop work until the account is current." Follow up with an email so it's in writing per contract.
- 60 Days **Accountant**: Email to known address, including invoice for work since previous bill. "Payment is now more than a month overdue. Our work on the project has stopped, and we are attaching our final invoice. Unless we receive payment in full for the prior invoice and for this additional bill within seven days, we will close out the account, place a lien on your property (if applicable) and refer these invoices to collections."
- 70 Days **Accountant**: Confirm with project manager that no additional work on the project is being conducted. Refer entire account to collections and lien the owner's property, if possible.

Ask yourself
Review the A/R steps listed above and respond: do we often consider this approach to be "... a custom More honor'd in the breach than the observance,"[1] as Hamlet put it?
What impact does it have on a firm if firm leaders and accountants fail to follow A/R procedures such as these?
Based on the sample project progress report in Appendix G, what is your understanding of how a project manager tracks overall project performance?

Accounting Philosophy

At the core of some publications and reference works about architectural accounting practices, we may find the concept *net operating revenue*, or a similar phrase with the same meaning. The accounting methodology associated with this term suggests—

1. Deducting consultant costs and a few other minor expenses from gross income received and calling the remaining income *net operating revenue*
2. Basing financial statements, progress reports, and profits on the trimmed-down *net operating revenue*, leaving consultants minor other expenses out of the equation

110 | 16 *Business and Financial Management*

Project and firm profits are then determined by subtracting all salaries and expenses attributable to each project and the overall firm from this *net operating revenue* number.

Net operating revenue accounting is practiced by many architecture firms. In comparison to basic business accounting, where gross revenues less gross expenses are the simple formula for profits, this more complex *net operating revenue* accounting approach is difficult to implement with standard accounting systems and has substantial drawbacks.

For example, a firm principal might not realize that the amount of money represented by a 12% profit target, based on gross revenues, represents a much higher number than a 15% profit on *net operating revenue*. Depending on a firm's consultant costs, even a 10% profit in basic business accounting terms could well exceed a profit of 15%, stated in terms of *net operating revenue*.

These figures reveal two important points:

1. Using *net operating revenue* for accounting and business planning is a good way to think you are setting profit sights high while actually aiming for appreciably lower returns than you may realize
2. As should be clear, variability of consultant costs can have a major effect on firm financial performance. Yet, *net operating revenue* accounting leaves those costs entirely off the table and out of the conversation.

Ask yourself

Can you test the above proposition on net operating revenues and profits using mathematics? The following equations provide a road map.

p = profit percentage

g = gross revenues

c = total consultant fees

e = other expenses (nonreimbursable*, including payroll)

P = total profits ($)

* For budgeting, we may properly leave reimbursable expenses out of our calculus because they are in essence a simple pass-through; each expense is joined by a matching reimbursement. Any potential financial benefit we might realize from a negotiated markup on these minor expenses is small enough to be negligible.

Net Operating Revenue Accounting:

$$p = 1 - (e / (g - c))$$
$$P = p * (g - c)$$

Example: *$1M gross revenue, $315K total consultant fees, $590K other expenses:*

$$p = 1 - (\$590K / (\$1M - \$315K) = 1 - (\$590K / \$685K) = 1 - 0.8613 = 13.9\%$$
$$P = 13.9\% * (\$1,000,000 - \$315,000) = 13.9\% * \$685,000 = \$95,000$$

Simple Accounting (Gross Revenue)

$$p = 1 - ((e + c) / g)$$
$$P = p * (g)$$

Example: *using the same revenue, consultant fee, and other expense numbers as above.*

$$p = 1 - ((\$590K + \$315K) / \$1M) = 1 - (\$905K / \$1M) = 1 - 0.905 = 9.5\%$$
$$P = 9.5\% * 1,000,000 = \$95,000$$

In both of these examples, the dollar value of profit earned is the same ($95,000), but two things are worth noting: the calculations for simple accounting are much easier and the percentages used to express an identical profit value are quite different. In the first case, an architecture firm records the profit as 13.9%; in the second, profit is calculated at 9.5%. In reviewing these examples—

Ask yourself

- *What, if anything, is the impact (using these two approaches) of labeling this very same amount of profit as equaling a higher or lower profit percentage?*

- *Some architects have suggested a firm shouldn't bring consultant costs into its accounting because consultant fees aren't really part of the architect's fee. What are the pros and cons of reflecting consultant fees in financial reports and calculations?*
- *Do you think considering consultant fees when calculating project and firm performance would tend to have any impact on selecting consultants and negotiating their fees?*

In summary, *net operating revenue* financial performance tracking and reporting leaves one of the largest portions of an architect's expenses (consultant fees) unmonitored, unreported, and unaccounted for. It is as if to suggest that the architect has no control over consultant fees—that these are a given and can't be managed—so the architect shouldn't concern herself with them in assessing firm or project financial performance.

The full fee represents the architect's scope of services and the work on which a profit is properly earned. Accountants outside the profession generally recommend that architects and allied professionals seek profit on their entire fee, not just on the portion used to pay for direct labor of employees and overhead expenses in the architect's own office.

It is worth remembering that the architect's risks and responsibilities related to the work of his consultants is not limited to administrative and coordinating efforts alone. If a consultant fails to meet its standard of care, the architect is the one that will be sued by the owner for breach of contract.

Additional Resources

The Architect's Handbook of Professional Practice

      7.1   Navigating Economic Cycles

      7.2   Financial Management Overview

ProPEL, ACSA Professional Practice Education Library (Videos for Classroom Use)

      https://propel.yuja.com

      Firm Finance Unit | Lessons 1 through 5

      Fees Unit | Lessons 1 through 6

Author's Note

Net operating revenue *accounting*

Several years ago, my partners and I set out to improve financial management at our firm. Step one was to hire a controller. When we interviewed three leading candidates, I asked each what they thought of the *net operating revenue* approach to accounting. Each candidate was quite familiar with general business accounting. None of the three was familiar with the *net operating revenue* way of looking at the books. When I described it in similar terms to those contained in this chapter, I asked each of the candidates whether they thought that was a better way to determine project progress, profits, and losses than the more common accounting method used by other businesses.

Each of the candidates thought about it; to a person, each said no. Looking at the overall picture was better. We ought to include consultant costs in our approach to assessing financial performance. Accordingly, we set up our new system and reporting using the accounting model commonly used in businesses of all types. That is how the financial tools presented in this volume are structured.

Note

1 Hamlet I.iv.15, 16

17

Business and Human Resource Management

Quality

Just before his retirement, the founder of a large and successful architecture firm told me the practice of architecture gives us three chances to get it right: in *design*, in *documenting our design*, and in *working with the contractor during construction* to make sure he builds what we were looking for.

Design

An architect can and should work to design a project so thoughtfully and intentionally that everything about the design is clear, that it all fits together in obvious ways. If the intent is so obvious a contractor can't miss it, he'll get it right, even if the architect does a poor job of documenting things or is of little help during construction.

Documentation

If the design isn't clear, it is possible for an architect to do the most careful job imaginable documenting the work through construction documents that are properly detailed, noted, referenced, and dimensioned. The contractor will be able to build exactly what was intended. Yes, painstaking documentation will do the job, but standout documents take far more work than it does to get the design right in the first place.

Construction

Now, if an architect missed the mark in design and didn't resuscitate the project through careful documentation, she has one last chance to salvage the effort. She can make extraordinary efforts on-site to hold the contractor's hand, spoon-feeding him what should have otherwise been apparent, either by virtue of good design or extraordinary construction documentation. The architect's efforts during construction will take much longer and cost her far more than either of the first two options. Although such babysitting may be necessary to salvage a poorly designed and documented building, it will very likely eat up all the profit the architect planned for, and then some.

Considering these opportunities to get it right, costs for being fastidious about *design*, the first opportunity to get it right, are acceptable. If we wait for opportunity number two, *documentation*, to invest our efforts, costs go up steeply. But if, instead, we keep on waiting to do our job until *construction*—our third and last chance, our work becomes a salvage operation. Our costs multiply exponentially. If our goal is to make project success inevitable (while still making some amount of money), careful design efforts at the start are paramount.

Forever Practice: The Architect at Work, First Edition. Jim Nielson, FAIA.
© 2025 John Wiley & Sons, Inc. Published 2025 by John Wiley & Sons, Inc.

Business Risk

Attention to our responsibilities during design, documentation, and construction influences not only our profits but also our professional risks. To manage risk, when, perhaps, quality efforts flounder or are disputed, a successful architecture firm turns to a suite of insurance products. To keep from accessing that insurance; it is wise to implement a robust program of training, standards, quality assurance, and quality control. To that end, **Chapters 18 and 19 *Getting It Right I and II***, of this book focus on best practices to improve the quality of a firm's instruments of services and avoid getting into trouble.

With respect to insurance, AIA owner-architect contract documents enumerate the major types of policies owners generally ask for and architecture firms usually carry. These include commercial general liability, automobile liability, worker's compensation, employers' liability, and professional liability (errors and omissions) insurance. Limits, other than perhaps for automobile and worker's compensation policies, are typically based on what owners require, although a firm may carry insurance above and beyond those requirements.

Not mentioned in AIA Document B101 Owner-Architect Agreement, but quite common for large projects on a fast track, an umbrella or wrap policy is something an owner may obtain for one or more projects together. This type of policy typically consolidates coverage for all contractor, architect, and consultant parties and facilitates expedited conflict resolution since all parties are covered by the same insurer. Design and construction work for games-time facilities at all competition and training venues of the Salt Lake 2002 Winter Olympics, for example, employed multiple design firms, consultants, and contractors, all covered under a single wrap policy. By all appearances, this massive effort did not give rise to a hint of a claim against anyone. If there were disputes, it was something that could be handled inconspicuously; nothing created a hurdle that affected the readiness of Olympic venues.

Chapter 20 What About Risks? addresses types of risks an architect and a firm may face, along with specific steps to mitigate a firm's exposure.

Human Resources

Payroll has already been mentioned in **Chapter 16 Business and Financial Management**. In this section, our attention turns to human resources, a part of architectural practice that, like many other aspects, may be accompanied by risk. When a firm faces challenges in human resources practices, engaging the services of an employment attorney, if possible, may be extraordinarily worthwhile. When hiring counsel is out of the question, a firm might instead contact the nearest office of an organization such as an employer's council and make arrangements to review sensitive personnel matters with one of their employment law attorneys.

Hiring an Architectural Employee

It was around the year 2020 that Indeed.com finally figured out that when an architecture firm puts up an employment listing for an architect, this solicitation was not a search for a high-tech worker that calls himself an architect. (Around the turn of the millennium, Bill Gates rebranded himself as *Chief Software Architect* for Microsoft. Lest there be any confusion, in spite of that aspirational job title, Gates was never licensed to design a building.)

Some online job boards do better than others, but at least there is hope now that when an architecture firm puts up a job posting, the firm won't be flooded by applicants from the IT sector. It is, however, still important that a firm writes its employment advertisements carefully. Some applicants and employment agencies still don't get it.

Online recruiting tools work reasonably well, but if a firm is not interested in applicants that would have to move across the country, it should limit the reach of its ads or simply choose not to consider applicants from outside its target area. Some firms have success advertising through AIA chapter and local online posting services. Such services may be available at no or low cost.

Although this may be a last resort, a firm may also choose to become an active poacher and raid other firms. One way to do this is to pay current employees a finder's fee. Raiding other local firms may make the marauding firm a pariah; even in bigger cities, the architectural community is relatively small. But depending on how busy other firms are when a company needs workers, poaching could help a firm find capable team members quickly.

When in need of experienced staff members, a firm may also decide to grow its own. That includes getting employees while they are in architecture school or just finishing, training them in the firm's way of doing things, moving those that are quick studies into management or design, as needs and talents match up, and helping them get licensed. Of course, if a firm's workload demands are immediate, it may not have *time* to grow its own employees from the ground up. Nonetheless, if firm leaders give dedicated recent graduates a chance, they might just be amazed at how quickly these future architects step in and contribute.

There are certainly other possible ways to shake the trees for new staff members: besides offering bounties to staff members, as mentioned previously, a firm may advertise outstanding benefits, attend job fairs, particularly at nontraditional schools and venues, and make the firm as noticeable as possible to that invisible, potential hire.

Ask yourself
What job hunting resources have you used the most? What forms of recruiting are you most drawn to?

Benefits

If the firm is known for unusually good benefits, that may be enough by itself to attract applicants. Benefits complement salary or wages. But not always as one might expect. A rich health insurance benefit, for example, for employees and family might not only be understood as discriminatory by those with no spouse or family, but it also may not be seen by all current and prospective employees as being worth as much as you spend on it.

Ask yourself
What makes benefits attractive is how much they are valued by prospective job seekers, especially cohorts that are currently joining the profession.
Which of the following would recent graduates entering the profession consider most valuable?
Which other benefits would merit your consideration of a job offer?

- Health insurance benefit for the individual
- Health insurance benefit for the individual and family
- Health insurance paid fully by the company
- Dental and vision coverage
- Disability insurance benefit
- Life insurance benefit
- Flexible spending accounts or medical savings accounts
- Eight paid holidays
- Vacation: 1 week, 1st year; 2 weeks, years 2–4; 3 weeks, years 5–9; 4 weeks, years 10+
- One week per year sick leave, rolled into vacation. Together considered PTO.
- One week bereavement leave in addition to the above at death of parent or grandparent
- Paid family leave
- On-site childcare
- Sabbaticals

116 | *17 Business and Human Resource Management*

- 401k retirement accounts with 1:1 match for first 3% of salary, ½:1 match above 3% up to 5%
- Firm gives time off and pays 80% [100%?] of all costs for each section of the ARE® you pass
- Firm provides current NCARB + Kaplan (or similar) study guides
- Education assistance
- Professional license fees
- Membership in AIA, NCARB record fees
- Profit sharing
- Wellness benefits
- Flexible work arrangements
- Free sodas and snacks
- In-house company charity for employees in need

Challenges

Managing complaints, accusations, and potential terminations effectively depends on informed input and careful consideration. Hasty decision making on such matters may put a firm at risk of legal consequences. And layoffs almost always affect employee morale. Experienced legal counsel is often indispensable.

Terminating Employment

Terminating an employee the firm considers ineffective requires careful documentation of a staff member's performance, including clear records in his personnel file documenting that:

- The employee has been put on notice repeatedly, over an extended period of time, of the need to improve
- He has been given ample opportunity to improve
- His performance over the course of many months (or probably years) has been monitored objectively following such notices
- Performance has not sufficiently improved

Even for firms operating in at-will employment states, such documentation must be extensive, valid, and legally defensible. And regardless of state at-will employment laws, many employees (often more than half) may be members of federally protected classes. In such cases, clear requirements and prohibitions apply.

Ask yourself
What is a protected class? Which federally protected classes apply to employment?

Legal review of proposed personnel actions is critical. Often, necessary documentation may be incomplete or missing entirely. Lack of such documentation and evidence may occur because of hesitancy on the part of firm leadership to put anything that could be considered negative in an employee's file.

Misplaced compassion—omitting pertinent information from an employee's personnel file—may hamper the ability of a poor employee to learn from difficult experience; it may also limit what a firm can do to deal with problem employees effectively. If recordkeeping is poor or if it leaves employees unaccountable, such lenience may make it so a firm is unable to let an underperforming employee go. Inability or unwillingness to hold staff members accountable may cause firm morale to suffer, undermine top performers, and put the firm at risk of losing them as they flee what they may come to think of as a sinking ship.

Without sufficient records of poor performance in the past, a firm is left in the position of starting the process at step one, putting the employee on notice, providing opportunities for improvement, and documenting how the employee responds. This is a process that can take months or years. Whether done from day one or only later when adverse personnel actions seem warranted, the work of documenting an employee's actions, providing notice, and monitoring performance must be undertaken consistently and religiously.

Be aware that, in many cases, letting an underperforming employee go during a firm-wide reduction in force reduces a firm's potential exposure to the risk of employment discrimination claims. Usually, the need to cut employees is considered sufficient justification for terminating a staff member's employment. But a reduction in force typically remains a minefield. The logistics of conducting a broad reduction in force require careful consideration. Morale for staff that remain and for leaders making the decisions and delivering the news is a perennial issue. To combat downward morale spirals, some firm leaders ask employees subject to reduction in force termination to leave immediately after the interview in which they are notified. Departing employees may then be invited back on the weekend (with pay) when the office is closed, to collect belongings.

As part of an effort to mitigate issues related to reduction in force terminations, a firm should consider offering severance pay. How this is handled may be addressed in employment agreements, if these are in place. Typically, though, these payments may be thought of as parting consideration for contributions to the firm over time. They might range from one week's pay for terminated employees that have been with the firm for a year or two to three or even four weeks' worth of severance pay for those terminated that have been with the firm for a decade or more.

Finally, firm leaders responsible for conducting reduction in force interviews must be prepared for gut-wrenching conversations or even confrontations. A leader's kindness, compassion, and forthrightness are never needed more. Yet, it still might not be enough.

Complaints and Accusations

Employee grievances, particularly accusations of harassment, must be investigated rigorously and never ignored.

As a starting point, firms are obligated to establish proper policies and provide annual training on acceptable and unacceptable behavior in staff and management interactions with each other. This training must address actions that some may not recognize as unacceptable, especially behaviors that may create a hostile work environment. The training should also provide clear direction on how to file a complaint and who to file it with, together with protections for the one complaining and an alternative communication path in case of allegations against the one normally intended to receive complaints for the firm.

Most important in all of this is fair and expeditious investigation, decisive disciplinary or administrative action in response to any policy violations, and communication about complaint status and actions taken, given promptly to the person that filed the complaint. For a healthy staff environment, it should not happen (as it too often does) that the one that filed the complaint reports many months later that, so far as he knows, the initial complaint was never addressed.

Ask yourself
Let's say you are a firm leader (or will be one someday) and an employee comes to you with the following complaint: "I am getting more and more uncomfortable about my interactions with so and so. He stops by my desk several times a day to talk. He wants to talk for maybe a half hour. He looks me up and down. He doesn't stop or gawk at the desks of any of the other female employees. Lately he's taken to giving me little gifts. When I tell him 'no thanks' for a gift or I need to get back to my work, he won't go away. It's a huge distraction, and I'm beginning to feel threatened."
Regardless of what role you might imagine for yourself in this story, where would you go for guidance? How might you respond? What action should you take?
Consider those same questions if you were in one of the other roles described in the complaint.

Chapters 18 and 19 *Getting It Right I* **and** *II* are next. They focus on things firms can do at every stage of the game to ensure quality work, to get it right.

Additional Resources

The Architect's Handbook of Professional Practice

    Chapter 8   Human Resources

    Chapter 16   Risk Management

ProPEL, ACSA Professional Practice Education Library (Videos for Classroom Use)

         https://propel.yuja.com

         Failures Unit | Lesson 1 Expect Failure; Be Willing to Take Risks

Author's Note

Reduction in force

A message I wish every up-and-coming firm leader would take to heart is that if you become involved in hiring people for your firm (typically a very positive and enjoyable experience), the flip side of this responsibility may be *letting someone go*, a duty that is extraordinarily difficult.

During the Great Recession, as we called it, even though I always had another principal by my side in these cases, I was still the one with the unwelcome task of conducting more than one reduction in force interview. Beginning in late 2008, we just didn't have the work to keep everyone employed. When we finally got on a solid footing after two of three years of struggling, our firm was less than half the size it had been. During one of these reduction in force interviews, I was touched by one young employee that tried to reassure and console *me*. She expressed empathy for my having to deliver such difficult news.

This generous colleague was the one losing her job, yet she reached out and made an honest effort to help me feel a little better about the difficult task I was charged with carrying out. I wished our firm's circumstances would have allowed us to keep her, but I had no doubt that this thoughtful and compassionate emerging professional would thrive wherever she ended up in her search for new employment.

18

Getting It Right I

Practice makes perfect, doesn't it?

I'm not sure about that, but an architect is not expected to *be* perfect. Also, an architect will often not be held responsible for the financial impact of reasonable miscues. Why is that? In the purest sense, an architect's construction documents are documents that convey advice. When the weather forecaster advises that it will be cold tomorrow and recommends a sweater, one doesn't file a claim if that sweater isn't needed.

The remedy for an architect's error is often limited to revising the drawings. This is sometimes true even if the mistake is discovered after work is in place. As a matter of practice, licensed architects should impress upon the client the requirement to carry appropriate contingencies to pay costs associated with unanticipated conditions, as well as issues caused by any of the parties on a project: AHJ, owner, contractor, owner's consultants, or architect. For a new construction project, an owner is commonly encouraged to have a contingency equal to 5% of construction costs. For a renovation or remodeling project, a contingency of 10% is often recommended. Such contingencies are part of the reasonable cost of building.

Additions or corrections paid through contingency funds become part of the building. Their value accrues to the owner. If an owner isn't willing to carry a contingency and cover reasonable errors or defects, she may hold the belief that she can look to members of the team, including the architect, for the funds to cover reasonable unanticipated expenses. The architect's risks of a claim under such conditions are, therefore, greatly multiplied. When a prospective client takes this approach, it may be appropriate to consider the risks and give the project a pass.

Regardless of circumstances, the architect has no more guaranty of avoiding a claim than anyone else on the team. Knowing that when a member of the project team experiences a claim, everyone suffers, it is prudent to help team members out of trouble as best we can, especially the contractor.[1]

A thoughtful architect will say to contractors at the outset: "We all screw up. If you make a mistake and end up in trouble, I will work to design a reasonable way out of the mess for you without undue expense. I won't charge extra for my efforts in this regard. And if you find a problem with our drawings, let's talk. You will probably have a better idea than I will for an effective, low-impact solution."

All this being said, the key issue here is how to make our contract documents better so we will be less likely to find ourselves in a conversation with the owner and contractor about a problem *we* may have caused.

Ask yourself
Based on your understanding and in your experience, what does it mean to make our contract documents better?

Forever Practice: The Architect at Work, First Edition. Jim Nielson, FAIA.
© 2025 John Wiley & Sons, Inc. Published 2025 by John Wiley & Sons, Inc.

Inventing Ways to Do Better

Each of the following headings deserves in-depth discussion, maybe even a chapter of its own, but as a starting point, the following is a list of ways architects improve the construction documents they produce:

Quality Assurance

Quality Assurance, or QA, is made up of standard, ongoing practices, procedures, and precautions. Once employees are properly trained, quality assurance is ongoing, as the work is performed.

For example, as part of QA, firm members might be coached to list key information on drawings only once and always in the right place (not an unusual goal for practitioners). The firm also helps employees understand what constitutes "the right place."

Staff might also be taught, whenever a reference mark is added to a sheet being drafted (Detail 4C/Sheet AE4011, for example), to find and then insert the correct reference that goes with the symbol *when it is added to a drawing*, not to put in an empty symbol someone might (or often might not) remember to populate later. Staff members could also be instructed not to add redundant, unnecessary, and telltale indications of incompleteness, such as "See Structural" or "See Specs." If such a reference within the set truly is helpful (a rather unusual circumstance), the one producing the drawings will include in the note the specific location in the specifications or consultant drawings (Framing Plan General Note 4/Sheet SE202, for example) to which the contractor is being referred for a critical piece of information. As noted in contractor playbooks for finding change orders, such as the one cited here, absent this degree of specificity, the drawing notation, "See Structural," is an open change order invitation; contractors are trained to recognize vague references of this sort as the kind of sloppiness on the architect's part that may signal incomplete information and is often an opportunity for the contractor to fish for extras.[2]

Staff should also be trained to *understand* the notes and references they include in documents. They should call out rated assemblies employed in their projects (with both fire ratings *and* sound ratings, where applicable) by UL listing or test number and the performance achieved by the assembly: *UL U336 System B, 2 Hour Rated, STC 66,* rather than *Sound-Rated Fire Assembly*. Architects should understand the requirements of pertinent assemblies in three dimensions and should show and detail the assemblies, as tested, in the construction documents.

As part of QA, team members might also be taught to ask questions about constructability: Can the contractor possibly build what is being drawn? In an effective QA program, firm leaders should expect office personnel to ask themselves questions, such as:

- "Is it really possible to install fasteners to the top portion of a lower roof where it comes in just below the eave of the roof above?" (There's no way to get even a palm nailer in there.)
- "Can we really expect construction workers to work a nut on a threaded rod all the way down from two stories above in order to support a suspended walkway?" (This question should have been asked in design and in shop drawing production for the Kansas City Hyatt Regency, where failure to employ this specific, impractical threaded rod detail was blamed for a deadly walkway collapse in 1981 that led to 114 deaths and more than 200 additional injuries.)[3]
- "Will wastewater actually flow from this basement toilet fixture to the sewer line 200 feet away, whose flow line is just two feet lower than the drain at the fixture?"

Channeling her inner skeptic, an architect will think of question after question.

Ask yourself
What is the top takeaway from your reading about quality assurance? How important would you say it is?

Training

Ongoing training is an indispensable component of an effective QA program. Design and curriculum requirements for such a program are generally straightforward and readily researched. Also, given the type of leadership and mentoring capacity common among architects, conducting such training is not necessarily problematic. The largest obstacle that causes failure of ongoing architecture office training programs is long-term follow-through.

The major contributor to this lack of necessary follow-through is a management approach often referred to as firefighting. Firefighting happens in response to the vicissitudes and short fuses of a stream of successive projects coming through an office pipeline. This planning and management strategy is akin to putting out whatever fire is burning the hottest. If architects thinks of everything as a fire, we may not ever see as much urgency in the matter of regular training as we do in the case of a project deadline in danger of being missed.

No. We put training on hold. We put out fires. And even though training could improve the quality of a firm's work products, mitigating risk and paying ongoing dividends in production throughput, firefighting, if it is the default, may lead a firm to suspend the very thing that would minimize deadline problems in the long run. What a firm loses through this myopia is the critical training that would help firm members avoid fires in the first place.

Ask yourself
Who is responsible for a firm member's training?

Standards

Standards may have to do with the size of fonts and types of symbols used on office drawings, the preferred way of dealing with RFI responses and meeting notes, the way a firm documents and disseminates records of construction deficiencies, the preferred way to detail a construction set, or the accepted approach to punch list review and certification. As with training development, when times are tight, creating and documenting standards often takes a backseat to pressing production work.

In some firms, a hazard associated with the ebb and flow of focus on standards is that in lean times, staff members assigned to lead out in developing and implementing standards may, by nature of this substantial administrative (and nonbillable) assignment, be seen as contributing less to producing the firm's deliverables. They might, therefore, end up in a position of particular vulnerability, should firm owners need to cut staff while maintaining the critical workforce needed for short-term production needs.

Processes

Staff will perform better if they are taught to understand how a project goes, from beginning to end. They will do their work better if they understand who generally does what, when. In good firms, junior staff receive real-world training in the way things work, especially in a specific setting. In the very best of firms, these processes are reinforced for emerging professionals through experience firsthand. Future architects come to learn how things should go down by working with clients, consultants, and in-house peers while a project is on the boards, and then adding one-on-one interactions with contractors and subcontractors during construction.

A new graduate's preparation depends on both 1) training and 2) hands-on experience. To be truly of benefit, the training must be thoughtful and consistent. And experience must not be micromanaged. The emerging architect must demonstrate that she is worthy of trust. To support true learning, firm leaders must grant him that trust, which will enable the prospective architect and future leader to move to the next level—by doing.

Ask yourself
Can you think of any reasons standards and regular processes (ways of doing things) that may be important to an architectural practice?

Direction

If a firm's employees are to succeed in finding ways to do better, the direction received from supervisors will be crucial to their success. The paragraph above included a brief reference to micromanagement, as well as trust. The image of giving an employee as much leash as is needed—even sufficient rope to get himself in trouble—portrays an agonizing dilemma for some. Delegating responsibility, with authority, and giving staff members latitude to do things differently than the director would (as the young staff member strives to put the training he has received into practice) involve risks that some firm leaders simply feel are too high. After all, in everything the inexperienced employee attempts, the firm's reputation may be at stake. Yes, a young employee might take actions that are contrary to firm standards out of ignorance, but a firm principal ought to be able to mitigate such mistakes with a simple explanation to a client or contractor.

The flip side of the question is this: however high the risks may be when firm leaders turn their employees loose early in their careers, the risks of not doing so are failing to build a culture of trust, as leaders continually micromanage employee actions and thereby undermine the professional development and independence of a promising new generation. Without such domineering, these emerging professionals might well become equipped to carry on firm leaders' legacy one day.

Ask yourself
What do you think are some of the reasons many people have difficulty delegating responsibility to young staff members?

See the discussion in ***Chapter 19 Getting It Right II***, for more about quality assurance and quality control.

Additional Resources

The Architect's Handbook of Professional Practice

   Chapter 12   Quality Management (Note that the handbook uses the term "quality management" for what is referred to here as "quality assurance.")

ProPEL, ACSA Professional Practice Education Library (Videos for Classroom Use)

   https://propel.yuja.com

   Lean Unit I Lesson 2 How does Lean Fit (or not fit) with Design (Note: this unit has excellent recommendations for how to make quality assurance reviews a valuable design feedback loop.)

Author's Note

The manager of QA training and standards

   For a firm and a designated staff member to succeed in quality assurance training and standards development, both firm and employee must believe that these efforts are equally as important as production of ongoing projects.

   Belief sometimes falters.

   For example, when our firm suffered a downturn and could see no way forward without layoffs, we made the difficult decision to let the staff member go that had been working extensively (and effectively) on office standards. We understood that standards were invaluable long term, but unfortunately we concluded that letting an only partially billable employee go would increase the ability of our remaining staff to meet our commitments to projects still on the boards.

Notes

1 In construction, as with many other endeavors, a principle proven repeatedly is that when dirt is flung in the direction of any team member, there is usually plenty of dirt to go around. The reason: no member of the team is perfect; if someone files a claim against one team member alone, that team member will usually file counterclaims against everyone else. Such risk spreading happens predictably when the various parties involved in the project have good insurance (and therefore deep pockets). I have seen firsthand how helping a team member avoid a conflict is a powerful risk management tool.

2 Civatello, Andrew M. (2002). *Contractor's Guide to Change Orders: How to Resolve Disputes and Get Paid.* BNI Publications, Inc. P. 73. Section "5.5 Incomplete Design," in this guidebook, which is used as a training manual to teach contractors how to seek, obtain, and get paid for change orders, reads, in part:

> Notations like "See Specs" instead of "See Section 05500" or "See Structural Plans" instead of "See 4/S3" are clear indicators that an assumption was made that somebody provided the relevant information. They indicate that [another] somebody did not take the time [to] do his or her homework and verify that the supplementary information was included at a particular location in the plans or specifications. The assumed information is just as likely to be missing altogether.

This is just one example of a contractor guidebook for uncovering change orders that points out examples in construction documents of telltale signs of a possible change order justification. Studying the opponent's playbook, as contained in contractor change order guidebooks is a worthwhile way to improve architectural document quality.

3 https://sma.nasa.gov/docs/default-source/safety-messages/safetymessage-2008-05-01-hyattregencywalkwaycollapse.pdf?sfvrsn=eaa91ef8_4 (accessed October 23, 2024)

19

Getting It Right II

This chapter continues our discussion about quality assurance and turns then to quality control (QC). We begin with a conversation about the foundations of an architect's work in design and construction. This narrative leads inevitably to detailed investigations of the *internal document review* process at the heart of quality control.

Design

Design is a big part of the phase we call *Schematic Design*. But it is not everything. The SD phase also includes many other things, such as:

- Client meetings and coordination
- Preliminary consultations with design engineers
- Development of visualization tools to communicate design concepts
- Establishing basic project scope, including square footage, floor plan adjacencies, basic massing, and overall building sections
- Making initial recommendations about exterior materials
- Evaluating and describing preliminary structural, mechanical, plumbing, and electrical systems to be included
- Preparing a rough, per square foot opinion of probable construction costs
- Reviewing all such choices with the owner to obtain initial feedback and ongoing confirmation as the design progresses

Design itself becomes an even smaller part of the *Design Development* phase. Like the phase that preceded it, this part of the work also includes a lengthy list of documentation, presentation, coordination, and owner meetings, together with more complete drawings and preliminary work on project specifications.

Some have protested that at the end of *Design Development*, design is finished. Indeed, as its name suggests, most of the work in the *Construction Documents* phase has to do with documenting design decisions that by this point have already been made. Experience makes clear, though, that at the beginning of this phase, some design issues typically remain to be solved. To a degree, design work even continues during bidding and into construction.

If an architect is calling things as she actually sees them, she will tell you that pure design work, as a portion of all services provided by architects on a typical project, may make up ten percent or less of the architect's overall scope of services, but some aspects of it will extend over the entire course of a typical project.

Regardless of the percentage, pure design makes up a relatively small part of an architect's work. Yet, this part of the professional's efforts is often what architects are known for. What about an architect's reputation for producing an exemplary, carefully coordinated, and well-detailed set of drawings and specifications? Does any fame come from that? No. Design is noticed first.

The fascinating thing about design is that just about everyone in the business wants to focus on it. As discussed in **Chapter 11 Architecture and Related Fields**, in an initial conversation with future leaders of a firm

---

Forever Practice: The Architect at Work, First Edition. Jim Nielson, FAIA.
© 2025 John Wiley & Sons, Inc. Published 2025 by John Wiley & Sons, Inc.

19 Getting It Right II

in transition, all but one of these newly anointed leaders spoke of wanting to lead design work for the firm. The one leader that did not claim design as his domain had something else in mind. What he really wanted to do was manage the practice to create opportunities; he wanted to mentor emerging professionals and help them do the most with those opportunities, including giving them wings to design.

From the time an architect is first asked to run a project, he may find his greatest satisfaction in assigning a recent graduate to work through a design challenge. With even the simplest design responsibilities on their to-do list, emerging professionals may give 110%—more than they would for any other task. A leader reviews their work, mentors them, and guides them. He provides the continuous design oversight as discussed in **Chapter 11**, so resulting design work will be internally consistent. He understands from experience that if he continues in the path of delegating and entrusting real responsibility of any kind, a concept broached in **Chapter 18**, to those that are near the beginning of their careers, he will encounter only very few occasions when he needs to step in and pull those responsibilities, including design efforts, back.

Production

Only a few firms choose to specialize in production, but this is generally where most of a project's fee is earned. It is the hard work of producing documents for construction. Production is something architects need to get good at, *maybe* even try to enjoy.

Improving production has already been mentioned more than once in this book. Furthering that emphasis, the following overview covers one of the most important efforts architects employ to ensure quality work before they sign, seal, and deliver their instruments of service.

Internal document review is a move beyond quality assurance, to quality control. As reported, quality assurance is the process everyone on staff is expected to follow, to do things right the first time. Quality control is the periodic and comprehensive checking to see that quality assurance is actually happening. Quality control tells us when the process falls short. QC results in corrective action, where needed. Internal document review begins with redlining. Highly complex reviewing procedures might demand three or four different reviewers and back-checkers, each working with a different color marker or highlighter. For most projects, though, architects use red. As redlines are corrected, a staff member may highlight them in yellow to show completion, a process sometimes known as "makin' orange."

In preparing, reviewing, and marking up a set of drawings, or even a part of it, the job captain or project architect, together with the project manager or peer reviewer, must check the set comprehensively. The checking process includes review protocols such as the following:

Internal Document Review (Mid-phase Review)

Begin with a Skeptical Eye

Whether a review happens in the middle of a phase or near the end, a reviewer should start with the assumption that everything she sees is wrong. Seriously. Make the drawings prove to you that things are correct. "Oh, this is a detail showing the frame of the overhead door" is not the right sentiment.

"That detail is probably referenced incorrectly." Or "I'll bet it's not called out in the door schedule. I'll check!" That's better.

Follow Every Reference

Each reference must lead to the appropriate detail, section, enlarged drawing, or other item indicated. Dead ends are not OK.

Read Every Note

If the notes started out as boilerplate from another project, at least a third of them will probably be wrong or inapplicable. Read them and delete or tailor the notes as needed.

Check Every Dimension String

Since these are usually generated from electronic files, we have a strong tendency to overlook a review of dimensions. *Beware.*

People often move a wall just a hair or pick up a dimension reference point and modify it. These things may happen inadvertently, but they can wreak havoc in the field. Make sure grid-to-grid and overall dimensions are logical, round numbers. They ought to be something like this: 30'-0". They should not be 29'-7 5/8". *Never!*

Use Checklists

Excellent checklists may be purchased or downloaded for free. Much of what an architect needs may be found in *Section 12.3 Checklists* in *The Architect's Handbook of Professional Practice.* (See "Additional Resources" at the end of this chapter.) Checklists will help the reviewer think about key requirements, some of which one could easily miss. Examples include:

- Are stairs designed with rise and run that will make it possible for the contractor to meet code? *By now, an architecture student should realize that designing stairs with precisely a 7" rise and an 11" tread will make it impossible for the contractor to meet code. In cases calling for the level of precision implied by those stair dimensions, without exceeding the code maximum, the architect ignores real-world construction tolerances. He disregards those physical limitations at his peril.*
- Where ICC 117.1 applies, do doors have 18" of clear space between the latch edge of the door and any obstruction?
- Does the building require one or more standpipes? Are they provided, meeting requirements?
- Is the transformer located as close as possible to the main switchgear, minimizing the length of costly secondary feeders?
- Is the fire sprinkler fire department connection located as required by the AHJ?
- Is the structural system upgraded for heavy internal loads, such as areas of compact shelving?
- Are starters/variable frequency drives for the mechanical system motors included in the electrical drawings, in the mechanical drawings, in neither, or in both? The project needs one (just one) for each piece of equipment.
- Are water lines, sewer lines (sanitary and storm), gas lines, and electric conduits shown on the drawings? Do the pipes and raceways that stub out from the building align with their *counterparts on-site drawings* (including site electrical) so they can continue offsite from there?

    (Be forewarned that locations for these utilities, as shown on building and site sheets, almost never line up, sometimes with costly consequences.)
- Do panel loads match scheduled requirements of HVAC, lighting, elevator, and owner equipment loads?
- Is the fire alarm control panel located as required by the AHJ?

Review Holistically (Knowing What to Look for)

Both the person in charge of producing a document set and the reviewer should cultivate the ability to go beyond the checklist and review every drawing, looking for notes, dimensions, and portions of drawings that don't make sense. The recommendation about having a skeptical eye is the starting point for such a review.

The reviewer that hasn't worked on the project has an advantage at this point. She should begin without any orientation on the project, like a contractor seeing the documents for the first time. If it's easy to connect the dots, the documents are generally good. If the references are circular and the notes are opaque, not so much. This dot-to-dot exercise provides a reviewer unfamiliar with the project with a quick sense of how much further and how much more thoroughly she will have to dig.

Before, during, and after an internal document review is conducted, the staff member responsible for overseeing document production must continue to pursue ongoing quality assurance efforts. In addition, once a review is completed, he must incorporate review comments, redlines, and other corrections identified during previous reviews. Progress since an earlier review is the first thing to check in a subsequent review.

19 Getting It Right II

Internal Document Review (End-of-phase Review)

Back Check

Leaving a paper trail showing actions since the last review is essential. An architectural employee correcting a CAD file based on hand-drawn redlines should create an ongoing physical record, with a highlighter, of corrections made. This is makin' orange, as mentioned earlier.

Whether production staff use this paper process or an audit trail built into a digital model, an architect's office must preserve prior corrections and verify in a subsequent back check that corrections noted previously have, in fact, been completed. Doing so allows the reviewer that follows to cross previous issues of concerns off the list and focus on new ones.

Quality Control

End-of-phase reviews represent quality control in its most important incarnation. This is particularly true at the end of the Construction Documents phase. After completing a thorough back check, conducting a new quality control review is critical. If possible, an architecture firm should use a peer reviewer different from the one that was involved at mid-phase. The process is the same as outlined above; however, a new reviewer is likely to pick up different issues. It is essential that the process include full final drawing and specification reviews, comprehensive coordination checks between the products of all consultants and between drawings and specifications, a clear record of corrections needed, and detailed communication with the job captain or project architect responsible for the documents.

The end result of effective quality control is:

- Finding and eliminating problems in a set of contract documents
- Crafting documents that represent the wishes of the owner effectively
- Improving written communication with the contractor so he will be able to build effectively
- Reducing exposure to potential claims substantially

Additional Resources

The Architect's Handbook of Professional Practice

    12.3   Checklists

Author's Note

Internal document inconsistencies

It was on a large project that I encountered one of the biggest document inconsistencies I have seen. As consulting architect, our firm had responsibility for some parts of the work, but not for the drawings that precipitated the following problems:

Substantial concrete foundations at a multistory stair tower were built and installed following drawings included in an early concrete package. Months later, when steel for the stair tower superstructure arrived on site, it didn't match up with the concrete. This structural steel had been fabricated based on a later steel package. The bust between what had been built and what was now supposed to be installed was several feet, requiring big adjustments (such as re-engineering and then lengthening, or splicing, large steel beams—a task not easily accomplished). The immediate schedule impact was measured in weeks, not days. Costs added up to tens of thousands of dollars.

Avoiding construction impacts such as these is the intent of quality assurance and quality control measures, such as those discussed here and in ***Chapter 18 Getting It Right I***.

20

What About Risks?

It would not be possible to put together a comprehensive description of all the risks a design professional might encounter. This book, however, points out many of the roadblocks architects may face in practice. It also suggests strategies for avoiding them. It is not my intent to paint a discouraging picture for current and future practitioners; I know from experience that professional practice can be immensely rewarding.

The practice of architecture is truly not all doom and gloom. A concept that I believe applies to the challenges of the architect's essential calling comes from the words of an old radio broadcaster.

Paul Harvey passed away in 2009 at age 90, not long after his last broadcast. He had started nationwide radio news and comment broadcasts in 1951 and had been on the air in Chicago for several years before that. I heard Paul Harvey speak at a conference I attended in the 1990s. As I remember it, he suggested that notoriety is connected to the unusual, to things that depart from the norm. Such things catch our attention and are therefore newsworthy. So, he told the crowd, the frequent reporting of bad news is actually a sign of good in society. He suggested we should be grateful that what the news reports is the bad stuff. Watch out, Paul Harvey said, if good things ever become newsworthy enough to be the major focus of news reports.

In our collective experience today, most of what architects do is more salutary than diabolical and, therefore, not newsworthy enough to be noted.

More Reward than Risk

I contend that the profession of architecture is largely positive and rewarding. Even though I assist with legal cases, I find that disputes and claims are the exception, not the rule. Problems and setbacks, of whatever cause, do happen, but from what I have seen, most architecture firms, once established, find a way forward. This has generally been true during my practice, even during the Great Recession and other financial downturns. As Paul Harvey suggested, however, if actions or circumstances sink a firm, leaving calamity in its wake, the story might catch our attention because such an implosion would be atypical.

Like being aware of bad news, it is worth knowing about risks, as long as we don't become convinced that threats to our firms and to ourselves are the predominant condition of our profession. Some blunders an architect might make are much more serious than others; however, often, it is not always easy to know which is which. At the point we consider taking a step in what may be the wrong direction, we might not even realize that we have suddenly transported ourselves into the middle of a minefield.

The list below includes many widely differing examples of actions by architects that contributed to, rather than resolved, problems. Some may be counterintuitive. Several of these instances led to disagreements or disputes that were resolved quickly. Others led to legal claims. Many had significant financial repercussions. A few of these circumstances are discussed in other chapters of this book. Note that none of the lists in this chapter is

Forever Practice: The Architect at Work, First Edition. Jim Nielson, FAIA.
© 2025 John Wiley & Sons, Inc. Published 2025 by John Wiley & Sons, Inc.

20 What About Risks?

exhaustive, but each list includes a range of actions and situations of the sort that, depending on circumstances, might affect an architect's risk.

Ask yourself
To seasoned practitioners, some of the anecdotes presented here may seem routine. Nevertheless, everyone in the business or entering the field would do well to consider the following occupational hazards.
How could the actions listed in the next section have an impact on a potential dispute?

Potential Occupational Hazards

- Agreeing to a design schedule that is overly optimistic and cannot be met
- Supporting, proposing, or pursuing changes in the project's approach to code compliance without reviewing things with the AHJ
- In architectural drawings, showing outdoor concrete walking surfaces with slopes of less than five percent, even though spot elevations on civil grading plans depict some of these same concrete surfaces with slopes exceeding five percent, which would make them ramps
- Failing to keep thorough written project records
- Proposing a specialty consultant (acoustical engineer, food-services consultant, elevator consultant, or similar) for work the architect does not have the ability to do, having that part of the proposal rejected by the owner, and then making the attempt to complete the scope even though the team lacks the necessary expertise *(This issue may be much bigger than the architect thinks.)*
- Building a stramp (combination stair and ramp) without the detectable indication on the top of treads directly above nonuniform risers[1]
- Observing a contractor mistake and, rather than insisting that they correct the problem, working to make allowances, which will likely ripple through the job, often with far larger consequences than fixing the original defect would have had
- Failing to note or specify the correct length of drywall screws to be used for attaching gypsum board panels to an acoustical resilient channel, having left that critical information out of the documents, failing to bring the issue to the contractor's attention during the construction phase, and failing to watch for the condition in the field *(Oddly specific, but this is a recurring and costly problem.)*
- Proposing a material or assembly needed to achieve necessary performance, but backing off when the owner objects due to cost
- As directed under contract, providing only limited services on a project, but not performing other project services a third party felt the architect was (or should have been) required to perform
- Building a sloped walking surface with a grade steeper than 5% without handrails *(That would be a ramp.)*
- Building condominiums with plastic rather than cast-iron waste lines
- In designing a landmark development for a developer recognized for successful work around the globe and understood to be extraordinarily wealthy, proceeding quickly through construction documents (creating over $1 million in unpaid invoices) even though no payments had been received since the early stages of work
- Ignoring a contractor's question about a product, then telling him just to read the specifications
- Airing a disagreement with a D-B teammate in an owner meeting rather than bringing it up internally
- Refusing to make a special trip to a jobsite to help a contractor establish a critical bearing elevation not given directly in the documents
- Rather than allowing for owner input along the way, holding back schematic design documents until they were ready for presentation at the end of the phase
- Performing additional services the owner requested without first securing approval for added fees

How to Mitigate Risks

The following are just a few of the things a firm can do to reduce its chances of experiencing a dispute or claim:

- Don't start a project until you have a contract
- Provide conscientious training, quality assurance, and quality control practices for your firm
- Follow up on late payments immediately and continuously
- Listen to project team members, particularly the owner and the contractor
- When asked a question, do not be afraid to say, "I don't know"
- Be clear and factual in your communications, but do not betray confidences
- Process pay applications fairly and as quickly as you possibly can
- Always discuss a contractor request for information before responding
- If a sensitive issue or situation needs discussing with another project team member, have the conversation face-to-face, so the other party can experience your constructive tone of voice and approachable body language. If an in-person meeting is not possible, the next best thing is a phone call. Tone of voice will still add to the communication. Do not conduct the discussion via text or email. If the other party is self-conscious or feels threatened, she might, for example, impute an intolerant tone to what you intended as neutral or supportive communication, changing her takeaway significantly and thereby minimizing prospects for a helpful resolution

If a Claim Is Lodged?

- Call your errors and omissions insurer immediately as soon as you learn about a potential claim
- In case of a claim, also speak with an attorney, who may be furnished by your insurer
- Be prepared to pay your full deductible and see your insurance rates go up the following year

About the Contract

Dealing with contracts effectively may be the most important risk-management tool a firm has. A contract is almost always better than no contract, particularly if you approach contracts in the following manner:

Have a list of contract must-haves and a list of ought-to-haves and negotiate accordingly. If your client rejects even one of your must-haves, treat it as a dealbreaker and walk away. If you take a hard line, it's possible you'll get a phone call from this prospective client conceding on the point and asking to resume negotiations.[2]

Items you might consider putting on these two lists are listed below. First, the must-haves, with explanations of each. The ought-to-have list comes after that. It includes headings without explanations, leaving an opportunity for further research by the reader.

Must-haves

Establish what every contract your firm signs absolutely must have, such as:

- An agreed-upon scope of services
  Most contracts are stipulated sum agreements. An undefined scope of work doesn't match up with a defined fee. If the owner can't come up with a scope, steer clear. If an architect really wants to work with this client, she should only agree if the owner will pay hourly without a not-to-exceed limit. In a situation like this, the owner may need the

132 | *20 What About Risks?*

architect's professional assistance to determine what the scope is. The architect does this on an hourly basis. Once the scope is established, the architect has a basis for making a fixed fee proposal for the balance of the work.

- A waiver of consequential damages
  Owner and Architect agree not to make a claim or file suit against the other due to consequential damages, which are damages that happen as a consequence of direct damages. Consequential damages can be much greater than direct damages and would include things like hotel room rents not received due to delays while construction defects were being remedied. If such damages were not waived, they would not likely be covered by errors and omissions insurance.

- An enumeration of the standard of care that is consistent with common law
  Watch out for any attempt to elevate the applicable standard of care above what the law requires.

- Mutual indemnification provisions between owner and architect
  In this part of the contract, the architect and owner each say to the other: I will hold you harmless and defend you in any claim against you that is the result of my actions. For the architect, besides having a hold harmless provision of this sort, it is absolutely necessary that the contract has identical language by which the architect grants indemnity to the owner and vice versa. In an agreement, properly written, there will be two indemnification clauses, usually one after another in sequence. The two paragraphs appear identical, but the names of the parties are switched.

- Clarity about who is responsible for construction means, methods, techniques, sequences or procedures, or safety precautions or programs
  Hint: it is not the architect.

- Placement of authority to stop the work solely with the owner
  Hint: Also not the architect.

- No requirement to certify anything beyond the architect's knowledge, services, or responsibilities under the agreement
  Many contracts have been proposed that require the architect to certify that the work of the contractor was completed in accordance with the contract documents. Others have asked the architect to certify that the contract documents complied with all applicable code requirements.

  The architect must not agree with either, or anything similar. The first certification requirement proposed above asks for representations that go beyond what an architect can possibly know. The second requires the architect to state that her services exceeded the applicable standard of care.

- A requirement that the owner not withhold pay unless the architect has agreed to the deduction or has been found liable for corresponding damages
  For a client to withhold pay in circumstances other than those noted above is a breach of contract. The concept here is that if the owner disregards the agreement, the contract clause in a typical contract template is sufficient for the architect to put the client on notice that the work will stop. The architect cannot afford to set up terms that allow the owner to withhold pay on a whim. Such terms would leave the architect with little contractual basis for stopping the work.

  "I won't pay you," the client pouts, "but, Ms. Architect, you still have an obligation to continue your work." Clients would love that!

- A standard of care definition the is consistent with common-law.
  See ***Chapter 9 The Architect's Standard of Care***.

- Ability to charge interest on past-due payments
  The function of interest charges on late payments is to bring a delinquent client, who sees the amount due rising higher and higher, to the bargaining table. At this point, the portion of a bad debt a deadbeat owner will pay depends on negotiations. In these negotiations, a savvy professional will hold out for full payment, including interest. When she has pushed the tardy debtor as far as she possibly can and senses the negotiations are almost at a breaking point, she says, "OK, I know I'll get in trouble with my partners for this, but I'll agree to waive half

of the interest charges if you'll pay within the next 10 days." If he pushes back, the final offer might then be to waive all interest charges if the slacker pays within the next week. If he accepts that and pays within seven days, the original invoice is paid in full, before interest charges are applied.

Interest on overdue invoices represents one thing: leverage that may be used in negotiations in order to get paid.

Ask yourself
If the starting point in all this haggling had been the original invoice amount, would the settlement amount have been payment in full for the original bill or would the architect have had to make concession, agreeing to partial payment?

Ought-to-haves

This should be a list of your next highest priorities, the things you really want but might negotiate under certain circumstances. These could include:

- A fee you can earn a profit on
- Net-30 payment terms
- The survey provided by the owner
- The geotechnical engineer hired by the owner
- Participation in all phases of the project, including construction phase services
- Responsibility for obtaining and paying for the building permit (as a reimbursable expense) is assigned to a party other than the architect
- A time limit on the architect's continuing scope of services after the date of substantial completion
- Architect should retain her copyright, merely conveying a license to the owner to use the design solely for a specific project
- A retainer the owner must pay before the architect begins scheduling the work
- A waiver of subrogation
- A limitation of liability

Ask yourself
Do you know what each of these things means? Can you explain why these contract provisions are important?

Responding to Risk

To conclude this chapter, allow me to share a reference to a legendary account of how one professional responded to phenomenal risks. The story is not about an architect; it is about an architect's consultant facing the sudden realization that a major structure he designed might be at risk of failure. It recounts the decisive response of the structural engineer for the Citicorp Center (*Figure 20.1*, now the Citigroup Center) when facing tangible concerns about its lateral-force-resisting system. The risk of structural failure was based on issues with his own engineering, taken together with field changes he had not known about and concerns about the coming hurricane season. The story is available online, in the May 21, 1995 issue of the *New Yorker*.[3] It reads like a novel (and may seem almost as long). When I came across it at the time it was published, I could not put it down.

Figure 20.1 The Citicorp Tower.

Notes

1 https://codes.iccsafe.org/content/IBC2021P2/chapter-10-means-of-egress#IBC2021P2_Ch10_Sec1011.5.4.1 (accessed October 30, 2024). International Building Code 2021, § 1011.5.4.1 Nonuniform Height Risers.

2 In 1992, I tried to haggle with Omar, a wood-carver in Jerusalem, over a small olive-wood sculpture I wanted to give my parents. Omar wouldn't come down to the number I wanted, so I got in a cab and returned to my hotel. Most evenings I would see Omar at the hotel offering free cab rides to his woodcarving shop. My last day there, I asked him if he still had that sculpture and if he might consider parting with it for $20 (my original offer). He made a show of reluctance but finally agreed. I gave him payment in cash, and he went ahead and shipped it to me. Moral of the story: even the shrewdest negotiator is quite likely to reconsider when you are willing to walk away from what you feel is an unfair agreement.

3 https://www.newyorker.com/magazine/1995/05/29/the-fifty-nine-story-crisis-citicorp-center The website skips the paywall and gives you full access, at least for the first couple of times you link to it. (accessed October 30, 2024)

We'll call this the village green of Pine Valley.

Part VII

Community

Chapter 21, which makes up *Part VII*, considers the theme of giving back. An architect seeks to build community because she understands how a vibrant community lifts and builds her. A citizen architect seeks ways to advance the interests of the public *and* of the profession. An architect builds community by becoming an architect-developer and healing disadvantaged neighborhoods. Another mentors emerging professionals, enabling them to give back as well.

21

Giving Back

Community is the soul of architecture. Without a public involvement, architecture would be much like a tree falling with no one to hear it. Just as some may say the tree, unnoticed in the forest, would make no sound, others may insist that architecture unappreciated in society would be of no consequence. Whether tree and architecture are unheard of or unappreciated, a society unable to draw on the ennobling effects of meaningful architecture would be less of a community.

One might be tempted to think only of how communities benefit from architecture; but without question, architects also benefit greatly from community. Most feel an obligation to repay.

A recent architecture school graduate runs for election to his city council. Across the nation, architects serve in state legislatures. Some become council members for large cities. Others participate in public policy as mayors and county councilors, landmarks and planning commission members, school board members, ad hoc committee leaders, and community organizers.

These are some of the more noticeable examples of architects giving back to their communities. Through less visible community service, pro bono work, and association with nonprofit organizations, architects regularly volunteer untold hours in support of:

- Low-income housing
- Renovations for those in urgent need
- Emergency accessibility improvements for community members that cannot afford design assistance
- Support to make it possible for people to clear regulatory hurdles for their projects
- Help for people new to the construction industry with building permits and inspections
- School enrichment design activities
- Student career fairs
- High school job shadowing and internships
- Canstruction®, a sometime competition where architects and contractors (usually D-B teams) donate tons of canned goods after constructing the most fanciful of sculptures with those cans before delivering them to local food banks (*Figure 21.1*)

Besides nonprofit work and volunteering, architects are known for offering volunteer services to their clients to make it possible to do a little extra in design and construction to further community interests. With the architect's leadership, the project team may decide to:

- Add a public gathering place on site connected to community trails
- Establish building massing to protect or reinforce important viewsheds
- Reinforce a street with a building wall and place parking behind

Forever Practice: The Architect at Work, First Edition. Jim Nielson, FAIA.
© 2025 John Wiley & Sons, Inc. Published 2025 by John Wiley & Sons, Inc.

Figure 21.1 *Canstruction* "Peas on Earth." *Source:* Big-D Construction. Used by permission.

- Reshuffle a site plan to prevent a structure from shading an existing public park
- Step in to coordinate the work of different landowners and entities on key properties when others are not leading out. (See *Example #1* in **Chapter 1 Caring About the World We Live in**. The fact that Tom, the architect that cared so much in that example, was willing to step in, may have been unwise from a business planning perspective, but the results of his intervention remain an improvement to this day.)

Finally, when presented with a regulatory or entitlement hurdle, a thoughtful designer turns those setbacks to the project's advantage. For example, years ago, when the D-B firm, Jersey Devil, built a home in Baja, Mexico, the group encountered a design requirement that didn't fit their offbeat sensibilities: all homes must have sloping tile roofs. Have a look at what they did with that (*Figure 21.2*).[1] They dubbed the project Casa Maraposa (a presumably intentional misspelling of *Butterfly House* in Spanish). Whether or not one appreciates this unconventional design, it is an example of thinking in different ways, satisfying community requirements, and still generating something memorable *and* functional. Importantly, this unconventional design facilitated the collection of rainwater in a central cistern.

Figure 21.2 *Casa Maraposa*, Baja, Mexico, Jersey Devil. *Source:* Jersey Devil.

Developer

Like our renegade design-builders at Jersey Devil, one thing architects can do is become developers and focus on areas of a city where development is needed when no one else is stepping forward to do it.

Budding architect-developers often channel their inner Jonathan Segal. For years, Segal has bought property, sometimes in neglected parts of San Diego, negotiated with the city from a position of strength (because they need housing and know what he can do), and developed housing in places where it may be lacking. Other developers watch what he does and rush in wherever he starts. The places he touches become some of the most sought-after in the community. Apparently, Segal has managed to hold onto most of his projects. He stays involved.

Ask yourself
Review Jonathan Segal's website,[2] including Figure 21.3.[3] Look for articles about him by others as well. Answer this question above all: In what ways does he make a difference in his community?

Mentor

Architects ultimately have many opportunities to guide and mentor young people, architecture students, emerging professionals seeking licensure, and fellow architects with less experience than they have. Because she cares about her community, an architect will lead out in learning what makes communities better. And she will help those that choose the path of architecture to pursue it with an awareness of all that it entails.

As an architect moves into leadership in an architecture firm, wherever and whenever she possibly can, she will offer employment—flexible employment—even to architecture *students* so that they can afford to attend school and complete their education program, all the way through capstone studio. She will then gladly sign up to be an AXP® supervisor, advising those she assists on the best way to sequence their efforts, helping her mentees find ways to get needed experience, following up to make sure they meet their responsibilities, and signing off on experience completed. She will help people prepare for the licensing exam, both through financial support to help with study materials and through individual coaching and informal seminars she sets up to help examinees down the stretch. Whether those she works with end up as architects or not, she builds community by mentoring.

Figure 21.3 *Mr. Robinson*, **a mixed-use project** by Jonathan Segal, FAIA. *Source:* Jonathan Segal.

AIA College of Fellows

Fellowship represents AIA's highest membership honor. It is awarded for service to the profession, the environment, and society, having broad impact. It recognizes giving back to the community and emphasizes:

- The duty to elevate the profession
- The duty to safeguard the environment
- The duty to build the community

A member may be nominated in one of six categories or objects. In addition to the candidates' general duty to build community, many of the category descriptions below make further reference to and are awarded in recognition of a record of substantial community service.

Fellowship Objects of Nomination

Object 1: To promote the aesthetic, scientific, and practical efficiency of the profession
Sub-objects: Design, Urban Design and Planning, Preservation
Object 2: To advance the science and art of planning and building by advancing the standards of practice
Sub-objects: Practice Management, Practice Technical Advancement
Object 3: To coordinate the building industry, and the profession of architecture.
Sub-objects: Led the Institute, Led a Related Organization
Object 4: To ensure the advancement of the living standards of people through their improved environment
Sub-objects: Public Service, Government, Industry Organizations
Object 5: To make the profession of ever-increasing service to society
Sub-objects: Alternative career, Service to Society, Volunteer work with organizations not directly connected with the built environment
Object 6: To advance the science and art of planning and building by advancing the standards of architectural education and training
Sub-objects: Education, Research, Literature
See the AIA Fellowship home page and related links for additional information.[4]

Ask yourself
Membership in the AIA College of Fellows recognizes substantial service in many ways; it also affords many opportunities for community building. What type of service appeals to you most, whether or not you ever end up with that extra letter after your name? How will you serve your community throughout your profession?

Additional Resources

The Architect's Handbook of Professional Practice
Chapter 4   Public Interest Design

Author's Note

Building community
Community building is of critical importance to architects. It matters to me. It probably matters to you, too.

Developer
My business partner and I set out to follow Jonathan Segal's lead in a marginalized neighborhood of our city. We purchased a half-acre parcel on lower Main Street that had been home to a print shop, followed by an ethnic grocery store. After that, the structure sat vacant for years before burning down, leaving just a shell. We designed and built a successful project on the site with 20 townhouses. Some might call our efforts gentrification, but the alternative was a burned-out vacant lot sporting nothing but an orphaned billboard.

That project has led to others. After a long entitlement process, we now have a similar project under construction in another part of town. The project is in a very favorable area, but it is on a parcel that was also home to a dilapidated building.

Educator
When I retired, I began teaching architecture as an adjunct professor. Years ago, many of the professors in my own professional program were or had been practicing architects. I figured teaching would be a way to give back something of what they had given me. But as I wrote in the dedication at the beginning of this book, I've gained more as a teacher than I can ever return.

This is the nature of service and community building. We begin with the idea of giving, but if we serve selflessly, in the end, we are the ones that reap the benefits.

Notes

1 https://www.jerseydevildesignbuild.com/img/gallery/corazon/cm2.jpg (accessed October 18, 2024)
2 https://www.jonathansegalarchitect.com/ (accessed October 18, 2024)
3 Project: https://www.jonathansegalarchitect.com/mr-robinson Image: https://images.squarespace-cdn.com/content/v1/5c9c3de8523958850083387d/1563564829821-XQEEQGTFIRHFQI4M05P7/Mr-Robinson-by-Jonathan-Segal-017.jpg?format=2500w (both accessed October 18, 2024)
4 https://www.aia.org/design-excellence/awards/fellowship (accessed October 18, 2024)

And what is it you want?

Part VIII

Client

At its core, **Part VIII** deals with client interactions, which is where the work of a successful practice begins. Every client brings different experience and expectations to a project. The architect must be prepared to deal with entities, both public and private, with owners that have funding from different sources, and with clients whose expectations of the architect vary widely. This wide range of clientele will ask for individual (possibly one-of-a-kind) project types, using distinct and possibly client-generated contracts and individualized scopes of services.

The delivery method selected by the client also has a material impact on what the architect is expected to do and how he does it. The demands of many clients (even experienced ones) may exceed the services the architect is contracted to perform. How the architect deals with such expectations can make the difference between a profitable, successful project and a losing proposition.

22

One of a Kind

An architect works with many different clients during his career; he may not encounter the same one twice. While he will get along easily with some clients, others will be more challenging. It is not uncommon for a firm leader to need to step in to resolve challenges with clients that are furious about how they had been treated by others in a firm, never mind that the problems may be mostly of their own doing.

When serious problems arise, clients may refuse to continue working with the assigned architectural project manager. They may threaten to sue or not to pay the architect's invoices. The breakdown usually centers on lack of communication—an inability or unwillingness, on the part of the client, architect, or staff member, to listen.

A few lessons an architect would do well to heed when working with difficult clients:

- Listen well and satisfy the client's demands to the extent possible within the scope agreed on
- When they ask for services not included in their contract, here's the script the architect should use *every time*: "We will be happy to give you a proposal for that."
- Finally, when the owner tries to bully the architect (as some will) and seeks to avoid its responsibilities as client (such as making payments according to the contract), the architect must be professional and point out what the contract requires of them, noting that he will have to stop work, for example, if his firm doesn't get paid

Clients vary in financial capability, temperament, and construction experience. The client or owner a firm may contract with could be:

- A small company doing a 10,000 SF tenant finish in an old building they got a deal on
- A public research university with a set of established design standards and a 25-person facilities department
- A D-B contractor teaming with the architect on a construction type such as food processing that the contractor knows well but with which the architect has little experience
- A burgeoning high-tech company that built a new building five years ago, has since expanded into leased space, and is now looking to consolidate its dispersed staff into a single headquarters facility with office and manufacturing space
- Some other unique client, whose blend of experience and ideas could be the impetus for a one-of-a-kind project

An architect's experience negotiating an agreement and working with the owner will be markedly different in each of the above cases. Differences in construction experience may lead the owner to assume a smaller or larger role for itself and assign more or less primacy to the contractor, often at the expense of the architect. With little experience in how things work best, the owner might also attempt to take a much larger role than is anticipated in AIA contract documents. Some clients may also resist making decisions and become difficult to reach.

In any such cases, as with less-familiar delivery methods as outlined in *Chapter 23*, specific differences in the way scope is assigned to each team member should be established in the agreement, when parties are on their best behavior, rather than left to be sorted out later, when construction is going poorly or relationships are deteriorating.

Forever Practice: The Architect at Work, First Edition. Jim Nielson, FAIA.
© 2025 John Wiley & Sons, Inc. Published 2025 by John Wiley & Sons, Inc.

22 One of a Kind

With a more experienced owner, one may face a request to use a client-generated agreement. Often, such agreements ask the firm to accept provisions its insurance will not cover. When firms receive such an agreement, a prudent architect turns it over immediately to his professional liability insurance agent for comment. Architect and agent then pour over the agreement in detail. An agent can clarify what is insurable and what is not. One of the most powerful negotiating tools an architect has when he goes back to a client that has asked him to consider such a contract is to inform him explicitly of the provisions he's asking for, which cannot be covered by his firm's insurance.

"Neither my company nor any of the owners have the financial resources to settle a claim with you on these matters on our own," you might tell him. "So, if I were to execute the agreement as written, you simply wouldn't have coverage in these areas."

The architect should then offer to rewrite these clauses in ways consistent with the firm's liability coverage and with the applicable standard of care. An insurance company or an attorney experienced with construction contracts can help here. A smart architect goes into the first round of negotiations with clauses rewritten to the firm's (and insurance company's) liking already in his back pocket.

Another possible outcome of negotiations about an owner-generated contract is that the owner simply won't budge. And let's assume the architect wants the project. (Or his business partner does.) In one such case, the client, a developer, wouldn't even read the AIA contract proposed. Too many words. The developer countered with a three-page letter contract intended for subcontractors. The architect sent it back with the 15 or 20 most important provisions from thc original contract he had proposed inserted. Still not happening. When architect and owner talked by phone further, the architect told him, as suggested above, in some cases he would be left uninsured under the proposed contract.

"Give me your top ten," the developer said. The architect sent him ten. Still too many. So, he tried five. Nope. Three or four? OK. Among the architect's top four was a limitation of liability, something insurance companies recommend strongly but most owners won't accept. At this point, though, the owner gave up and accepted the architect's four biggest revisions, all appended to his simple letter contract, using language the architect's insurance agent helped him with. It wasn't everything, but it addressed the firm's biggest concerns.

Scope of Services

Chapter 9 The Architect's Standard of Care reviewed in detail the legal standard we are held to in our work. In our different team roles—particularly during construction—clients and contractors may confuse the architect's standard of care with her scope of services. In fact, the architect's standard of care does not bind the architect to any particular list of services that must be provided on any particular project. No. The architect's standard of care applies to the architect's performance fulfilling whatever scope of services her contract requires.

Scope Always Varies

Services an architect is hired to perform are different on every job. Consider these examples:

- An architect worked as a consultant to a landscape architect on a freeway project. The landscape architect worked for the engineering firm designing the freeway. Neither architect nor landscape architect was responsible for coordinating consultant work or construction administration. The architect for this project had a narrowly defined and carefully circumscribed scope of services.
- An architect mentioned in a previous chapter worked on a large public facility downtown. The city's civil engineer for adjacent road and sidewalk work asked this architect for input on traffic signal and streetlight coordination. The architect's sense of civic duty did not create an obligation for him to assist. He understood

that by offering freelance input, his efforts would probably not be covered by his firm's professional liability insurance.
- Finally, when serving as architect of record on several projects for the local Transit Authority, an architect's specific scope of services on these complex projects dealt only with the shelters and platforms at each station. He did not have responsibility for overseeing or coordinating the work of the engineer that hired his firm. The fact that he was producing architectural documents for facilities whose long-term viability depended on carefully engineered rails and structures close by did not in any way bestow responsibility on him to take charge of or play any role in the design or coordination of those structures or rail appurtenances.

These three examples describe only a few of the carefully defined and sometimes limited roles architects may be asked to fulfill on a variety of project types. An architect's scope of services is always tailored to specific owner, contractor, and project needs. Over the course of an entire career, an architect may work on hundreds of projects, including repeat designs of the same prototype in different locations. Considering all of these efforts during a long career, an architect will not likely be part of any two projects with precisely identical scopes.

Defining the Architect's Scope of Services

Definition of the architect's role begins with the professional services agreement negotiated with the client, but legally it may also be established or modified by direction from the client and by procedures adopted in the course of the project. The architect's scope may also include or exclude virtually any service a client and architect agree should be in or out of the scope. An architect may accept responsibility for many additional services, but he should make sure that he is able to perform the additional duties assigned competently, that the services will be covered by insurance, as appropriate, and that he will be paid for the work.

To provide an idea of the kinds of services we might consider, here are some items I have seen *excluded* from what some may consider an architect's standard scopes of services:

- Construction Administration
- Design team leadership
- Cost estimating or opinions of probable cost in any form
- Coordinating the work of design engineers
- Conceptual design
- Complete design services up to and including the Design Development phase
- Construction Documents

In addition, services that are sometimes *added* to baseline scopes of services are items such as:

- Full-time on-site representation
- Detailed cost estimating
- Civil engineering (provided by a consultant) and associated coordination
- Landscape architecture (provided by a consultant) and associated coordination
- Feasibility studies
- Facilities programming
- Market research
- Econometric studies (generally assisted by a consultant)
- Public involvement exercises
- Development of branding, business development, and fundraising materials
- Bond election support

Initial negotiations for every project include the practice of confirming, adding, and removing work from the architect's scope of services normally included in published agreements. No standard scope or standard of care exists independently of such negotiations. Therefore, in addition to its limitations of reasonableness, time, location, and circumstance, the architect's applicable standard of care is also limited to the scope of services actually provided. This further limitation can be stated as follows:

To the extent a client and architect agree on a scope of services, including architectural work (services included in the architect's scope of work, for which the architect is under contract, that the architect actually performs, and for which he received consideration), those services must be performed in accordance with the applicable standard of care.

Pro Bono and Detective Work

The architect is not obligated to provide services voluntarily that she has not been contracted to perform. The architect also has no mandate to discern the existence of and act on the contents of communications not shared with the architect. And the architect is not asked to be a detective or to conduct surveillance to discover the status of communications, concept development, or construction preparations to which she is not otherwise privy; the architect is not required to read minds. Assertions and professional conclusions based on the premise that "the architect should have known!" have no bearing in an evaluation of an architect's performance in accordance with the applicable standard of care.

Additional Resources

The Architect's Handbook of Professional Practice

    17.1   Agreements with Owners

    17.3   Owner-Generated Agreements

ProPEL, ACSA Professional Practice Education Library (Videos for Classroom Use)
        https://propel.yuja.com
        Fees Unit | Lesson 6 Examples and Implications

Author's Note

A difficult client

One time, in a conversation with a belligerent client who had not paid our firm's final bills, I waited until he was done screaming and then pointed out firmly, yet professionally, that our AIA owner-architect agreement disallowed withholding payment unless a claim against the architect had been substantiated in a recognized dispute-resolution process or the architect had agreed to the withholding in writing. I told him where to look in our agreement to find that provision. Since no agreement to forego payment or dispute-resolution process had happened or was even pending, I told him he was failing to meet his obligations under contract; it was our intent, therefore, to turn his overdue invoices over to a collection agency and file a claim against his company for breach of contract, if necessary.

Our firm received payment in full within a week.

23

Delivery Methods and the Client

Often the client dictates the scope of an architect's services, in part, through the choice of project delivery methods. Owners opt for different project methods based on what they believe will best serve their needs. In practice, delivery methods may affect an architect's relationships with the owner and contractor and the architect's scope of services. Delivery methods generally fall into the following common groupings:

Traditional Design-Bid-Build

In Design-Bid-Build delivery, the design team produces detailed plans and specifications, contractors bid the job, and the successful bidder builds it. Due to the absence of contractor cost feedback prior to bidding, this method is the most prone among common delivery approaches to coming in over budget. The architect's role with this traditional delivery method includes leading the team right from the beginning. Depending on contractual provisions and contractor or owner preferences, the contractor may take on overall project team leadership once construction work gets underway.

Design-Build

Since they often have greater financial resources, in many cases, contractors are the ones that lead large D-B projects. As D-B, the contractor hires the architect. Contractor, architect, or even subcontractors may hire the consulting engineers. The D-B method usually involves an agreement by the D-B team to accomplish a given scope for a price agreed to up front. By contract, the Design-Builder (contractor) has the tools to ensure the budget is met. Among those tools is D-B subcontracting.

To support D-B subcontracting, architects may convey basic requirements to subcontract bidders without prescribing details that might add costs. Instead, the team may look to bidders for independent creativity, entrepreneurship, and initiative to provide the needed results at the lowest possible price. For portions of a project, shop drawings produced by D-B subcontractors may end up taking the place of detailed construction documents. In the end, if all goes well, the subcontractor furnishes and installs the work successfully, at the price the contractor was looking for.

In contractor-led D-B delivery, the contractor leads the team from the outset and the architect works for the contractor. Turning to a term contractors sometimes use, the architect may *skinny up* drawings (for further development by bidders) when asked to do so by the contractor. Complying with this request generally means showing key concepts and dimensions for part of the work parametrically, not going into the detail that would be required for a Design-Bid-Build project.

Forever Practice: The Architect at Work, First Edition. Jim Nielson, FAIA.
© 2025 John Wiley & Sons, Inc. Published 2025 by John Wiley & Sons, Inc.

Without the project leadership role in Design-Bid-Build delivery, the architect's responsibilities and control over the project are reduced.

Construction Manager/General Contractor (CM/GC)

CM/GC project delivery generally includes CM-At Risk and CM-As Advisor methods. Depending on the market, CM-At Risk (with a Guaranteed Maximum Price or GMP) may be the predominant form of this delivery method. CM/GC (at risk) is similar to Design-Build delivery in some ways. Like D-B, the contractor provides cost estimating, constructability input, and schedule projections throughout design. At an agreed-upon point (based on a set completion percentage of the documents), the contractor prices the work and then agrees with the owner on a GMP. The GMP should include a sufficient contingency to account for items not yet shown in the drawings and specifications, which are usually incomplete at the time a GMP is set.

Although CM/GC differs from D-B, early contractor feedback, together with the possibility of up-front design interactions with potential subcontractors, may lead to the same type of contractor requests for simplified drawings to let the magic of bidder-designed contracting and subcontractor innovation work to keep prices low. Such requests are relatively common with CM-At-Risk delivery, in combination with a GMP, because this delivery method helps the contractor control costs to meet the GMP.

In a CM/GC project, the architect and contractor function as partners, each with a share of leadership and respective control. The architect's project leadership responsibilities fall partway between his role in Design-Bid-Build delivery and in D-B.

Integrated Project Delivery (IPD)

This collaborative delivery system typically brings owner, contractor, architect, and other team members under the umbrella of a single contract and a common insurance policy. Owners commit to invest the time and attention necessary to participate in collaborative design and construction processes from start to finish and to be available to make decisions without delay. Project teams may be co-located during key parts of the process so input from different members of the team may be both collaborative and instantaneous. For example, I was part of an IPD team for a large memory chip fabrication plant. While construction was underway, dozens of design architects and engineers had offices on site. Given team member proximity to each other and the integrated nature of the project, RFI responses were usually returned to the contractor in minutes, and the work proceeded. Rarely, if ever, did such a response take even an hour. As a corollary, key members of the owner team were consistently available and were empowered to make the big decisions immediately.

With IPD, a major reason work moves expeditiously is that in their interactions, team members experience little concern for liability issues. This lack of legal concerns frees up bandwidth that can be applied to better project design and development. More important than whether the team is co-located is whether participants exhibit effective collaboration—a key component of IPD that generally leads to substantial improvements in construction budgets and schedules.

Heightened requirements for early and continued owner involvement in the integrated process, plus demands for wrap coverage products not all liability insurers may offer, mean that IPD has traditionally been more common with large projects and a few specific project types. However, in the right circumstances, IPD shows promise for smaller projects of many types.

Leadership in IPD projects is shared broadly. Lines of communication are diffuse and multidirectional. IPD may not affect the extent of the architect's leadership responsibility. But it changes the nature of leadership for the overall team. An IPD organization tends to be almost flat, with shared responsibilities and little hierarchy. Unlike other delivery systems, the architect's (and virtually everyone's) leadership roles are characterized by consensus, participation, and collaboration.

Ask yourself
What impact does project delivery choice have on the architect's role in a design team?

Bidder-designed Systems and Components are Found in All Delivery Methods

Usually, the more bidder-designed components a project includes, the smaller the architect's role. Customarily, all delivery methods, including Design-Bid-Build, involve some subcontractor D-B (bidder-designed) scope. In a D-B project, a substantial part of the work may be bidder-designed. Bidder-designed scope in projects delivered using the CM/GC or IPD process often falls somewhere between that of Design-Bid-Build and D-B projects.

Of course, the varied nature of construction markets and general contractor preferences ensure a different scope of bidder-designed products and services on every project. Bidder-designed work on a project may range from fire protection (for most projects) to less common fare, such as ammonia refrigeration systems, gravity-retaining walls, custom wall panels, curtain walls with integral shading devices, and sound reinforcement systems. Depending on the project and on key team members' experience and preferences, almost any part of a contractor's scope may become a bidder-designed task.

Architect as Consultant Rather than Design Team Leader

Project delivery methods may dictate the architect's role, but other factors may have more impact. Regardless of delivery method, when the architect works as a consultant, rather than team leader, he takes on a smaller role. For example, as mentioned briefly in a previous chapter, infrastructure projects such as rail transit lines may use just about any delivery method. But in such projects, an architect (who is likely responsible for platforms and canopies) may report to an engineer. In such cases, much of the work an architect might typically design or oversee is built and administered either by subcontractors (bidders) or an engineer or other team members that hired the architect as a consultant. For example, the team leader, an engineer or contractor, is likely to have its own concrete specifications and maybe even a concrete crew. The architect's role is minimized; she calls out concrete at a station platform, for example, by drawing up the geometry and noting it as *concrete*. Coordinating structural requirements for canopies? Other team members have that covered, too. The architect's primary responsibility is to show the canopies' geometry and dimensions.

Challenges—Architect's Role: Case Study

In a recent claim involving the failure of a site structural system, the project delivery system and agreements used, along with early team leadership practices by owner and contractor, all combined to reduce the architect's scope of services and influence. The architect had no involvement in the defective construction associated with this claim. The architect also had no knowledge, authority, nor ability to mitigate the defective work.

Project Leadership

Early in the development of this project, the owner looked to the contractor for general project leadership. Often, on large projects, the architect leads a multifaceted team of consultants.

But the mere presence of an architect on a team does not make her accountable for work of the team, about which she receives no information.

Who holds the reins of leadership, exercises responsible control and is ultimately responsible? This is determined based on assignment, agreement, and operational practices adopted by the owner and those to whom he assigns leadership roles.

The architect's client—the D-B, or contractor in this example case, functioned as the team leader, conducting business often assigned to an architect on other projects and frequently doing so without involving or informing the architect.

Role Limitations, Based on the Actions of Others

This project experienced a failure of a site structural system. Leading up to that failure, the architect's role in this project had been limited as previously described. Case documentation noted below demonstrated clearly that, with respect to this site structural failure, the architect's role was extraordinarily constrained:

- The architect was not assigned responsibility by contract to prepare or oversee any design or documentation related to the special structural systems for dealing with large site grades and therefore did not do so
- Meeting minutes showed that the contractor led discussions of these structural systems separately from agenda items about what the owner and contractor treated as architectural items
- The contractor selected the site structural systems used, informed team members what had been priced, and directed the project team to design and construct accordingly. No member of the project team questioned the contractor's authority to make these decisions unilaterally
- The architect was not consulted nor involved in such direction by the contractor

Consequences of a Diminished Role

The project described above experienced major defects resulting in outright failures and leading to multi-million dollar claims. Owner and Contractor made claims against all major parties, including the architect. Written records made by those involved demonstrated that with respect to the failed structures, the architect's diminished responsibilities made it impossible for her to exercise any design oversight to ensure delivery of a fully successful project. The architect's usual role in leading the design team had been seriously abridged by the owner's assignments, agreements, and operational practices adopted.

Ask yourself
What difference does it make if the architect leads the design team or not? Why might it make a difference?

Additional Resources

The Architect's Handbook of Professional Practice
  Chapter 9   Design Project Delivery

Author's Note

Hired by the engineer

My firm was hired by a civil engineer to be the architect for a water treatment plant. The engineer handled not just infrastructure and horizontal development but also designed the equipment, tanks, and process piping that filled the building. This was a successful project, for which our firm, as architect, played a minor role. I led the team that designed the shell to go around all the equipment engineered by the engineer leading the team. Responding to the special requirements of water flow and equipment within the building, we created a distinctive look for the plant that water district officials loved. Major parts of the work, however, including metal roofing, windows, door hardware, and special coatings, were contractor-, engineer-, or bidder-designed. And, in response to the needs of the engineer we worked for, we included only very little detailed design information in our construction documents for these parts of the work. We reviewed the few submittals associated with our work, but we were not involved in or even aware of submittals for many items designed by others.

Last chance to get it right.

Part IX

Construction

Construction administration is the focus of ***Part IX***. Through appropriate and thoughtful decisions and actions during this phase, the architect has the opportunity to finish a strong project out successfully or rescue one that has been previously troubled. This effort begins by setting up communications and processes with a contractor effectively, respecting the contractor's approach, and making sure that instructions are handled properly and in writing. It continues with cooperation on site and with closeout procedures that follow the conditions of the contract as completely as possible.

Two factors affect things along the way. The delivery method used for a project (Design-Bid-Build, D-B, and so on) lays a few key ground rules for the architect and contractor that need careful consideration and discussion. And the architect must pay special attention to the parts of the contractor's work that are bidder-designed. From drawings and specifications to submittals and site visits, this distinction brings with it fundamental challenges. And it affects the architect's scope.

24

Getting Started

As noted at the end of ***Chapter 17 Business and Human Resources Management***, if a project isn't designed well and construction documents are not airtight, our work during construction represents our last opportunity to pull the project out of the fire. But if we have waited this long, making things right will be no easy task.

With respect to the project overall, the architect's success and effective risk management depend a great deal on the contractor's success. Here, in ***Part IX***, are recommendations for what the architect can do during construction to help both owner and contractor succeed.

Assisting with Contractor Selection

Assisting the owner with contractor selection is a key architect responsibility. It helps the owner determine who will build the project. If the client wishes to negotiate directly with contractors based on qualifications, the architect's involvement may include giving recommendations for construction firms to interview. If the delivery method the owner chooses requires selecting a construction manager, the architect may help the client prepare a solicitation for qualifications and basic construction management fees. He may then be asked to recommend firms the client could interview. Finally, for a stipulated sum contract or Design-Bid-Build delivery method, the architect helps the client prepare bid instructions. A client may also ask the architect to prepare a list of recommended contractors the owner could ask to submit bids for a project.

The recommendations an architect prepares may be based on experience with contractors, conversations with other architects, or general research. The architect may even conduct interviews with contractors independently and maintain a list of preferred contractors, perhaps based on both experience *and* interviews. An architect serves her clients best if she is able to recommend competent contractors to them with a consistent record of integrity.

Ask yourself
What fees would a solicitation require contractors to include in proposals for basic construction management services?
What factors would an architect consider in evaluating contractors to recommend as bidders?

Contract Documents and the Conformed Set

Short answer for this section: don't think about preparing a conformed set without additional compensation.

The documents put out to bid should be labeled *contract documents*. They might also be called *construction documents*. It isn't a good idea to label them as *bid documents*, even if the client requests this. The name *bid documents* suggests that when bidding is done, the architect will turn them into *construction documents*.

Forever Practice: The Architect at Work, First Edition. Jim Nielson, FAIA.
© 2025 John Wiley & Sons, Inc. Published 2025 by John Wiley & Sons, Inc.

158 | *24 Getting Started*

These naming conventions suggest gathering all instructions given by addendum, modifying the drawings, and coordinating things so everything covered by addendum (often in abbreviated fashion) is fleshed out and reflected accurately and completely, with new dates and an updated table of contents. The contractor would already have been given all of these instructions. Reissuing the set, a task that is not part of basic services, means expending time and effort. In addition, the possibility of unintentionally omitting something in the transition creates potential problems during construction and significant liability for the architect.

If our client requests this added scope and the architect can't talk the client out of it, the architect should prepare a proposal to provide a *conformed set* as an additional service. This is an industry term for a set of drawings prepared after bidding and negotiations are complete, as discussed above.

Bidding and Negotiation

The architect's role during competitive bidding and negotiation is to make sure that everything she says and every change she makes is communicated to every contractor preparing bids or negotiating for the job. Changes made are included in *addendums*. These documents modify the contract documents and are binding on those bidding on or negotiating for the job. Substitution requests should be considered only if the proposer can demonstrate that they will make the project cost less, be completed sooner, or be of improved quality. Only if proposed substitutions or other changes are incorporated into the project by addendum should bidders base pricing on them in bids or proposals.

Contractors bidding or negotiating for the project should put requests for bidding information or clarifications in writing. If time constraints dictate a verbal conversation, the architect may discuss possible clarifications or solutions with contractors but should caution them that unless a change or clarification addressing the issue makes it into a written addendum by the deadline found in the bid instructions, the party seeking the contract must bid the documents as he understands them and may not rely on verbal communications from the architect.

For private clients, the architect may prepare a bid tabulation where bids can be arrayed as they are read. The owner and architect review the bids at the location of the client's choosing and at the date and time of bid opening. They compare base bid amounts (including allowances) and determine the apparent low bidder. If bid alternates or unit prices have been solicited in the contract documents and priced, and if any budget dollars remain, the architect assists the owner in evaluating which, if any, of the bid alternates or unit prices to approve or budget for. Then, the group arrives at a tentative final construction cost.

Public clients generally have standard forms and procedures for bid openings.

The construction cost at this point is tentative, pending potential negotiations, value engineering with the apparent low bidder, and costs for any owner-directed changes in the general contractor's team. The apparent low bidder is typically required to submit a list of major suppliers and subcontractors within 24 hours, after which the owner (and often the architect) reviews with the contractor any requests for changes to subcontractors. Directing subcontractor changes is relatively uncommon and is typically only done when the owner or architect has experienced very poor or untimely performance working with a proposed sub on one or more past jobs. It also comes with a cost, which may mean a budget overage or a desired alternate left out of the job. The reason for the added cost is that in almost all cases, the subcontractor that will initially have been included in the bid will be the contractor's lowest bidder in that trade. If the owner rejects that subcontractor in favor of another, the delta between the two bids is added to the base bid amount.

After basic pricing has been worked out (which might go on for some time, particularly if value engineering is needed), the owner negotiates and executes an owner-contractor agreement. Once the contractor has also signed the agreement, the owner provides a notice to proceed and the contractor schedules the work.

Ask yourself
How do the architect and the owner review questions, prepare addendums, compile bid tabulations, determine the bid alternates to accept, and evaluate possible subcontractor changes?
Would an addendum ever be issued after bids are opened?

Preconstruction Meeting

The preconstruction meeting marks the start of construction. The architect should be there. Specifications generally include a comprehensive list of agenda items for the meeting, from hours of operation and site fencing to temporary utilities (usually including portable toilets). The meeting generally covers how the contractor will run things, including information about meetings, submittals, RFIs, change orders, and pay applications.

The architect should come prepared with an agenda covering the suggested topics. The contractor may want the architect to run the meeting. Sometimes the contractor runs it. Either way, the architect is there to answer questions or, if something important doesn't get mentioned, to bring it up for dicussion.

Preconstruction Conferences for Individual Trades

The most common of these preconstruction conferences, and often the only one on a job, is the pre-roofing conference. So many trades on the roof of a building need coordination (mechanical, plumbing, electrical, horizontal glazing, sheet metal flashing, roofing, and often structural steel) that it is easy to find a way to blame another party. An experienced architect once described the pre-roofing conference to me this way:

> "You get all the liars up on the roof and you hear what they have to say. And maybe after they've told all their lies in public, when things go wrong, they may not have quite as many stories to tell about why it went wrong."

We're all pretty good at saying what we know people want to hear.

In all seriousness, though, the purpose of preconstruction conferences is 1) to make sure each subcontractor involved fully understands its scope *and* 2) to ensure that subcontractor personnel meet their counterparts personally—those with whom he'll have to coordinate.

Coordination is what makes it possible for each subcontractor to do what they do without getting in the way of all the others' work. If subcontractors have met the people, *including* the general contractor and the architect, this interaction with others working on the same part of the same project helps lead to the realization that they all have to cooperate to make things happen. With these things in mind, there's a better chance of working together to forge a successful outcome.

On rather large projects, general contractors will sometimes hold preconstruction conferences for trades other than roofing.

Ask yourself
In some large construction management projects, subcontractors are hired over time, as the job is bought out. Although these new hires miss the initial preconstruction conference, could their own individual preconstruction conferences fill the gap?
What does it mean for a job to be bought out?

Project Meetings/Site Visits

It is a good idea to schedule project meetings and site visits so that they coincide. An architect almost never has enough fee to go back twice each week all the way through construction. In pricing fee proposals, architects will often assume one site visit/project meeting each week for the duration of construction. That tends to be a good average.

With that average in mind, it is wise to work with the contractor to plan site visits/project meetings at the outset a little less frequently than once a week. Doing so leaves room in the architect's budget to add in a site visit (or even two), between times, as needed to support project progress during the height of construction activity.

AIA contracts typically contain language about the architect visiting the site at intervals as appropriate to construction progress. As is clear when considering a contractor's typical S-curve, representing cumulative expenses (a very good proxy for work progress) over time, the amount of work generally accomplished each week during the opening months of a project can be expected to be only a fraction of what will be done each week halfway through the job. (See *Appendix H Contractor's S-curve* for examples of how sophisticated contractors plot project progress in terms of pay requests and time spent.)

During the busiest construction season, an architect may be called to the jobsite to respond to unanticipated contractor needs more than once in a week. If the architect stops by the job weekly when little is happening early on, all these visits may eat up fee needed for this extra attention when construction is hopping. In fact, an agreement will often stipulate a fixed number of visits. Going to the site more often should be reimbursed as additional services. However, if it appears that the architect went to the jobsite more than necessary at the outset, it may be difficult to get the client to pay for any extra visits when the contractor really needs them.

Ask yourself
What are the implications of the contractor's S-curve? What does the chart mean to the architect?
Also, what if the architect runs out of fee to visit the jobsite? Is she obligated to continue construction administration activities?

Additional Resources

The Architect's Handbook of Professional Practice
    10.9   Construction Phase Services

Author's Note

Lots of preconstruction conferences
On a large project I worked on, the contractor held preconstruction conferences for each group of trades as soon as the work was bought out. I attended these meetings; they were remarkably valuable in establishing contact within a related cluster of subcontractors, together with much-needed connections between these new members of the team and the general contractor and architect. These connections were critical in eliminating the anonymity that might have otherwise resulted on a job they were just joining, where typically more than 1,000 people were working on a given day.

25

Put It in Writing

Throughout construction, the architect, contractor, and owner exchange key documents relating to design intent, contract documents, and scope, as outlined in this chapter.

Items used to make sure that what the contractor has planned will meet the design intent are generally referred to as **submittals** and include samples, product information, and shop drawings.

The architect may respond that submittals do not meet the design intent, that they will if minor corrections are made, or that they are acceptable as submitted. Submittals are not a vehicle for making substitutions; they are a double check that the contractor's proposed products, systems, and methods meet the requirements and quality standards shown and specified.

Neither submittals nor the architect's comments thereon change the contract documents. If the contractor wishes to make a substitution for a product, system, and/or method required by the drawings and specifications, the contractor must initiate a document that will change the contract. This could be an RFI, as described later in this chapter, but most straightforward would be a Change Request for architect and owner review. If the request is acceptable, the architect may then direct the contractor to include the revision in a change order (perhaps together with several other approved change requests) for signature, thus modifying the product or assembly, plus any or all of the above: contract price, time, and quality standards.

As noted previously, in order to be considered, a substitution request, before or after bidding, should give the owner an advantage in cost, time, or quality. Accordingly, a change order implementing a contractor-proposed substitution request should include a credit, reducing the contract cost, a revised completion date, agreeing to complete the work sooner, and/or documented improvement in project quality.

Ask yourself
Would there be any reason (and what would such a reason be) for an owner to approve a substitution request proposed by a contractor that provides the owner with no advantage over the original contract document requirement?

Deferred submittals, such as fire protection drawings and pre-engineered building design documents, are reviewed for consistency with design intent. These are also reviewed concurrently by the AHJ for code compliance review and incorporation into the project permit. For more information on deferred submittals, see **Chapter 27 Bidder-designed Work**.

Documents used to clarify and modify contract documents and contractor scope include requests for information (RFIs), architect's supplemental instructions (ASIs), and proposal requests (PRs). A contractor may also initiate a Change Request, either in response to an unanticipated and unforeseeable condition or receipt of one of the documents listed here.

An *RFI* is the contractor's method of requesting information or clarification regarding something in the contract documents he considers to be unclear.

Forever Practice: The Architect at Work, First Edition. Jim Nielson, FAIA.
© 2025 John Wiley & Sons, Inc. Published 2025 by John Wiley & Sons, Inc.

162 | *25 Put It in Writing*

An architect should never respond to an *RFI* without first discussing it with the contractor. The contractor's request could be the result of an issue in the contract documents. It could also be due to a mistake on his part that he needs to find a reasonable way out of. Either way, as architect and contractor discuss the contractor's issue, the architect should not begin by dictating a solution.

The reasons for this approach are:

1. The contractor has just brought the issue to the architect's attention but will have been thinking about a solution for some time beforehand—longer than the architect has had to ponder the problem
2. In many cases, the solution will center on constructability, which the contractor knows much more about than the architect

If an architect shoots a freshly revised drawing or sketch back to the contractor without going over things with him first, the architect's input may just give the contractor something more to be puzzled about.

And when a contractor is puzzled, things usually cost more.

If the contractor includes a proposed solution with an *RFI*, the architect might need to redirect the builder's approach a bit to salvage important design considerations. But discussing that approach with the contractor, together with the architect's design concerns, may result in a better, more expeditious approach than either would have come up with, working alone.

Ask yourself
"If the contractor is puzzled, things tend to cost more." Why would that be the case?

An *RFI* creates a binding change to the contract documents. The architect should generally avoid adding anything to the contractor's scope that cannot reasonably be inferred from the documents. If something is not clear in a given situation, the contractor is almost always still obligated by contract to provide a complete and functional assembly; however, in situations that generate an *RFI*, the details of how to accomplish some part of what the contractor is required to do may appear in the documents in a manner that is less than useful. For this reason, a thoughtful architect starts the conversation about an *RFI* with the question: "Mr. Contractor, what do you suggest?" Or, "What had you been thinking about doing here?"

Contractors have the right to counter an *RFI* response with a change order request, particularly if they see the response as adding scope. Let's say that a piece of trim is shown, even though the documents don't describe the nature of the trim piece exactly. If the architect responds to the contractor's *RFI* on the subject with an elaborately detailed, two-part custom molding, the contractor might request a change order for the entire assembly drawn up in the *RFI*. A contractor will usually not include in his proposal an offsetting credit for the minimum he would have been required to provide for basic functionality as originally drawn.

So again, we start by asking him what solution he already had in mind (based on what his contract requires and what is shown in or can reasonably be inferred from the documents). Maybe we can live with that and avoid a change order.

Ask yourself
How do RFIs and related claims for payment fit into the context of complete and functional assemblies?
How and why might it be useful, when reviewing an RFI with a contractor, to ask, "What had you been planning to do here?"

The number of RFIs issued by a contractor can often be a leading indicator of claims ahead. For example, a 2017 construction dispute over a project in a resort community began with a contractor performing successfully for about a year before making a costly mistake. When the builder began hearing talk of construction errors, however, things quickly turned hostile, with the contractor blaming the owner and design team. Although the drawings and project team had not changed, as a litigious environment took hold, the flow of contractor RFIs (many of which began to focus on trivial things) more than doubled.

Ask yourself
Why should we pay attention to how many RFIs a contractor issues and whether many of them seem frivolous or unnecessary?

An ***Architect's Supplemental Instruction (ASI)*** is like a reverse *RFI*. It is initiated by the architect to convey the same kind of information frequently dealt with in an *RFI*. Based on its classic definition, an *ASI* is a clarification of something the architect notices that should have been explained a little better in the contract documents. In the best of all possible worlds, an *ASI* will contain clarifying information without changing the contractor's scope. However, when predicting how a contractor will respond, the architect is not the best mind reader. As with an *RFI*, if a contractor doesn't think the response is consistent with the intent of the drawings, he may answer with a change order request.

Many architects, perhaps unsure of how a contractor will see supplemental instructions, will usually issue information in *ASI* form, rather than guiding the contractor down the change order path by way of a ***Proposal Request (PR)***. An *ASI* leaves the possibility of a change order request in the hands of the contractor, who understands the project cost structure more thoroughly than architect and owner ever will and is well positioned to explain the effect of an *ASI* on the scope of work. A contractor change request for what he sees as an extra does not change the fact that the owner and often the architect negotiate with the contractor before change order requests are finalized or approved.

As noted, *PRs* from the owner (prepared by the architect) are generally less common than *ASIs*. In practice, the only consistently valid purpose of a *PR* is to provide a vehicle for a specific, clear request from the owner, asking the contractor for a price to add construction scope that is, without question, not part of what the contractor originally bid.

For example, the following communication would certainly warrant a *PR*:

> *The owner requests that the contractor provide a price to provide office furniture for the project, in accordance with the attached new drawings:*
> *AF001   First Floor Furniture Plan*
> *AF002   Second Floor Furniture Plan*
> *The work is to be completed in accordance with the attached new specifications section:*
> *Section 12 51 00 - Office Furniture*

Finally, with respect to changes to the work, an architect would do well to avoid relying on ***Construction Change Directives (CCDs)***, if at all possible. With this instrument, the owner compels the contractor to do work he hasn't priced yet, and about which he may have shown reluctance. Before signing a *CCD*, the parties will have agreed, ostensibly, on a method of calculating payment for the change. In fact, a *CCD* often lays the groundwork for a claim the contractor may initiate later on, seeking payment that may be many times prevailing bid prices for the added scope of work.

This is what happened in a case involving a contractor that had priced and performed work on a couple of change orders without incident. When the project encountered problems, however, the contractor began claiming it could not figure pricing timely. This happened first on one *PR* and then on another. The owner considered it important to keep the work moving and agreed to construction change directives. The contractor ultimately treated each of the ten or twelve *CCDs* as a blank check, demanding payments that were more than double A/E estimates of their value, or more. The contractor used these demands to counter the owner's construction defects claims.

Changes to a contract for construction come in many ways and often hit roadblocks. But for construction to be successful, payment for work that has been agreed to and performed must happen like clockwork. An architect shouldn't mess with ***Pay Applications***. Pay requests are, and always will be, the lifeblood of contractors and those that work with them, from suppliers of off-the-shelf products to custom fabricators, from laborers to corporate executives, from material delivery and storage, to the site superintendent's salary (and pickup truck). Timely action on pay applications is required for everything that is furnished and installed.

With a fixed-fee contract for construction, the schedule of values is set in advance; the line items of the pay request are percentages set against line-item totals. It is a straightforward assessment to look at the completed concrete work, all but some sidewalks, and agree that that trade is 92% done. The architect might say, "It looks like 95% to me, but the contractor only claimed 92%. I'm OK with that." She may then look at the steel on site, together with the amount erected, and say, "Yes, that looks to be at least 60% complete, as stated."

The architect reviews each line item in this manner. This review usually takes place on site with the contractor present. The architect asks a few questions. The contractor explains. In almost every instance, work in place at the time the architect reviews the request is further along than what is billed. This pattern stems from the fact that contractors generally require subs to turn their invoices in a week or more ahead of submitting the pay application.

If everything looks OK, the architect signs. (The signature field on the AIA form is called the "*Architect's Certificate for Payment*"; it should only be signed by a licensed architect.)

The owner then countersigns and arranges for payment. In a practice that has become increasingly common in recent decades, the owner or financial institution that distributes funds ensures that payments are passed through to subcontractors and suppliers. They may do this by cutting joint checks to each subcontractor, payable to both the subcontractor or supplier and the general contractor.

Pay application processes will differ based on the owner and delivery type. But whatever the process, handling pay applications is a function an architect must ***never*** leave undone. If he has a question about anything, he discusses it with the contractor. If something needs to be corrected or too much seems to be billed for a specific line item, the architect may change amounts on a pay request, attaching an explanation. Better still, the architect asks if the contractor would like to make the change and re-issue the form. That is generally the contractor's preference.

As always, don't change a pay application unilaterally. To build the best possible relationships on a jobsite, the architect should always talk with the contractor first.

Additional Resources

The Architect's Handbook of Professional Practice

5.1   Architects and the Law (Blue box text: Backgrounder, "Project Documentation," Pp. 178–180)

Author's Note

Another approach to pay applications

I did construction administration for a large CM/GC project that had an effective process for handling pay applications. A designated construction team representative, a technical representative of the owner, and I sat down each month to go over individual subcontractor and supplier pay requests one by one. The three of us would go through these pay applications, discuss them, ask questions, and agree or disagree with the proposed amounts. We sometimes discussed changes in an amount billed. When we agreed that changes were needed, the general contractor would convey our decision back to the affected subcontractor or supplier. A couple of days later, the contractor then delivered a consolidated pay request for the whole project, incorporating previous changes. Each of us signed the consolidated pay application presented by the general contractor. The owner then arranged for payment.

26

Delivery Methods and the Contractor

The project delivery method chosen by an owner affects the contractor's incentives. The choice of delivery method also affects the relationships between owner, contractor, and architect:

As a starting point (and it may not be diplomatic to point this out), a major contractor incentive in a ***stipulated sum Design-Bid-Build*** project is to seek as many change orders as possible. Low-bid contracting may leave the successful bidder with so little margin that he cannot absorb any of the common financial setbacks on a project. The contractor might also have won the bid by leaving something out (inadvertently, we will assume). If that is the case, for the contractor, the project may be a losing proposition from the start.

A small renovation project for a public agency offers a case study. A purchasing department received bids for a small project that were spread quite widely. Bids ranged from less than $80,000 to over $130,000, based on construction costs at the time. These bids were, of course, supposed to reflect the same scope of work. Several were clustered together near the architect's estimate, but the apparent low bid was a full $25,000 below the next lowest. The purchasing agent made the following observation:

> Experience has taught me to take the difference between the low bid and the next low and divide that number by two. That is the minimum dollar value of change orders I expect.

For this project with these bids, this official was saying, the agency could expect change orders well in excess of 15% of the contract total—much more than they considered acceptable.

Of course, it is not OK to shop bids or play one bidder against another. Except as otherwise permitted in the bid instructions (to make a substitute in place of a subcontractor the owner found unacceptable, for example), one may not ask a contractor to change its bid. One thing that is usually permissible, however, is to inquire whether a very low bidder would like to withdraw its bid for any reason: "Did you miss anything?" "Are you confident you can perform?"

The purchasing agent asked those questions. Nope, they weren't withdrawing. They said they were good.

In this instance, considering the official's concerns over the prospects of change orders, the architect reviewed the design history of the project and made a suggestion. The budget for this remodel/renovation had started at $100,000. As estimated, the agency's top two priorities used up that full amount. But they had abandoned their next priority—re-carpeting the building. That line item was estimated at about $20,000. The architect suggested to the purchasing agent that if policies allowed, they should ask the contractor, as part of value engineering, to price a change order to replace the carpet. The agent agreed. The contractor priced it, and the work was added to the contract. (Understandably, since this was a change order, the cost of the added work was a bit higher than the previous estimate for that scope.)

Although the contractor never said so, this change order gave the builder a somewhat larger margin on the project overall. The project went smoothly. There were *no* other change orders—a rarity in Design-Bid-Build contracting—especially with a contractor that left so much on the table.

Forever Practice: The Architect at Work, First Edition. Jim Nielson, FAIA.
© 2025 John Wiley & Sons, Inc. Published 2025 by John Wiley & Sons, Inc.

166 | *26 Delivery Methods and the Contractor*

Relationships in Design-Bid-Build follow familiar patterns, but one wrinkle is worth noting. Contracts for this delivery method intentionally cast the architect and contractor in adversarial roles. Early in the project, though, the contractor hasn't been chosen, so the architect and owner tend to forge close ties.

When the contractor enters the picture, a strong owner-architect connection may make him feel as if it is two against one. It is at this point that many contractors begin trying to drive a wedge between architect and owner. They may denigrate the architect's understanding of construction or the quality of her work products:

> "These drawings are terrible."
> "We've been hampered by numerous design errors."
> "If they could just review the drawings one more time, fill in all the gaps, and correct all the problems, we'd have a better chance of meeting our schedule."

These are all things contractors have been known to say. Of course, the architect's work wasn't perfect, but it probably met the standard of care. If an architect produced the same documents for a contractor-led D-B project, the contractor might bring legitimate concerns to the architect's attention internally, but in that case, the contractor would never convey criticism of the architect to the *owner*.

This brings us to **D-B** contracting (most frequently contractor led). To get a job, contractors oversee a project and control costs tightly, but they often need a good architect to bring a compelling design to the table. To address cost issues, while still promising a stunning building, a D-B proposal may include a list of things the owner would like to have but may not be getting (at least not the whole wish-list), due to budget constraints. In essence, the contractor may say, "You asked for this, but we're giving you that. Isn't it beautiful? And here is the price. Trust us. It will be fine."

For the client, a D-B proposal can be a minefield. She has, in effect, purchased a complete scope and maybe a design that is mostly complete. With most contractors that specialize in this delivery type, if the client wants to re-design anything or add something she forgot, changes are extra. And these extras—even if they are fundamental and happen early in the D-B process—come at change order prices.

At the same time, for the architect working for a D-B contractor it turns out to be much easier to get paid for extra design work than in any other delivery method. Every D-B change request goes out to every subcontractor, including the architect (to the contractor, just another subcontractor, I guess), for pricing. The architect submits a fee; everything, including the architect's fee, gets rolled into the change request to the owner. In other delivery methods, it is the architect's task to approach the owner separately to get paid for extra design work related to change orders. And architects aren't typically as good (or as successful) as contractors are in wrangling extra pay for extra services. (We should ask matter-of-factly and as a matter of course, just as contractors do.)

Relationships in D-B are different from Design-Bid-Build. The architect usually works for the Design-Builder or contractor. The contractor's aim is often to do the very minimum to satisfy owner's requirements. The architect desires to provide good design and to ensure that construction meets the owner's expectations. She must balance that aim against price constraints set by the contractor. Professionally, the architect must also review the work of the contractor. The architect's professional duty, if not her contract, compels her to keep and publish a list of construction deficiencies, for example. As noted previously, keeping this list is generally not appreciated by the contractor—typically the one that signs the architect's checks. Despite needing the architect's participation in the punch list walk and assistance in creating the list of corrections later on, it is not uncommon for a contractor partner to direct the architect not to maintain an ongoing list of construction deficiencies.

A third delivery method is *construction management*. Its more common form in my experience is **construction management at risk**. The construction manager (CM) is hired shortly before or after the design team is selected. The two work as partners. In this version of the delivery method, the CM usually goes on to become the general contractor. Expressing this dual role, this delivery method is often referred to as Construction Manager/General Contractor (CM/GC).

Before construction begins, a CM provides design assistance in the form of cost control, scheduling assistance, and constructability guidance to the architect. Given this lead-off partnering component in CM/GC delivery, it is less common than in Design-Bid-Build delivery for the contractor to work to undermine the owner's confidence in the architect. In terms of relationships, CM/GC projects include many of the advantages of D-B work (principally the early involvement of the contractor with design), which can help render the architect's designs more feasible. However, this method also eliminates some characteristics of D-B delivery. Specifically, in a CM/GC project, contractor incentives to control design and focus on costs are reduced. Design decisions may be less fettered. Costs may be higher.

Regarding finances, the CM's cost control responsibilities offer nuanced incentives. Because construction costs often fluctuate widely and unpredictably, it is generally prudent, where possible, to add an independent professional cost estimator to CM/GC teams, if possible. Doing so also balances the different parties' approaches. Drawing on both contractor and independent cost estimates, both parties perform a pricing exercise at each phase. When the owner and design team compare these two separate estimates, the numbers often don't match. An extended conference with both estimators ensues. The powwow continues until they reach a consensus.

The independent estimator, drawing on his own extensive database, endeavors to represent, for each line item, the expected low bid in an open price competition. The CM/GC, on the other hand, may come up with slightly higher numbers, turning to its own library of bid data to predict an overall price point it is confident will not be exceeded.

Not all parties may agree with (or admit to) the following statement, but the CM/GC's estimating approach, if not weighed against a professional independent estimate and adjusted accordingly, may serve the builder's own interests. It may open a window for a good showing later: as the job is bought out, costs will tend to come in lower than conservatively estimated. The CM/GC estimate may also facilitate earning a portion of a larger leftover shared contingency. That contingency, if determined in response to a rather conservative CM/GC estimate, could end up higher than actually needed. Accordingly, more ends up being left to share. In many CM/GC contracts, the owner pays the builder 30–40% of any shared contingency left unspent.

For the contractor, perhaps more than anyone involved in a project, the choice of delivery type is all about incentives.

Ask yourself
This chapter has reviewed three major types of project delivery. What are these three delivery types?
What are the pros and cons of each?

Working with the Contractor

When working with contractors, an architect will usually not have much repeat work with the same construction firm. Even if so, he'll most likely work with different personnel each time. Though cast members change, an architect must build the best relationships she can. Why? Even in large cities, we are all part of a rather small industry; word gets around.

When interacting with contractors, keep these things in mind:

- An architect should *never* let anyone on the construction side hear him say, "Just build it the way I drew it," or words to that effect.
- If the contractor is raising issues with something in the drawings or specifications, an architect must start from the assumption that the contractor is not incompetent or dishonest. Most likely what the design team has put in the documents doesn't make sense to the contractor. It could be that our documents are less brilliant than we think.
- An architect must respect the contractor's input, using language that goes something like this, "Here's what we're after with this detail. What would you recommend we do to make the concept work?"

168 | *26 Delivery Methods and the Contractor*

Ask yourself
Why shouldn't the architect insist that the contractor just build things as the design team we drew them?

Here are a few more tips for the architect during construction:

- On the jobsite, act like the guest that you are. Yes, we generally have a right to be there, but the architect should be careful about asserting that right. This is the contractor's turf, and we should respect that.
- Coordinate visits with times that are convenient for the contractor. Ideally, you and the contractor should walk the site together. Either way, you should prepare and circulate a written document of your observations, but it will work so much better if you have an opportunity to discuss things before the contractor gets your written report.
- No matter how unpopular it makes you, the architect's standard of care will usually require that you maintain and share an ongoing list of construction defects, with things marked off as corrected. This corrections list should be a regular attachment to the architect's site reports. Each report should summarize the status of the list with language such as, "Two items have been added to the corrections list this week; three are observed as having been completed. The list now includes 14 items, three of which have been on the list for more than a month." When the contractor requests a substantial completion list, the architect asks the contractor to add to his punch list any items remaining on the architect's construction defects list.

Ask yourself
Why is it important to maintain a list of construction defects?

Additional Resources

The Architect's Handbook of Professional Practice
> Chapter 9   Design Project Delivery
>> 10.9   Construction Phase Services

Author's Note

Working with the contractor

One time, I picked up an architect at the airport who was presenting at a local AIA conference. When I opened my trunk to load his luggage, he saw my beat-up hard hat, complete with a bunch of stickers for rigging companies and steel fabricators. "I'm from Chicago, and I build!" he said. "It looks like you do, too."

Yes.

I've seen architects show up on jobsites with wingtips, spit-polished hard hats, and a dry-clean-only dress coat. I always felt that if I wanted contractors to consider me as somebody they could turn to with an important question, I needed to look like someone comfortable with a hammer or a Sawzall. In addition to that hard hat, which I've worn for more than 30 years, my attire on site consisted of old boots, worn jeans, fraying insulated work gloves, and a faded Carhartt.

As we are reminded in this chapter, during construction, you *are* on the contractor's turf. It's a good idea to be approachable. In my opinion, that includes looking the part.

And yes, I do know how to use a reciprocating saw. And, because I've worked as a framer, I can drive a nail about as well as anyone.

27

Bidder-designed Work

In virtually every project an architect is a part of, some of the work provided is designed by the company that bids and provides the work. At permit submittal, drawings addressing these portions of the work generally lack sufficient detail for determining code compliance. So, plans examiners require that deferred submittals be turned in after the permit is issued. Deferred submittals include drawings, details, specifications, and calculations communicating the contractor's completed, engineered designs for bidder-designed work.

Subcontractor Scope Items that Are Generally Bidder Designed, Regardless of Delivery Method, Include:

- Fire Protection and Fire Alarm Systems
- Metal-plate-connected Wood Trusses
- Pre-engineered Metal Buildings
- Modular Buildings

Bidder-designed scope items above are listed based on how often they occur in buildings:

- Fire Protection and Fire Alarm Systems

    Fire protection and fire alarm systems are a key part of most buildings. Almost without exception, these systems are bidder designed. Design team responsibilities for sprinkler systems include determining and communicating hazard levels, code and owner insurance requirements, available fire flow and pressure, and special density requirements from the AHJ. The design team may also establish guidance for specific locations and spacing of sprinkler heads and other devices. Fire *alarm* guidance from the design team may include directions on the type of system, system capabilities (including fire sprinkler interactions), locations of panels and pull stations, if applicable, aesthetic requirements for device locations (without compromising function), and building uses with special visible and/or audible notification requirements. For projects that include a smoke control system—also bidder designed—the panel and sequence of operations for that system are integrated into both the fire alarm control panel and also the building management system.

    Subcontractors design these systems, submit them to the AHJ and the design team for approval, and then install what has been approved by both. Beyond reviewing and approving these deferred bidder-designed submittals, the major role of the design team is to coordinate locations and available space in and around a building for devices, sprinkler heads, fire department connections, panels, riser assemblies, standpipes, cleanouts, and indicator valves (as applicable).

Forever Practice: The Architect at Work, First Edition. Jim Nielson, FAIA.
© 2025 John Wiley & Sons, Inc. Published 2025 by John Wiley & Sons, Inc.

Ask yourself
Review each of the items for which the design team "coordinates locations and available space," as listed in the last lines of the paragraph above.
Do you know what each of these things is and what it does?
Is there a connection between bidder-designed work and Design-Build project delivery?
Can you explain your answer to this question?

Other scope items that are generally bidder designed include:

- Metal-plate-connected Wood Trusses

    Sometimes referred to as pre-engineered wood trusses, these are the wood trusses used for roof structures in many wood-framed residential and commercial projects. These structural members are designed and custom built for the span and configuration shown on the architect's drawing. These are not used exclusively for pitched roofs. They may be produced with parallel chord configuration, commonly used for low-slope roofs. Trusses are delivered to the jobsite, together with any prefabricated blocking needed, ready for installation.

    Historically, builders in the United States built roofs one piece at a time, using rafters, ridge beams, collar ties, ceiling joists, and purlins. Building such a roof required experienced craftspeople. Around the middle of the twentieth century, home builders in the US started using jobsite-built trusses. These critical structural elements had top and bottom chords, splices as needed, and a pattern of diagonal web members. They were not engineered but were rather put together based on experience and common sense. Geometry was intuitive. Connections and splices depended on a whole lot of nails, but no one could tell you exactly how many. Today, roofs for most homes in the US are framed with pre-engineered metal-plate-connected wood trusses.

    The architect's design work for metal-plate-connected wood trusses is limited to overall shape, slope, and any special geometry needed. In some cases, an overall roof plan may be all the fabricator needs. Truss geometry shown in the architect's drawings usually doesn't need to show web members or call out the structural pattern of the truss (i.e., King Post, Howe, etc.). Such decisions are up to the supplier's engineer.

Ask yourself
How have approaches to roof framing changed in the last hundred years? Why?

- Pre-engineered Metal Buildings

    We usually turn to pre-engineered metal buildings for agriculture, military, industrial, vehicle maintenance, recreational, and technical education shops and facilities. I've also seen them used for churches. And they were considered for the Speed Skating Oval for the 2002 Olympic Winter Games.[1] The design team's scope of services for a pre-engineered metal building generally includes complete foundation and slab design (including tie beams below grade or other means of dealing with the horizontal thrust of three-hinged arches), grid layout, building geometry, window and door locations, lighting and mechanical systems, utilities to serve the structure, building envelope specifications, code analysis, and coordination with building engineering, both before bidding and after receiving the deferred design submittal for the engineered structure.

    In my experience, design team effort for a structure of this type is around 60% of what it would take to complete full design for a similar conventionally framed building.

- Modular Buildings

    Modular buildings are used as flex space for schools, public agencies, temporary facilities for mass gatherings (such as a rock concert at Central Park), and office space for industrial plants, among other things. These structures share most of the characteristics of pre-engineered buildings, but they generally also arrive on the jobsite complete with mechanical, electrical, and lighting systems.

    The design team is responsible for laying out interior partitions, windows, and doors for the fabricator, building access routes (ramps and stairs) for building floors a few feet above grade, and providing site utility connections and support structure for the modular buildings to connect to. Other than site construction, permitting and inspections are generally complete before the modules are moved to their locations on site. In my experience, the level-of-effort required of the design team for a structure of this type is roughly 25% of what it would take to complete full design for a similar conventionally framed building.

Design-Build Projects and (CM/GC) Projects Often Include Additional Bidder-designed Construction Items.

Examples of the range of bidder-designed work encountered during my career are listed below.

In Design-Build Projects:

100,000 SF state office building
- Light shelves, including material selection and engineering for shelves and supporting structure
- Terrazzo flooring
- Millwork from old-growth fir reclaimed from a 1904 railroad trestle

Memory chip fabrication facility (Design professionals working on the project called the project build-design— only partially in jest. Actually, the delivery method was IPD.)
- Pumphouses
- Tunnels
- Conduit banks
- Electrical substation
- Full building cladding system

110,000 SF freezer building (−10° F)
- Shrinkage-compensating concrete (with armored joints 100' on center)
- Ammonia refrigeration system

Higher-education satellite campus
- Retaining wall
- Locally quarried quarzitic limestone adhered stone veneer
- Stone benches

University academic library
- Glass fiber-reinforced concrete column covers and spandrels
- Curtain wall system with integrated sun shading

Technical school campus building
- Curtain wall system with integrated sun shading
- Polished concrete floor system
- Custom aluminum wall panel system

Military rocket fuel testing complex
- Frangible wall assemblies

High-technology company call center
- Tubular skylights
- Acoustic baffles

Public transit station shelters
- Custom steel plate wall and roof panels

National Guard readiness center
- Natural stone veneer cladding

27 Bidder-designed Work

Meat plant expansion
- Exterior insulated panels
- Walkable insulated ceiling system
- Drying houses
- Ammonia dehumidification system

In CM/GC Projects:

Hillside twinhome subdivision
- Extensive retaining walls

180-unit apartments and suites
- Exposed exterior column and railing system

21,000-seat religious auditorium
- Glass-fiber-reinforced gypsum ceiling panels
- Sound reinforcement/enhancement system
- Custom pipe organ (130 ranks)
- Locally quarried hand-set honed granite stone cladding
- Locally quarried random ashlar cleft-face stone masonry

70,000 SF Sewing plant
- Custom multi-utility floor boxes

University office laboratory buildings
- Sheet-metal building cladding system
- Terra cotta building cladding system

20-unit rowhouse development
- Cushioned Luxury Vinyl Tile flooring

Federal Metropolitan Planning Organization office tenant improvements
- Custom perforated metal wall panels

Summary

Bidder-designed or deferred submittal items share the following characteristics:

- Costs tend to be controlled
- The design team's work is minimized
- The design team's major focus is showing design intent, then coordinating the bidder's work with the work of other subcontractors on the project

Not too many generations ago, an architect's drawings depicted the basic volumetric aspects and appearance of spaces to be created. Where we might create hundreds of plans, sections, elevations, and details for a major building today, in the nineteenth century or earlier, twenty carefully crafted drawings might have sufficed. Putting it all together to make the architect's design a reality was the job of the builder, using a process similar to bidder-designed work today.

Generations ago, the architect was known as the master builder, perhaps having taken on this role after much training and experience as a stone mason. Having laid out plans for a great project, he worked with craftsmen that helped prepare meticulous and beautiful details, working in concert with these artisans to make the master's vision a reality. If there had been such a thing as a building official then, imagine his plan review comments on these amazing construction details, which could really only be considered deferred submittals.

Additional Resources

The Architect's Handbook of Professional Practice

9.4 Contractor-Led Design-Build. (See Paragraph and Sidebar on the subject of *Design-Build Subcontractors*, P. 546.)

Author's Note

2002 Olympic Speed Skating Oval, a Pre-Engineered Metal Building?

I headed up games-time buildout for several 2002 Winter Olympic venues, including the Speed Skating Oval. I hadn't been part of the design effort on the permanent structure, but a colleague of mine managed that project. What I share next comes from notes published by the New York office of Ove Arup, design engineer (as noted previously and referenced below). GSBS led the effort, with Arup as design structural and MEP engineer. Two local engineers of record also participated.

For budget reasons, the committee for the games asked the team to consider using a pre-engineered metal building for the enclosure, alongside any other design options. The team did just that. But the pendulum ultimately swung in the direction of an elegant suspension cable design: a structure relying on a series of masts and cables above the roof to carry its structure, like a series of suspension bridge decks lined up next to each other.[2]

Why did the most dramatic and evocative design win out? To span 310 feet, as required to accommodate the ice sheet and spectators, the haunched bents (or three-hinged arches) of a pre-engineered metal building would have forced the roof almost 30′ higher than would have been required by the suspension cable structure it was compared to. There were other options on the table, but integrating all aspects of the design and evaluating their impact on each other showed the suspension cable roof with the lowest overall (first and lifecycle) cost. The roof was lower than other options—far lower than the pre-engineered option. The lower roof selected required far less area of exterior walls, a smaller interior volume of space (whose temperature could more easily be controlled), and much less energy to keep the ice just the right temperature.

Smaller envelope, smaller heating/cooling system, smaller ice plant: GSBS/Arup's most stunning design concept was the winner. It came in on budget—a budget that was less than 10% of what Nagano Japan had spent on its own speed skating oval for the Olympics held four years earlier!

Partly because of all of these design efficiencies, to this day the building is still known for the fastest ice on the planet.

Notes

1 https://www.arup.com/globalassets/downloads/arup-journal/the-arup-journal-2002-issue-2.pdf, Pp. 29–35. (Accessed October 17, 2024)

2 This structure is discussed briefly in **Chapter 5 The Value of Green**, which also includes a photograph of the building (Figure 5.1).

28

Closeout

When a project is ready to close out, the architect begins by drafting a Certificate of Substantial Completion for review and approval. Once substantial completion is certified, it doesn't mean everything is done. It means the work is complete enough to be used for its intended purpose.

When the contractor tells the architect the project, or a portion of it the owner and AHJ have agreed may be accepted independently from the rest, is ready for substantial completion, the architect often humors the contractor by showing up briefly and, after seeing things aren't prepared, asking when he *will* be ready for a substantial completion walkthrough. That's usually how it goes down. Standard contracts, such as those published by the AIA, state that it is the contractor's job to prepare a punch list before the architect (or anyone else—owner, consultants, AHJ) shows up for the walkthrough. In the history of construction, I doubt whether it has ever been done that way. If the design professional is even aware of this contractor requirement, he may think about the process this way:

I am to review the contractor's list (if there is one) and add anything I think is missing. Just making my own list from scratch hardly takes more effort than double-checking and adding to the contractor's list.

Following this line of thinking, an architect or engineer usually steps in and does the contractor's job.

Whoever prepares it and whoever double-checks it, the list should include things that are incomplete, things that are damaged, things that are done incorrectly, and things that are missing. It's a list of pending corrections and completions the contractor still needs to take care of.

If, in the architect's walkthrough, he notices defects or incomplete items that will make it impossible to occupy the space or use it as intended, the walkthrough should end with a quick conversation to talk about trying again another day. However, assuming no dealbreakers emerge during the punch list walk, the architect's next step is to execute the certificate of substantial completion for the project (or portion thereof), append the punch list to it as soon as it can be written up, and establish a reasonable cost estimate for punch list corrections.

The architect and consultants needn't worry about being extraordinarily precise with this estimate. If there is any uncertainty in developing these numbers, it is prudent to err on the high side. One should also review estimates with the contractor before entering a total on the substantial completion form. The architect can and should be diplomatic in discussing this estimate, but the number is up to the design team. Regardless of how much is held back at substantial completion, the contractor will be paid the remaining contract value—all of it—when the project reaches final completion. The small amount held until then should not be a hill for anyone to die on.

Shortly after substantial completion, the architect may expect the builder's penultimate application for payment. Typically, the contract will provide that all remaining retainage be released with this payment, except for this substantial completion holdback, intended as a small incentive for the contractor to finish things up.

Be aware that a ***certificate of substantial completion*** and a ***certificate of occupancy*** (C of O), which may happen concurrently, are not the same. The AHJ issues the C of O, making it legal for the owner or user to occupy the space. The AHJ review is about life safety. The architect, her consultants, and the owner certify substantial

---

Forever Practice: The Architect at Work, First Edition. Jim Nielson, FAIA.
© 2025 John Wiley & Sons, Inc. Published 2025 by John Wiley & Sons, Inc.

176 | *28 Closeout*

completion, agreeing that things are far enough along for the space to function as intended. For this certification, the owner and design team focus on life safety **and** everything else.

Before it can be put into service, a project needs to have both certificates.

And *final completion*? In an ideal world, the contractor reports that he has completed work on the punch list. In addition to work in place, this completion includes mechanical systems test and balance work (and reports), finalized operation and maintenance manuals, and training of owner facilities personnel, among other administrative requirements. The architect and her consultants review the work and confirm completion. If the contractor has a payment/performance bond on the project, he furnishes a statement from his surety (the bond company) approving final payment.

With these requirements satisfied, the architect approves the contractor's final pay application, reflecting 100% payment of the entire contract amount, including all approved change orders.

In real life, however, the days and weeks (or even months) between substantial and final completion are sometimes characterized by fights over punch list items, demands for change orders never previously discussed or processed, claims for damages, and possibly lawsuits. Not every construction saga comes to this denouement, but far too many do. A project that winds down this way may *never* achieve final completion. And settling project disputes may require more time, effort, and even expense than will have been invested in the project to that point.

Such conflicts happen far more often than they would if all members of a project team—owner, contractor, and architect—did their best to create a successful project for everyone, to meet their individual contractual obligations, and to listen to each other.

So, good luck out there!

Ask yourself
What strategies will you employ to avoid conflicts among project team members, especially as projects conclude?

Closing Thoughts

A couple more thoughts to keep in mind. This book may have conveyed the impression that in the construction business, there are bound to be conflicts. While that is true in many cases, and the architect needs to know how to deal with them, it's worth remembering that the best conflict resolution tool is not to have a conflict in the first place.

Dealing with Conflict

In our free-market society, we all want to get ahead; we tend to seek the upper hand for ourselves. Conflicts are inevitable. Below are a handful of suggestions for how an architect may thrive in this environment:

- Know the contract. Don't be afraid, in the most professional manner possible, to share an understanding of a particular responsibility assigned to the architect or contractor by contract. The architect should also not be afraid to cite the contractual responsibilities of parties she is discussing an issue with.
- Do not take things personally. (Easier said than done. I know.) It may be hard to believe, but a person yelling at someone may not really be mad at that person. Yes, the one yelling is unloading on the nearest human. But stop to consider. This aggrieved person may be mad at his boss for signing the contract he did; he may be mad at someone working for him that screwed up; he may be angry at a city inspector. The architect is way down the list of his troubles, but there he is—a convenient target.

- Listen. Listen. Listen. Don't be turning your attention away from what a frustrated party is saying in order to formulate a response while the other party goes on and on. There will be time to decide what to say next.
- Concede and apologize sincerely for mistakes you and/or members of your firm may have made.
- Consider any creative solutions in advance that might possibly address the concerns you're aware another party has.
- *Never* raise your voice. (Good luck with that!)
- If another party is treating your firm unfairly, make sure he knows who/what is impacted by that treatment: a favorite consultant, one of the firm's employees he likes, or the firm's financial ability to continue to provide him with the support he needs.
- For those in a leadership setting, discover and cultivate one or more key individuals that excel in clear thinking and diplomacy. If a firm has an employee with these skill sets, it would do well to use her as a fixer for fractious projects and relationships. It might be a good idea to send her in place of or in support of the team member regularly assigned to a project.
- Try to understand where the other party is coming from. Suppose her company is losing money on this project. She may feel responsible. Unless she can push some of the blame onto the architect or some other project team member, she may think that she will suffer a career setback or even lose her job over the problems she sees.
- Treat resolution of conflicts as business decisions. Firm leaders need to understand when it makes sense to give in or settle, rather than standing on principle.
- In conflicts, always assume a simple misunderstanding before assuming ill will.

Finally, How Much Do I Understand About Construction?

For most of us, the answer is *not a lot*. Remember that. The contractor has forgotten more things about construction than an architect may ever learn. He knows how things go together and what works. If the architect lets him, the contractor can *help* the architect help *him* (the contractor) deal with whatever confusion architectural drawings may have caused.

Trust me, an architect's instruments of services will often cause contractors a great deal of confusion.

But to the point: how much does an architect know? Let's start at the beginning, with on-the-job vocabulary. The list of construction jargon below includes terms most contractors know. But architects? See how you stack up.

Ask yourself
Can you explain the following construction terms and concepts, along with their importance in construction? (No fair looking them up.)

- Shore
- ACI
- Full pen weld
- Prism test
- Formsaver
- TCNA
- Mortise lockset
- Sputter coat
- Crown
- Crazing
- Fiberglass reinforced thermoset resin panels
- Structural glazed silicon
- Screw shore vs. friction shore
- Parting stile
- SMACNA
- Desilvering
- Titanium dioxide
- Eight-inch lift
- Janka scale
- Engineered pick
- Vertical duo cabinet door
- Form liner

28 Closeout

- Flat lock
- Rectified
- Terne coated
- Rebar lap
- Nylon 6 6
- Surface barrier
- Spectrally selective
- Densifier
- Astragal
- Stinger
- Blower door test
- Recessed fire sprinkler head
- Oil canning
- Reshoring
- CH Stud
- Rebar cage
- Camber
- AWI
- Cushion edge
- Hook
- Vapor drive
- Deck bearing
- Handed hardware
- Scabble
- Pyrolytic
- VFD
- Tremie
- Embed
- Muffin monster
- Fresno
- Rain screen
- Dance floor
- Bee holes
- Shaft Liner
- Thyristor

Additional Resources

The Architect's Handbook of Professional Practice

9.2   The Architect's Role in Construction Manager-Constructor Project Delivery (Conflict Resolution, P. 521)

10.1   Managing Architectural Projects (Blue box text: Backgrounder, "The Effective Project Manager", Pp. 601, 602)

10.10   Project Completion and Post-Construction

Author's Note

Always assume a simple misunderstanding before assuming ill will

A memorable interaction during construction of a 100,000 SF office building for a state agency early in my career ended up with a name of its own. The project manager for the construction company on the project was great to work with, one of the best. But that didn't stop a misunderstanding.

Walking the job one day, I came across a widespread issue related to doors. Maybe it was something about hardware, about alignments or adjustments, about the way frames were prepped for hardware, or maybe about wood door slabs with mismatched grain. I don't recall.

At any rate, I walked the entire project, cataloged each issue related to doors, and wrote a draft memo with a schedule covering each issue. I included the usual project contacts on the draft, but I didn't send it to them. I sent my draft memo with a cover letter addressed only to our fine construction project manager. This is a draft, I told him, of an important issue. I suggested he and I review and find a way to resolve things before sending anything to anyone else. The cover letter was clearly marked as a DRAFT, but the attached memo was not. My bad.

This was the mid-1990s, so the draft report and cover letter arrived by fax, of course, on separate sheets of paper. Not long after I had sent the cover letter and draft memo to our construction manager (and to him alone) for his thoughts, he returned a blistering reply, copied to every one of our project contacts. Why had I sent this out to the whole world, he demanded, without talking with him first? I hadn't. It seems the memo had gotten separated from the cover letter, and he had not seen my message telling him the whole thing was a draft and suggesting we talk about it before proceeding.

Not having realized that he thought the letter had gone out, in my first response I thought to myself, I guess I misjudged; I didn't realize just how antagonistic our construction manager could be. My frustration about what I assumed he had done was apparent in my hasty, irritated reply. The cycle continued as our contractor responded again, and consultants and agency coordinators chimed in to see what was wrong. Things didn't calm down until I realized the whole thing had been caused by a misunderstanding—of my own making.

By the time of our next project meeting, the construction project manager and I had realized what had happened. Working together, the two of us had also come up with a plan of action to deal with these worrisome doors, whatever that was about. And we'd sent out a joint note to the entire team attempting to explain our misunderstanding. The only mention of the issue in that next site meeting came from the agency's deputy director, who asked if *Door Wars* (her name for the kerfuffle) was behind us.

Rooftop appendages at Hudson Yard, NY.

Part X

Appendices

Part X Appendices includes additional information cited in *Parts V Project*, *VI Firm*, and *IX Construction*. These resources flesh out the information presented there and include mockups of tools architects often find useful in project and practice management.

A

The Facilities Program

The following outline shows what is often included in a facilities program. The program laid out here relates to a large academic building, but the process and the resulting document are usually quite similar, regardless of project type.

I. INTRODUCTION
Team: Who prepared the program?

Timeframe: When was this done?

Process: What did the work include?

- Conduct meetings and workshops with stakeholders
- Establish vision and goals
- Map existing organizational structure
- Identify issues with existing facility systems and infrastructure
- Explore and evaluate options for reorganizing operations
- Identify proposed space needs
- Develop individual outlines of each type of space
- Establish required adjacencies and preliminary blocking and stacking diagrams
- Outline existing and proposed connections to surrounding context: circulation, systems, and technology
- Seek expert input and incorporate requirements specific to the project type
- Develop cost models to sift priorities and adapt project needs to the available budget
- Develop preliminary visual concepts for identifying facility massing, together with the building exterior and interior
- Address issues related to future planning

II. PHILOSOPHY
The vision for the new facility is... With this vision in mind, the following purposes and goals were established:

Planning

- Create a visually open facility through which users may navigate easily
- Utilize the main level as the retail, food service, and Information Commons zone from which one can easily find other services and activities
- Arrange departments in a way that facilitates synergy among like functions
- Maximize gathering, lounge, and study space within the footprint
- Locate service points and gather the most needed functions in an intuitive pattern
- Eliminate barriers (real and perceived) to disabled persons
- Enhance users' connection to outdoor areas

Forever Practice: The Architect at Work, First Edition. Jim Nielson, FAIA.
© 2025 John Wiley & Sons, Inc. Published 2025 by John Wiley & Sons, Inc.

Technology
- Provide locations for technology-rich information services for students, faculty, staff, and visitors
- Create an Information Commons that is more than a typical computer lab
- Ensure that the facility is as hospitable to technology as can be afforded
- Anticipate future technological development and plan for the flexibility to accommodate that development

Facility Environments
- Create collaborative work environments for staff, students, and users
- Create a variety of lounge environments
- Provide comfortable meeting and gathering spaces
- Develop spaces for inquiry, consulting, and conversation
- Provide group meeting and study rooms
- Develop high-technology zones
- Develop quiet zones
- Respond to the desire for a café
- Place the facility desk at the hub of the building
- Respond to the needs for acoustic control
- Create a space for exhibiting artwork
- Provide a zone within the building to accommodate extended hours service
- Provide natural light and upgrade finishes as the budget allows

Infrastructure
- Create a flexible facility that responds to current and future functional needs
- Provide mechanical and electrical systems that exceed standards for function and efficiency
- Provide the infrastructure necessary to service technology-rich environments
- Address fire protection and life safety needs
- Address structural and seismic issues
- Address accessibility (ADA) requirements
- Take advantage of opportunities to increase comfort and energy conservation opportunities

III. PROGRAM SUMMARY

Mission
The new building is intended to help the existing building fulfill its basic mission as it becomes a new and modern home. This new home will become an essential part of the campus's growth and a welcoming gateway to the campus.

The facility will be an attractive, modern building with a visually appealing and functional structure and convenient access to other campus buildings. Public services offered will play a vital role in creating a stimulating new image for the university.

Context
The new facility should fit within the context of the university's main campus. It should be a good neighbor to the buildings and campus around it, yet also remain distinctive. A suitable site has been selected to the east of another campus building. Landscaping should seek to reduce water usage but blend with the adjacent campus.

Energy, Environment, and Resource Conservation
A key planning idea in the programming process has been sustainability. The intent is to incorporate high-performance design that will provide maintenance efficiency and low operation costs. By doing so, the facility will provide the university with an opportunity not only to benefit from a high-performance building but also to promote and showcase the benefits of sustainable design.

Building

The facility will give the university the opportunity to enhance the current facility's mission to "offer exceptional services and assistance, utilizing current technology to enhance research and ensure intellectual freedom." The facility continues the ongoing outreach initiative by planning for spaces that:

- Are socially rich, blending a café-style atmosphere with the services of the facility
- Provide diverse digital resources with integrated research areas
- Include multiple types of learning environments that support the varied needs of undergraduate and graduate students

To strengthen the role of the facility on campus, the building must have a well-conceived floor plan. A later section of this document outlines the building's functional relationship and addresses the planning goals to create efficient, flexible, and engaging environments.

Summary Space List

The final part of the program document outlines the types and spaces needed in each room/area within the building. The building's total area will be approximately x gross square feet. The resulting net assignable area will be approximately y square feet (65% of the total). Consequently, approximately z square feet (35%) will be attributed to non-assignable areas—floor space occupied by public circulation, such as public lobbies and lounges, mechanical and electrical shafts and rooms, restrooms, wall thicknesses, and other undifferentiated uses. The section concludes with individual space outlines—detailed summaries of the specific requirements of each individual space or room. These individual space outlines, or room data sheets, represent the heart of the program.

The program contains fourteen primary divisions as identified in the space summary list at the end of the program. These primary space divisions consist of:

- Public Services
- Writing Center
- Entry
- Lobby
- Space Type 1
- Space Type 2
- Space Type 3
- Space Type 4
- Space Type 5
- Systems/IT Services
- Building Administration
- Building Support Spaces

IV. ADDITIONAL TECHNICAL REQUIREMENTS

These include information and details related to:

- Building and life-safety code compliance, including a detailed code analysis
- Structural, mechanical, electrical, technology, and acoustical requirements
- Possible design and construction phasing
- The recommended project schedule
- A conceptual construction cost estimate
- A discussion of how the new facility should fit in with the campus master plan

B

The Project Plan

A project plan includes:

- Project name and number plus the date of the plan
- Background information about the project, such as:
  - Construction budget
  - Project delivery method
  - Size of facility
  - Site features
  - Anticipated structural, mechanical, electrical, and plumbing systems
  - Consultants
  - Unique aspects of the facility
  - Fee amount and allocation (*Figure B.1*):
  - Design and construction schedule
    - Key milestones
    - Vacations/holidays, potential impediments
    - Groundbreaking
    - Substantial completion
    - Occupancy
  - Average and total architectural manpower needed by phase (see *Figure B.2*)
  - Profit target
  - Goals for the project
- Reasons the firm is doing the project, such as:
  - Good profit
  - Contractor relationship
  - Opportunity for new project type
  - Consistency with firm values and business plan
  - Prospects of repeat business
- Budget allocation of design fee
  - Profit
  - Expenses
    - Consultants
    - Travel
    - Photography
    - In-house printing

Forever Practice: The Architect at Work, First Edition. Jim Nielson, FAIA.
© 2025 John Wiley & Sons, Inc. Published 2025 by John Wiley & Sons, Inc.

188 | B The Project Plan

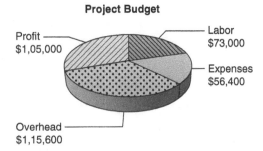

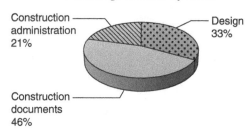

Figure B.1 Budget allocation of design fee—
The project manager evaluates the scope of work, the level of effort, and the design fee (as requested or negotiated) to plan the percentages of the fee that will cover all costs: labor, overhead, and other expenses (including consultants), along with the anticipated profit, which is the portion of the fee remaining after covering costs.

Figure B.2 Percentage of labor expended by phase—
The project manager determines the number of hours required to complete the project scope of services and establishes the percentage of work to be expended in each phase. Rather than the traditional project phases (Schematic Design, Design Development, Construction Documents (CDs), and Construction Administration (CA); this project only has a single design phase, plus the standard CDs and CA phases.

- Overhead
- Labor
  ○ Percentage of labor expended by phase
  ○ Level-of-effort by phase

Additional plan aspects:

- Listing of staff members that will work on the project
  - Tasks assigned to each staff member
  - Hours allocated for each task
    ○ Tally of hours matching total
    ○ Percentage of labor expended by phase and activity (*Figure B.3*):
    ○ Average manpower needed by phase
  - The average manpower tally makes up a key part of the design schedule, showing timeframes for completion of each task, as discussed in ***Appendix C The Project Schedule***

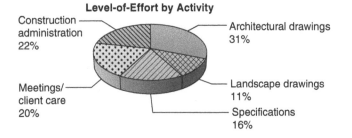

Figure B.3 Level-of-effort (Hours) by activity—
As part of the assessment of total hours required to complete the work, the project manager assesses the overall level of effort required for each of the major activities involved. For this project, the architect's scope of services included landscape architecture.

C

The Project Schedule

The project schedule may include detailed activities included in each phase of the scope or services. Or it may simply chart the overall phases. Activities and phases are displayed graphically, from start to finish, and in relation to each other. Gantt charts are most commonly used for design and construction schedules, with dates along the top and a bar or milestone symbol for each line item listed in order on the left, beginning at the top. Start and end dates are listed alongside activities and/or shown graphically in the body of the chart. See *Figure C.1* for an example of such an approach. The example includes simplified dependencies, represented by fine lines connecting certain activities. More on dependencies below.

A dependency is a graphic representation showing that one activity or milestone must begin or end before another starts. Based on these dependencies, most software used to create schedules has the capacity to evaluate data entered and determine the project's critical path. Based on information the scheduler builds into a design or construction schedule, some activities float freely. For these actions, completion can be delayed to a degree without causing the entire schedule to slide. But other activities (tasks such as permit submittal, initial earthwork, or steel framing) tend to be on the critical path. A delay of anything on that path results in a delay for the entire project.

Contractors generally use robust (and expensive) software to organize and run their projects and to create construction schedules. Less expensive or no-cost applications are also available to create schedules such as *Figures C.1 and C.2*.

To those familiar with them, detailed Gantt charts may communicate a schedule effectively, both in overview and detail, but to some stakeholders, Gantt charts will be unfamiliar. Over the course of a project, team members may come to understand such schedules, but it is often necessary to find an effective way to communicate the timelines of the architect's proposed work during the selection process—perhaps in that very first marketing interview.

For this purpose, architects may seek other ways of displaying the times their design work will start and end. A useful approach that has been used by some firms is a simple flow chart (*Figure C.3*). This example shows a pre-design proposal (for facilities programming). It is easy to follow, shows key activities for each phase of the work, and is not tied to specific dates.

The arrows on *Figure C.3 A schedule for the rest of us* show the progression from phase to phase. Timeframes are presented on the right side of the schedule. They are listed by weeks rather than dates, allowing for inevitable changes in the planned start date.

Schedules like these are an integral part of project management. They integrated into the project plan discussed in *Appendix B* and should be reflected in project planning outlined in *Chapter 13 Project Management*.

Forever Practice: The Architect at Work, First Edition. Jim Nielson, FAIA.
© 2025 John Wiley & Sons, Inc. Published 2025 by John Wiley & Sons, Inc.

190 | C The Project Schedule

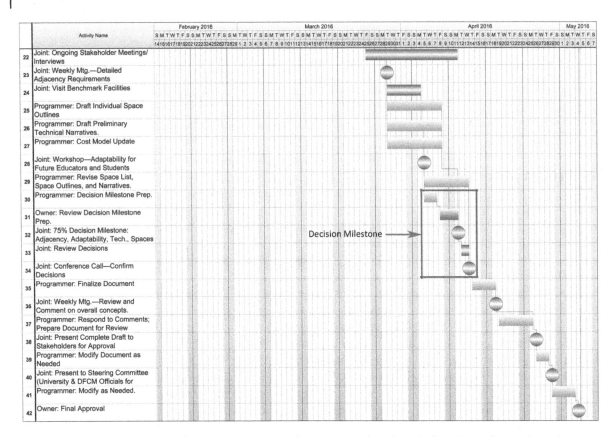

Figure C.1 Gantt schedule chart. This approach shows a simple progression of pre-design phases. *Source:* the author.

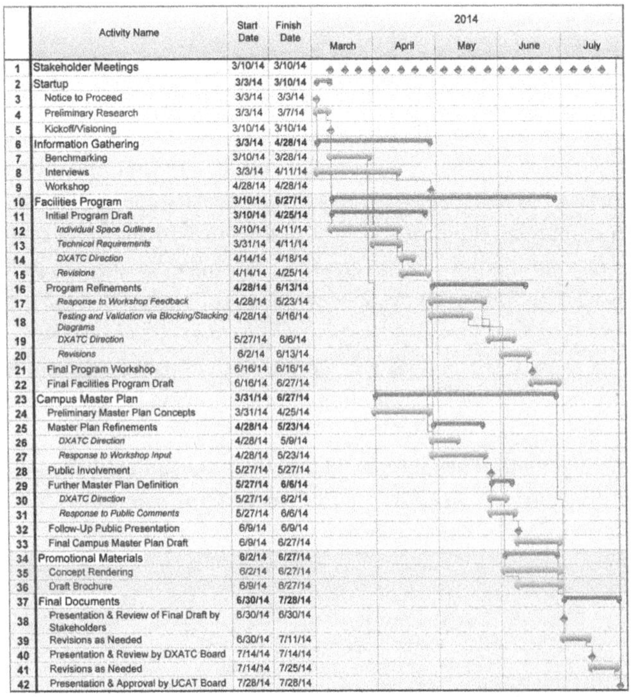

Figure C.2 Gantt schedule chart with more detailed dependencies. *Source:* the author.

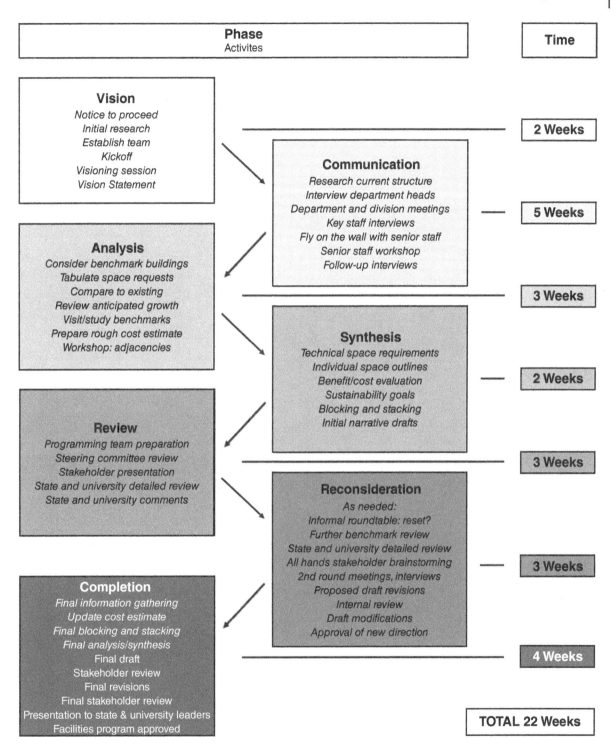

Figure C.3 A schedule for the rest of us may make it easier for an owner to visualize the process and its timing. A schedule the client understands may help win the job. *Source:* the author.

D

Breaking Down the Fee, Scope, and Schedule

If the fee is broken out by task, level-of-effort, and schedule, as mocked up here, when asked to cut the fee, the architect responds, "OK. Which of these tasks do you want us not to do?" (*See Table D.1.*)

Forever Practice: The Architect at Work, First Edition. Jim Nielson, FAIA.
© 2025 John Wiley & Sons, Inc. Published 2025 by John Wiley & Sons, Inc.

194 | D Breaking Down the Fee, Scope, and Schedule

Table D.1 Breaking down the fee, scope, and schedule

Scope			Design Principal	Managing Principal	Project Manager	Preservation Specialist	LEED® Specialist	Arch. Technician	Clerical Support	Consultants	Fee	Start	Finish
							Level-of-Effort (Est. Hours)				Fee	Schedule	
Part I													
Phase I – Planning and Schematic Design													
Scope Cluster #1: Program development and development of design													
	A	Task: Interview owner and potential user groups for program input	16	8	12	20	16	16	4	48	$15,540	7/21/00	8/1/00
		Deliverables: Interview notes, summary of program requests/ recommendations, list of project requirements, analysis of LEED® certification potential											
	B	Task: Develop conceptual design options	24	12	10	8	12	24	2	88	$19,980	7/21/00	8/8/00
		Deliverables: Conceptual floor layout possibilities, exiting and restroom options, conceptual architectural, structural, mechanical, electrical, and vertical transportation technical review and recommendations											
	C	Task: Begin preliminary discussions with city and regulatory agencies.	6	8	12	10	0	20	8	12	$8,440	8/4/00	10/10/00
		Deliverables: Meeting minutes, action items, preliminary entitlement feedback											
Scope Cluster #2: Definition of scope of work													
	A	Task: Conduct preliminary scoping discussion(s) with owner, stakeholders	4	4	6	4	4	0	2	8	$3,550	7/21/00	7/25/00
		Deliverables: Meeting minutes											
	B	Task: Update scope and fee from proposal	0	1	2	1	1	1	1	4	$1,220	7/25/00	7/29/00
		Deliverables: Revised scoping document, NTE fee estimate, and project plan											
Scope Cluster #3: Development of SD documents & computer rendering if requested													
	A	Task: Conduct weekly design meetings	24	18	32	28	12	0	10	48	$19,090	7/21/00	10/10/00
		Deliverables: Agenda, minutes, decision milestone reports, action item tracking	(Note: Meeting agenda items will cover all tasks under all scope clusters.)										
	B	Task: Undertake multiple iterative design explorations and revisions	48	32	96	120	32	180	24	320	$94,570	8/4/00	10/10/00
		Deliverables: In-progress design options and sketches, narrative system description updates											
	C	Task: Prepare Construction Documents for fire escape	6	6	24	24	0	120	24	60	$29,300	8/4/00	8/29/00
		Deliverables: Plans and specifications, permit and other city submittals	(Note: Dates may vary based on actual timeframe for bidding)										
	D	Task: Provide rendering if requested	0	0	4	0	0	4	0	24	$3,550	9/1/00	9/26/00
		Deliverables: Preliminary views, proofs, initial presentation rendering, one major revision	(Note: Optional Additional Service)										
	E	Task: Support owner's SD cost estimate, confirm budget	4	8	12	6	2	2	4	12	$5,550	9/1/00	10/10/00
		Deliverables: Meeting minutes, review comments on owner's cost estimate, value management recommendations											

(Continued)

D Breaking Down the Fee, Scope, and Schedule | 195

Table D.1 *(Continued)*

Part II											
Scope Cluster #4: Engineering discipline contracting and management											
A Task: Contract with engineers for	0	16	8	0	2	0	8	32	$7,330	7/21/00	8/15/00
Deliverables: Engineers' scoping documents, engineers' proposals, executed contracts											
B Task: Manage engineering disciplines	4	16	24	8	12	8	6	0	$8,660	7/21/00	10/10/00
Deliverables: Internal design decision milestone reports, coordination reviews of engineers' document submittals											
Scope Cluster #5: Evaluation of potential for residential use											
A Task: Develop and analyze potential layout options	10	4	6	16	4	24	8	28	$11,100	7/28/00	8/8/00
Deliverables: Multiple potential floor plan scenarios, discussion points											
B Task: Evaluate technical constraints of infrastructure	2	4	4	4	2	0	0	72	$9,770	7/21/00	8/8/00
Deliverables: Technical analysis reports											
C Task: Review feasibility of all options and provide decision support	6	4	8	10	4	2	6	12	$5,770	8/11/00	8/15/00
Deliverables: Pro and con analysis of each scenario and decision matrix											
Summary Fee, Phase I:	154	141	260	259	103	401	107	768	**$243,420**		
Phase II – Design Development and	*Fixed Fee, No Hourly Breakout*								**$594,210**		
Scope Cluster #1: Design Development documents										10/13/00	1/23/01
Scope Cluster #2: Construction Documents										1/26/01	3/27/01
Scope Cluster #3: Approvals and permits										8/4/00	5/15/01
Scope Cluster #4: Coordination with contractor & work packages										8/15/00	3/27/01
Phase III -- Construction	*Fixed Fee, No Hourly Breakout*								**$323,760**		
Scope Cluster #1: Construction bidding										3/23/01	5/15/01
Scope Cluster #2: Services during										5/18/01	6/18/02
Scope Cluster #3: Record										6/28/02	7/9/02
Scope Cluster #4: Project										6/7/02	8/6/02
(Note: End date is only an estimate. We will continue closeout activies as long as is necessary to meet the owner's needs.)											
Summary Fee, Total Project:									**$1,161,390**		

Source: the author.

E

Dividing up the Work

Based on NCARB practice analyses documenting the comprehensive practice of architecture in detail, architects working as a team decide who does what (and how much of it). This analysis estimates respective levels of effort and thus offers a useful starting point for negotiating a fair allocation of fees.

The first four pages of *Table E.1* address each of the tasks enumerated, considering allocation of responsibility and weighed levels of effort for each task.

The last two pages of the table use the data entered previously to display percentage responsibilities of both firms for each phase. Putting it all together, these pages apply the relative level of effort *of each phase* to tabulate the overall division of responsibility for the project.

In the example shown in *Table E.1*, this bottom line calculation shows the Architect of Record (AOR) as being responsible for 61% of the work; in this case, the the design architect's share would be 39%. See the table for an example of this analytical approach, which may help inform negotiations between an architect of record and an associate architect as the two decide on their respective project scope and fees.

Forever Practice: The Architect at Work, First Edition. Jim Nielson, FAIA.
© 2025 John Wiley & Sons, Inc. Published 2025 by John Wiley & Sons, Inc.

198 | E Dividing up the Work

Table E.1 Dividing up the work

	TEAM		Weight	Weighted Total	
	AOR	Design		AOR	Design
Part I					
DESIGN AND CONSTRUCTION DOCUMENTS					
1. Programming					
Identify qualitative and quantitative requirements for the program	25%	75%	5	1.25	3.75
Develop questions and a checklist for owner/user survey	25%	75%	2	0.50	1.50
Investigate and document user work processes	25%	75%	3	0.75	2.25
Interview users (groups and key individuals)	60%	40%	10	6.00	4.00
Conduct stakeholder workshops	50%	50%	6	3.00	3.00
Prepare functional relationship/adjacency diagrams	50%	50%	6	3.00	3.00
Calculate net and gross area requirements	70%	30%	3	2.10	0.90
Relate the budget and schedule to the program	55%	45%	4	2.20	1.80
Determine owner/client needs for phasing the project and for future growth and development	25%	75%	3	0.75	2.25
Analyze owner-supplied data and document programmatic implications	25%	75%	3	0.75	2.25
Specialty space programming	10%	90%	10	1.00	9.00
Produce program document	60%	40%	10	6.00	4.00
Total, Programming				**42.0%**	**58.0%**
2. Site and Environmental Analysis	TEAM		Weight	Weighted Total	
	AOR	Design		AOR	Design
Document and evaluate:					
Building location options on the site	30%	70%	10	3.00	7.00
Regulatory restrictions (e.g., parking, zoning, building codes, ADA) for the site	60%	40%	7	4.20	2.80
Natural conditions (e.g., topography, vegetation, climate considerations, orientation) on the site	60%	40%	6	3.60	2.40
Constructed conditions (e.g., infrastructure, building foundation)		100%	2	0.00	2.00
Access to utilities	70%	30%	3	2.10	0.90
Environmental hazards	60%	40%	5	3.00	2.00
Input from consultants (e.g., landscape architect, geotechnical engineer)	60%	40%	4	2.40	1.60
Input from groups with community interest (e.g., community organizations, historic preservation organizations)	70%	30%	6	4.20	1.80
Information from public agencies with jurisdictional authority (e.g., zoning, planning, building, fire)	80%	20%	4	3.20	0.80
Feasibility of alternate sites	40%	60%	1	0.40	0.60
Total, Site & Environmental Analysis				**54.4%**	**45.6%**
3. Schematic Design	TEAM		Weight	Weighted Total	
	AOR	Design		AOR	Design
Develop alternative conceptual design proposals that address the program	20%	80%	10	2.00	8.00
Evaluate engineering systems appropriate to the project	40%	60%	4	1.60	2.40
Prepare volume and area calculations and evaluate the cost of alternative design proposals	30%	70%	2	0.60	1.40
Prepare presentation packages, including drawings and models, to show the owner/client	40%	60%	6	2.40	3.60
Prepare a verbal and graphic presentation to communicate the intent of the designs to the owner/client	40%	60%	6	2.40	3.60
Review the selected schematic design with the owner/client and revise the design based on owner/client feedback	40%	60%	9	3.60	5.40
Coordinate consultants' activities relative to the schematic design	70%	30%	6	4.20	1.80
Specialty design	20%	80%	10	2.00	8.00
Incorporate relevant code requirements into the schematic design	40%	60%	5	2.00	3.00
Total, Schematic Design				**35.9%**	**64.1%**

(Continued)

E Dividing up the Work | **199**

Table E.1 *(Continued)*

Part II					
4. Engineering Systems Coordination	TEAM		Weight	Weighted Total	
	AOR	Design		AOR	Design
Research and assist in the selection of appropriate engineering systems	60%	40%	4	2.40	1.60
Assess sustainability issues	50%	50%	2	1.00	1.00
Evaluate the types of consultants required	50%	50%	1	0.50	0.50
Coordinate and verify the availability of adequate utilities	60%	40%	1	0.60	0.40
Evaluate engineering proposals and fee structures	80%	20%	2	1.60	0.40
Coordinate project information with consultants	80%	20%	2	1.60	0.40
Coordinate engineering system documents	80%	20%	5	4.00	1.00
Lab systems coordination	40%	60%	7	2.80	4.20
Evaluate space requirements and costs for engineered systems	70%	30%	4	2.80	1.20
Total, Engineering Systems Coordination				**61.8%**	**38.2%**
5. Building Cost Analysis	TEAM		Weight	Weighted Total	
	AOR	Design		AOR	Design
Prepare preliminary cost analysis	60%	40%	4	2.40	1.60
Investigate and prepare quantity calculations for selected materials	50%	50%	1	0.50	0.50
Evaluate life-cycle cost information in relation to specifications	50%	50%	6	3.00	3.00
Research value analysis opportunities	50%	50%	4	2.00	2.00
Evaluate and document scope/quantity/cost in comparison to materials selection and the preparation of specifications	50%	50%	5	2.50	2.50
Factor the current inflation rate and other economic variables into the cost estimates	50%	50%	1	0.50	0.50
Review non-construction project costs, including land acquisition, design, government approvals, project financing, and marketing, and how they impact building cost	50%	50%	1	0.50	0.50
Total, Building Cost Analysis				**51.8%**	**48.2%**
6. Code Research	TEAM		Weight	Weighted Total	
	AOR	Design		AOR	Design
Evaluate design alternatives based on code requirements	60%	40%	7	4.20	2.80
Research all applicable codes	60%	40%	6	3.60	2.40
Develop a life-safety analysis	60%	40%	4	2.40	1.60
Participate in preliminary meetings with code officials and make design adjustments to reflect compliance with relevant codes	80%	20%	8	6.40	1.60
Lab code research	20%	80%	8	1.60	6.40
Develop a list of required agency approvals during final project reviews	60%	40%	4	2.40	1.60
Total, Code Research				**55.7%**	**44.4%**
7. Design Development	TEAM		Weight	Weighted Total	
	AOR	Design		AOR	Design
Prepare design development documents from the approved schematic design, incorporating appropriate levels of detail in drawings and outline specifications. Coordinate and cross-reference documents	70%	30%	10	7.00	3.00
Participate in discussions with the owner/client regarding project scope, quality, and cost	50%	50%	3	1.50	1.50
Document decisions reached during owner/client meetings and evaluate their impact on the design program	70%	30%	2	1.40	0.60
Review the design development documents for conflicts between building systems and coordinate the work of consultants to resolve conflicts	65%	35%	3	1.95	1.05
Lab design development	20%	80%	7	1.40	5.60
Review the design development documents to ensure they conform to previously established requirements and meet applicable codes	30%	70%	3	0.90	2.10
Total, Design Development				**50.5%**	**49.3%**

(Continued)

200 | E Dividing up the Work

Table E.1 (*Continued*)

Part III					
8. Construction Documents	TEAM		Weight	Weighted Total	
	AOR	Design		AOR	Design
Create mock-ups of project drawing sets	80%	20%	2	1.60	0.40
Prepare a schedule for preparation of construction documents that includes milestone markers and reviews as appropriate	90%	10%	2	1.80	0.20
Prepare plan, elevation, and section drawings that clearly convey the design development documents and coordinate and cross-reference the documents, including the work of consultants	90%	10%	10	9.00	1.00
Document decisions reached at relevant project team meetings, and evaluate their impact on the development and production of the construction documents	95%	5%	4	3.80	0.20
Review the program to check for discrepancies between the design development and construction documents	20%	80%	2	0.40	1.60
Help the owner/client obtain required approvals and permits	90%	10%	2	1.80	0.20
Technical lab drawings	10%	90%	6	0.60	5.40
Using the owner/client operational requirements, develop a construction phasing plan	80%	20%	1	0.80	0.20
Total, Construction Documents				**68.3%**	**31.7%**
9. Specifications and Materials Research	TEAM		Weight	Weighted Total	
	AOR	Design		AOR	Design
Investigate product literature or question manufacturers' representatives to acquire information about materials for use in preparing specifications	70%	30%	8	5.60	2.40
Lab specifications	20%	80%	4	0.80	3.20
Prepare specifications for project	70%	30%	7	4.90	2.10
Total, Specifications and Materials Research				**59.5%**	**40.5%**
10. Document Checking and Coordination	TEAM		Weight	Weighted Total	
	AOR	Design		AOR	Design
Develop a list of all drawings and other documents required for the project, including brief descriptions of their contents	75%	25%	1	0.75	0.25
Cross-check products and materials called for in the specifications for consistency with corresponding terminology and descriptions in the construction documents	75%	25%	4	3.00	1.00
Coordinate all project drawings for accuracy of dimensions, notes, and abbreviations	75%	25%	9	6.75	2.25
Develop a schedule of lead times required for proper coordination with other disciplines	75%	25%	2	1.50	0.50
Cross-check all consultants' drawings with architectural drawings for possible conflicts and interference of plumbing lines, ductwork, electrical fixtures, etc.	25%	75%	10	2.50	7.50
Conduct final document review for compliance with applicable codes, regulations, etc.	25%	75%	10	2.50	7.50
Make revisions and corrections to project documents based on the results of project document checks	75%	25%	10	7.50	2.50
Total, Document Checking and Coordination				**53.3%**	**46.7%**
CONSTRUCTION CONTRACT ADMINISTRATION					
11. Bidding and Contract Negotiation	TEAM		Weight	Weighted Total	
	AOR	Design		AOR	Design
Prepare bidding documents and maintain the distribution register	90%	10%	2	1.80	0.20
Research and prepare an addendum to the bidding documents and write a notice announcing the change	75%	25%	8	6.00	2.00
Attend bid opening and assist in the bidding process	90%	10%	1	0.90	0.10
Assess requests for substitutions	65%	35%	6	3.90	2.10
Develop and illustrate a comparative analysis of bids	75%	25%	2	1.50	0.50
Compare bids with final project estimate	75%	25%	2	1.50	0.50
Total, Bidding and Contract Negotiation				**74.3%**	**25.7%**

(Continued)

E Dividing up the Work 201

Table E.1 *(Continued)*

Part IV					
12. Construction Phase—Office	**TEAM**		Weight	Weighted Total	
	AOR	Design		AOR	Design
Obtain information and submittals required for the notice to proceed	90%	10%	1	0.90	0.10
Manage, review, and coordinate the shop drawings, samples, and other items submitted by the contractor	90%	10%	10	9.00	1.00
Attend a preconstruction conference	90%	10%	1	0.90	0.10
Process change orders, requests for information (RFIs), and requests for clarification	75%	25%	8	6.00	2.00
Document conflicts that occur during the construction process, and propose alternative resolutions to conflicts	65%	35%	10	6.50	3.50
Review and approve applications for payment	90%	10%	3	2.70	0.30
Participate in verifying the punch list submitted by the contractor	90%	10%	6	5.40	0.60
Prepare a certificate of substantial completion	100%	0%	1	1.00	0.00
Total, Construction Phase–Office				**81.0%**	**19.0%**
13. Construction Phase—Observation	**TEAM**		Weight	Weighted Total	
	AOR	Design		AOR	Design
Take minutes at job site meetings	100%	0%	2	2.00	0.00
Review progress of work and attend meetings when appropriate to assess quality and performance	80%	20%	10	8.00	2.00
Document unforeseen conditions that arise during construction, and develop alternative solutions to resolve these problems	60%	40%	10	6.00	4.00
Verify completion of work itemized in monthly applications for payment	90%	10%	2	1.80	0.20
Verify the completion of punch list tasks	90%	10%	5	4.50	0.50
Total, Construction Phase–Observation				**76.9%**	**23.1%**
MANAGEMENT	**TEAM**		Weight	Weighted Total	
	AOR	Design		AOR	Design
14. Project Management					
Assess time requirements for all project tasks	90%	10%	4	3.60	0.40
Develop a project work plan that identifies tasks, responsibilities, personnel requirements, schedule, and budget	90%	10%	9	8.10	0.90
Manage consultants and review all contracts and billing approvals	100%	0%	10	10.00	0.00
Evaluate project work progress	90%	10%	7	6.30	0.70
Manage project reviews and coordination through participation in meetings	80%	20%	4	3.20	0.80
Prepare a schedule of client billings, and establish initial client invoices according to project contracts	100%	0%	3	3.00	0.00
Participate in and document the project closeout process	80%	20%	2	1.60	0.40
Help resolve any disputes that arise	90%	10%	5	4.50	0.50
Total, Project Management				**91.6%**	**8.4%**

(Continued)

202 | *E Dividing up the Work*

Table E.1 *(Continued)*

Part V			
SUMMARY	**Percentage Division of Phase**	**Portion of Entire Fee Each Phase Represents**	**Apportioned Percentage Points**
DESIGN AND CONSTRUCTION DOCUMENTS			
1. Programming		9%	
AOR	42%		3.78%
Design	58%		5.22%
2. Site and Environmental Analysis		2%	
AOR	54%		1.09%
Design	46%		0.91%
3. Schematic Design		9%	
AOR	36%		3.23%
Design	64%		5.77%
4. Engineering Systems Coordination		4%	
AOR	62%		2.47%
Design	38%		1.53%
5. Building Cost Analysis		1%	
AOR	52%		0.52%
Design	48%		0.48%
6. Code Research		4%	
AOR	56%		2.23%
Design	44%		1.78%
7. Design Development		13%	
AOR	51%		6.57%
Design	49%		6.41%
8. Construction Documents		26%	
AOR	68%		17.75%
Design	32%		8.25%
9. Specifications and Materials Research		4%	
AOR	59%		2.38%
Design	41%		1.62%
10. Document Checking and Coordination		5%	
AOR	53%		2.66%
Design	47%		2.34%

(Continued)

Table E.1 (*Continued*)

Part VI			
SUMMARY, cont.	Percentage Division of Phase	Portion of Entire Fee Each Phase Represents	Apportioned Percentage Points
CONSTRUCTION CONTRACT ADMINISTRATION			
11. Bidding and Contract Negotiation		3%	
AOR	74%		2.23%
Design	26%		0.77%
12. Construction Phase—Office		8%	
AOR	81%		6.48%
Design	19%		1.52%
13. Construction Phase—Observation		8%	
AOR	77%		6.15%
Design	23%		1.85%
MANAGEMENT			
14. Project Management		4%	
AOR	92%		3.66%
Design	8%		0.34%
TOTAL			
Architect of Record			61%
Design Architect			39%

Source: the author.

F

Employee Owned

The following outline is built upon an ownership transition plan adopted by a consulting engineer and shared with the author, who adapted and developed it further.

Guiding principles behind the plan include:
- Choosing not to provide a generous golden parachute for founders when they retire
- Building financial resources and leadership opportunities for those that will take over
- Seeking opportunities for future leaders to have a stake in the firm's physical facility
- Encouraging all employees to own part of the firm they work for
- Helping them to do so

Note: this plan includes deferred compensation paid by the firm: if such future commitments are not backed up by assets, annuities, escrow, or similar funds, it is then possible that based on these obligations, Generally Accepted Accounting Principles may recognize these obligations as liabilities on a firm's balance sheet, possibly complicating efforts to obtain a bank loan or line of credit.

Ownership Transition: An Employee-owned Firm

Common characteristics of architectural firm ownership transition plans
- Transition generates wealth for owners moving on
- It may not be legal for all employees to own stock
- Facility ownership benefits and builds capital for firm owners
- Stock (or partnership percentage) purchase
  - Ownership must be purchased
  - Emerging owners carry high cost
- Stock appreciates with firm financial performance
- Deferred compensation is typically not included in the plan
- Key leaders receive a sizeable retirement or buyout benefit

A different approach to ownership transition
- As described here, this plan is not organized to generate wealth for owners
- It encourages facility ownership to benefit the firm
- Everyone is given the opportunity to own a part of the firm
- Stock appreciation and repurchase have less of an effect on what owners take with them at transition
- The retirement benefit is modest
- Deferred compensation plays a larger role and is influenced by:
  - Corporate financial performance (best three of the past five years)
  - The individual's employment record with the firm

Forever Practice: The Architect at Work, First Edition. Jim Nielson, FAIA.
© 2025 John Wiley & Sons, Inc. Published 2025 by John Wiley & Sons, Inc.

206 | F Employee Owned

- The leadership position at retirement
- Deferred compensation is paid by the firm

Why this approach?
- Creates a culture of ownership
- Recognizes an individual's value to the firm
- Embodies an egalitarian firm structure
- Makes individual ownership transition costs affordable

Culture of ownership

"In the history of the world, no one has ever washed a rented car"

-Lawrence Summers, Former President, Harvard University

- Broad ownership opportunities recognize individuals' value to the firm
- Ownership opportunities are extended to everyone
- A carefully chosen legal structure provides that *anyone may legally hold stock*

Starting point
- Total firm employees
- Roughly one half of these are prospective stockholders (based on leadership position)
- Ultimately all employees ≥1 year of service will be invited to become stockholders

Egalitarian firm structure
- The firm has modest executive compensation
- The ratio of executive to non-executive pay is less than 1.7:1
- Every level of employee is represented on the Board of Directors

Affordable individual ownership transition costs
- Employees have no requirement to buy out retiring owners
  - By the time firm members are invited to become stockholders/leaders, they have already made significant contributions to the firm's bottom line
  - Asking them to pay a high price for stock is akin to asking them to pay twice

Deferred compensation
- Eligibility begins at a specific leadership level
  - Based on a formula
  - Paid out over five years
- The firm carries cost of this compensation

Ownership/leadership positions
- Shareholder
- Leadership position i
- Leadership position ii*
- Leadership position iii
- Leadership position iv
- Founder

  * Initial eligibility for executive compensation plan

Deferred compensation factors
Deferred compensation (subject to maximum payout amounts) =
- Three-year financial performance calculation ×
- Retirement factor ×
- Leadership position factor

Financial performance calculation
- Average firm net worth for top three of five years preceding retirement +
- Average firm pre-bonus profits for top three of five years preceding retirement

Retirement factor
- Maximum of 1.0 for normal retirement age and 15 year tenure in good standing with the board of directors as licensed professional or equivalent

Leadership position factor
- Leadership position ii: 5%
- Leadership position iii: 20%
- Leadership position iv: 50%
- Founder: 80%

Maximum payout amounts (relative concepts, not specific amounts)

Position	Maximum Payout
Leadership position ii:	$x
Leadership position iii:	$xx
Leadership position iv:	$xxx
Founder:	$xxxx

Deferred compensation example
Leadership position iv, after three years of modest profit

- Average firm top three of five year net worth: $xx
- Average firm profits, same period: $xxx
- Financial performance calculation: $xx + xxx
- Retirement factor: 1.0
- Leadership position factor: 0.5
- Max. position iv payout = ($xx + xxx) × 1.0 × 0.5 = $xxx
  (less than $xx + xxx maximum)

Deferred compensation example payouts for other positions are calculated based on corresponding leadership position factor, retirement factor, and firm financial performance calculations in their year of retirement.

Stock details
- Stock value doesn't float
- Value is set by board
- Currently $10 per share
- No plans to increase share price
- Participation is by invitation
- Shareholder/leadership benefits, including promotions, may result from participation

208 | F Employee Owned

Share valuation and transfer
- Method of valuation and value set by board of directors
- A future board may decide to allow stock price to rise and determine an updated basis for establishing stock valuation
- Not a significant component of retirement package
- Transfer by purchase, bonus/purchase, gift, or match
- Stock purchases may be financed and repaid for a period of up to 12 months through payroll deduction
- Firm stock ownership assistance program (SOAP)

Firm stock ownership assistance program (SOAP)

Purchase assistance:
- Minimum holdings: 25 shares
- When a prospective shareholder agrees to make an initial purchase of 25 shares, she purchases 10 @ $10/share and the firm provides 15 additional shares as ownership assistance at no cost. (Assistance bonus is considered taxable income.)

    Total investment: $100. Shares owned: 25. Out of pocket cost per share: $4.
- 1:1 match thereafter. (1:2 for shareholders not in leadership.) Firm match is considered taxable income.

Example: An employee at any leadership level elects to purchase an additional 25 shares @ $10/share. Firm matches that investment with a bonus of 25 additional shares, vested over 5 years. Additional investment: $250. Total investment to date: $350. Shares owned: 75. Out-of-pocket cost per share: $4.67.

G

The Project Progress Report

The report mocked up here is the single most valuable tool for firms to track their projects financially. It compares hours and billings to the project budget, along with current profit/loss and multiplier. Properly set up, most accounting systems can produce this report using real-world data. (See *Table G.1.*) Financial information in the table reflects a project part way through Design Development. In Schematic Design, now apparently completed, hours went slightly over budget, but overall expenses fell within the target amount.

Hours and expenses posted to the project so far account for just over 40% of the project manager's Design Development budget. Job-to-date profit, at three and a half percent, is on the low side, but if the team's design and documentation work has progressed to around 40% completion for Design Development, the project remains in the black.

Forever Practice: The Architect at Work, First Edition. Jim Nielson, FAIA.
© 2025 John Wiley & Sons, Inc. Published 2025 by John Wiley & Sons, Inc.

210 | G The Project Progress Report

Table G.1 The project progress report

Project Progress Report — For the Period 12.01.XX—12.31.XX

Description	Current Hours	Current Amount	JTD Hours	JTD Amount	Budget Hours	Budget Amount	Percent Expended	Balance Hours	Balance Amount	Effective Rate
Project Number XX-016 Gateway Hall										
Schematic Design										
Labor			295	22,848	280	22,560	101.28%	−15	−288	77.45
Overhead				62,831		62,040	101.28%		−791	
Total Labor & Overhead			295	85,679	280	84,600	101.28%	−15	−1,079	
Expenses										
Consultants				125,985		125,985	100.00%		125,985	
Other Direct Expenses				5,565		10,955	50.80%		10,955	
Reimbursable Expenses				1,200					−1,200	
Total Expenses				132,750		136,940	96.94%		135,740	
Total Schematic Design			295	218,429	280	221,540	98.60%		270,401	
Design Development										
Labor	167	12,024	240	17,499	558	43,069	40.63%	318	25,570	72.91
Overhead		33,066		48,122		118,440	40.63%		70,318	
Total Labor & Overhead	167	45,090	240	65,621	558	161,509	40.63%	318	95,888	
Expenses										
Consultants		54,971		81,650		188,978	43.21%		107,328	
Other Direct Expenses		4,579		6,450		16,433	39.25%		9,983	
Reimbursable Expenses		245		318					−318	
Total Expenses		59,795		88,418		205,411	43.04%		116,993	
Total Design Development	167	104,885	240	154,039	558	366,920	41.98%	318	212,881	
Construction Documents										
Labor					1,305	92,300	0.00%	1,305	92,300	
Overhead						253,825	0.00%		253,825	
Total Labor & Overhead					1,305	346,125	0.00%	1,305	346,125	
Expenses										
Consultants						404,952	0.00%		404,952	
Other Direct Expenses						35,214	0.00%		35,214	
Reimbursable Expenses										
Total Expenses						440,166	0.00%		440,166	
Total Construction Documents					1,305	786,291	0.00%	1,305	786,291	
Construction Administration										
Labor					590	4,115	0.00%	590	4,115	
Overhead						11,316	0.00%		11,316	
Total Labor & Overhead					590	15,431	0.00%	590	15,431	
Expenses										
Consultants						179,800	0.00%		179,800	
Other Direct Expenses						15,830	0.00%		15,830	
Reimbursable Expenses										
Total Expenses						195,630	0.00%		195,630	
Total Construction Documents					590	211,061	0.00%	590	211,061	
Summary										
Labor	167	12,024	535	40,347	2,733	162,044	24.90%	2,198	121,697	
Overhead		33,066		110,954		445,621	24.90%		334,667	
Total Labor & Overhead	167	45,090	535	151,300	2,733	607,665	24.90%	2,198	456,365	
Expenses										
Consultants		54,971		207,635		899,715	23.08%		692,080	
Other Direct Expenses		4,579		12,015		78,432	15.32%		66,417	
Reimbursable Expenses		245		1,518					−1,518	
Total Expenses		59,795		221,168		978,147	22.61%		756,979	
Total Project		104,885		372,468	2,733	1,585,812	23.49%	2,198	1,213,344	

Financial Analysis	Total Billed	Revenue	Spent	Profit	Profit %		Fee	1,713,500
Current	68,540	68,540	61,270	7,270	10.61%		A/R	82,000
Year to Date	179,200	179,200	172,015	7,185	4.01%		Unbilled	102,810
Job to Date	275,000	275,000	265,400	9,600	3.49%		Eff. Mult	2.92

Source: the author.

H

The Contractor's S-curve

The contractor's S-curve is a graph that correlates project spending with the project schedule. It helps visualize and track schedule performance at the 30,000 foot level. The contractor charts the original curve by plotting planned construction billing from start to finish. Throughout the project, the graph is updated with a second curve to show actual billings. Because numbers (prepared honestly) don't lie, nothing shows actual progress on a construction schedule better than a chart of cumulative billings over time. If the owner, architect, and contractor see that billings aren't keeping up with the projected pace of the work, they know immediately that if they want to be finished on time, they will need to play catch-up.

The project progress diagram is called an S-curve because of its shape reflecting anticipated billing throughout the project, as shown in *Figure H.1 Plan*. The path as plotted typically begins with a shallow but increasing slope, reflecting staging and mobilization as things get going. Progress and associated billings ramp up from there until they reach their maximum, about midway through the schedule. As work moves past the midpoint, construction activity and billing gradually slow a bit, before dropping more and more quickly as the project nears completion and closeout, and the work is finally done.

Most projects encounter unexpected challenges getting everything necessary completed on or before the appointed hour. When milestones aren't met, the cumulative work and billings lag can be charted. This slower path may resemble the dashed line added to the graph in *Figure H.2 Slippage*. Here, starting out too slow has caused the curve to fall below the original plan. While building at a slower pace than planned is not uncommon, doing so may make it virtually impossible to finish the project by the original completion date.

Facing schedule delays, some contractors promise that they will simply accelerate construction work and thus move their performance rapidly to where it needs to be for on-time completion. This is usually easier said than done.

Figure H.3 adds a curve (dotted line) showing a plan to speed things up big time and complete the project right on schedule. This graph shows what aggressive acceleration might look like. At its steepest, the optimistic pace needed to get back on schedule would represent almost $40 million worth of billing (about one quarter of the entire project) in a single month. To accomplish this might take as many as 2,000 full-time workers, all month long. For a contractor billing barely $10 million a month at the time, with no more than a few hundred workers on the job every day, changing course to ramp-up so swiftly would seem to be a statistical impossibility.

More often than not, when a contractor faces the situation diagrammed here, the outcome is not the Pollyanna make-up schedule presented in *Figure H.3*. No, experience suggests that what often happens in situations like this is the contractor picks up speed, exceeding the pace that resulted in slippage. And although the project doesn't finish up on schedule, it still ends up being completed earlier than the date it was headed for when the contractor was furthest behind. This course is shown in the dash-dot line added in *Figure H.4*. This figure shows a challenging, yet realistic, make-up trajectory for a contractor that has fallen behind, yet truly seeks to come as close as possible to the originally scheduled completion date.

Forever Practice: The Architect at Work, First Edition. Jim Nielson, FAIA.
© 2025 John Wiley & Sons, Inc. Published 2025 by John Wiley & Sons, Inc.

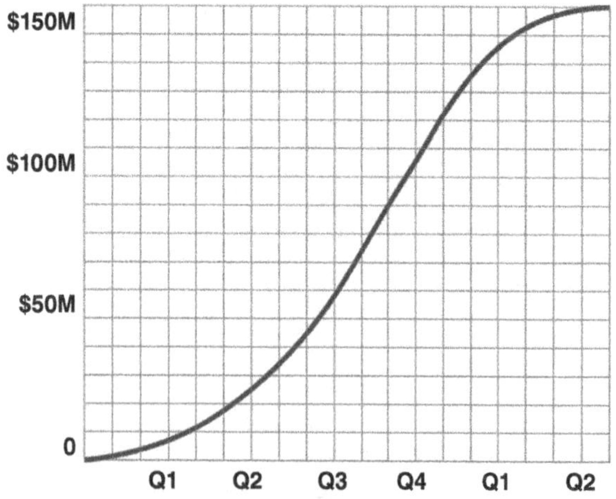

212 | H The Contractor's S-curve

Figure H.1 Plan This original curve plots the anticipated pace of billing (construction activity) against the contractor's proposed schedule. *Source:* the author.

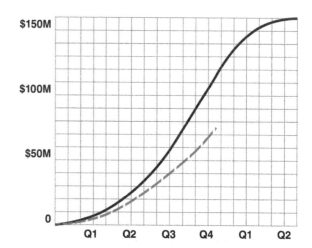

Figure H.2 Slippage In this theoretical example, the dashed line shows actual performance; the project is falling behind schedule. *Source:* the author.

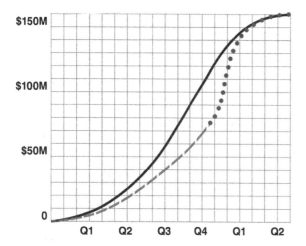

Figure H.3 Optimistic recovery plan The next curve added to the graph with a dotted line is the contractor's optimistic make-up plan. This revised plan requires ramping up construction activity substantially. *Source:* the author.

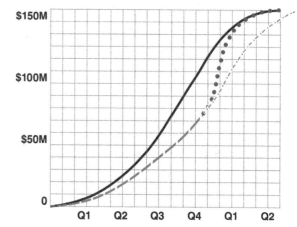

Figure H.4 Alternative ending The final line added (in dash-dot pattern) shows a more likely outcome: the pace of construction picks up some, but the project still finishes late. *Source:* the author.

If the contractor doesn't track progress in terms of cumulative billing numbers as shown here, the architect just might want to build this very same kind of chart, based on the contractor's original schedule and on cumulative total billings from the contractor's monthly pay requests. If the contractor has prepared a schedule of anticipated monthly billings, as owners often require, turn that into the initial plan or S-curve.

Index

Note: Page numbers in *italics* and **bold** refers to figures and tables respectively.

a

accounting 105
  accounts payable 107–108
  accounts receivable 108–109
  building blocks 107
  firm employee accounting responsibilities 106
  philosophy 109–111
  principal/owner accounting responsibilities 107
  project manager accounting responsibilities 106–107
  responsibilities 105–106
accounts payable (A/P) system 107–108
accounts receivable (A/R) system 108–109
accredited degree programs 43
addendums 158
allied careers 68
American Institute of Architects (AIA) 38–39, 50
  AIA College of Fellows 140
  Code of Ethics and Professional Conduct 53, 54
  contract documents 5
  contracts 160
  owner-architect contract documents 114
analytical approach 19
architect(s) 3–5, 41
  career as 36
  challenges 151
  as consultant 151
  contractual language 54
  direction 122
  improving construction documents 120
  leadership 137
  marketing claims 7–8
  obligation of professional association membership 54
  processes 121
  proclaim 19
  professional licensing requirements 54
  quality assurance 120
  responsibilities 48–49, 61
  rules of conduct for 33
  scope of services 147–148
  standard of care 50–51, 53, 55–56, 146
  standards 121
  state jury instructions regarding 56
  training 121
architect-contractor relationship 65
Architect Licensing Act Rule 49
Architect Registration Exam® (ARE®) 42, 43–44
architect's supplemental instruction (ASI) 161, 163
Architects with Attitude (AWA) 37–38
Architectural Experience Program® (AXP®) 42, 43
architectural firm ownership transition plans,
   characteristics of 205
architectural licensure
  ARE 43–44
  AXP 43
  becoming licensed 41–42
  education, experience, examination 42
  licensure and workplace 44
  NAAB-accredited degree 43
  NCARB record 42
  state licensing board 44–45
architectural practice, complexity of 37
architectural project manager 7, 77
architecture 3, 15, 16, 17, 33, *138*
  developer 139, *139*
  fellowship objects of nomination 140
  mentor 139

Forever Practice: The Architect at Work, First Edition. Jim Nielson, FAIA.
© 2025 John Wiley & Sons, Inc. Published 2025 by John Wiley & Sons, Inc.

214 | *Index*

architecture career and culture
  5 Things I Wish I Knew When I Graduated with My
    Architecture Degree 71
  Culture of Architecture Needs an Overhaul, Part I 71
  Culture of Architecture Needs an Overhaul, Part II 71
  Culture of Architecture Needs an Overhaul, Part III 72
  indicators for 72
architecture firm leaders 9
Architecture of Persistence, The 22
attitude of architecture 37–38

b

Bachelor of Architecture (B. Arch.) 43
bad debt 109
Belle, John 15
bidder-designed scope items 169–171
bidder-designed systems and components 151
bidder-designed work
  CM/GC Projects 171–172
  design-build projects 171–172
  subcontractor scope items 169–171
bidding and negotiation of contractors 158
bottom-up level-of-effort budget 83, **85**
breaking down fee, scope, and schedule 193, **194–195**
building scientists 19
business risk 114

c

Calatrava, Santiago 17–18
Canstruction® 137
care and feeding 69
career in architecture 59
Casa Maraposa project 138, *138*
celluloid architects 69
certificate of occupancy (C of O) 175
certificate of substantial completion 175
Citicorp Tower 133, *133*
closeout
  conflict, dealing with 176–177
  construction 177–178
CM-At Risk delivery 150
code of conduct as architects 48
Code of Ethics and Professional Conduct 50
communication 77
community 137
  building 141

competence 54, 55
Competency Standards for Architects 42
competency-based qualification 42
conformed set 157–158
ConsensusDocs® 39
construction 113, 177–178
construction administration 155
construction change directives (CCDs) 163
construction documents. *see* contract documents
construction management 166
Construction Management Association of America
  (CMAA) 39
construction manager (CM) 166–167
construction manager/general contractor (CM/GC) 150,
  166–167, 171–172
contract 131
  demands 67
  must-haves 131–133
  ought-to-haves 133
contract documents 157–158
  phase of schematic design 125
contractor 149
  assisting with contractor selection 157
  S-curve 211–212, *212*
  working with 167–168
contractor-led design-build delivery 149
conventional building *20*
coordination 159
core responsibilities of architect 61
  building 62
  communicating 62
  designing 62
  leading 63
  planning 61
  practice management priorities 64
  sustaining 63
cost model 20
CSI Project Delivery Practice Guide 39
culture of ownership 206

d

Darkin, Byron 16, 17
Davis Langdon 25
deferred compensation 206
  example 207
  factors 207

Index | **215**

deferred submittals 161, 169

delivery methods and client

  architect as consultant 151

  bidder-designed systems and components 151

  challenges 151

  construction manager/general contractor 150

  design-build 149–150

  diminished role, consequences of 152

  integrated project delivery 150–151

  project leadership 152

  role limitations 152

  traditional design-bid-build 149

design 10, 67, 113

  design-build contracting 166

  vs. management 68

design-bid-build delivery method 157

design-build (D-B) 149–150

  projects 171

  team 67

Design-Build Industry of America (DBIA) 39, 54–55

design development phase of schematic design 125

designer 8–9

developer-architect relationship 66

dispassionate professionalism and design-build 67

Do Architects Retire? (Darkin) 16

documentation 113

Dodge Construction Network 92

e

Economist, The 23, 30

effective architect 63

effective project manager 7

egalitarian firm structure 206

egress systems 41

employment, terminating 116–117

energy

  codes 23

  efficiency measures 25

Engineers Joint Contract Documents Committee (EJCDC) 39

enthusiasm 8

entitlement process 79

environmental control systems 26

environmental tobacco smoke control 29

ethical practice 48

experienced architects 4

f

facilities program 183–185

financial management

  accounting 105–111

  company, form of 103

  general business planning 104

  goals 104

  ownership, building 104–105

  succession planning 103–104

  tax planning 103

fire protection and fire alarm systems 169–170

firm 8, 89

  employee accounting responsibilities 106

  leaders 10

  management 91

  stock ownership assistance program 208

forms of contract 38

full-time employee (FTE) 83

g

Gantt charts 189, *190*

Gaudi, Antoni 17

general business planning 104

Go/No-Go decision 93–94

  Go/No-Go questionnaire **94**

Great Recession 118

green 25

  building green without wasting green 25

  high-performance building 30

  integrated design and adding triple-pane glazing to house 26

  specifics 30

greenwashing 25

gross revenue accounting 110

Guaranteed Maximum Price (GMP) 150

h

Harvey, Paul 129

heat recovery ventilation (HRV) 26

human resource management 114

  benefits 115–116

  business risk 114

  challenges 116

  complaints and accusations 117

  construction 113

  design 113

216 | *Index*

human resource management (*Continued*)
  documentation 113
  hiring architectural employee 114–115
  human resources 114–117
  quality 113
  terminating employment 116–117

i

indoor air quality (IAQ) 29
indoor environmental quality 29
initial decision maker 66
Integrated Marketing Systems 92
integrated project delivery (IPD) 150–151
internal document inconsistencies 128
internal document review
  back check 128
  begin with skeptical eye 126
  check every dimension string 127
  end-of-phase review 128
  follow every reference 126
  mid-phase review 126
  process 125
  quality control 128
  read every note 126
  review holistically 127
  use checklists 127

j

Jersey Devil 138–139
Johnson, Herbert 38
Johnson, Philip 15

k

Kemp, George Meikle 17

l

Latrobe Fellowship 22
leadership
  architect 137
  in architecture firm 139
  in design-bid-build delivery 150
  firm 9, 116
  in IPD projects 151
  position factor 207
  positions 206
  practices 151
  project 152
  responsibilities 56, 150
  substantial 15
  type of 121
  women 35
Leadership in Energy and Environmental Design
  (LEED®) 22, 25
  LEED 1.0 25
  LEED 2.0 25
  LEED-Accredited Professional 99
  LEED certification as proxy for sustainable
    buildings 25
Leboff, Grant 91
Le Corbusier 17
Lee, Evelyn 71
level-of-effort 83
licensing exam. *see Architect Registration Exam®*
  (ARE®)
life-cycle costs 21–22
life-safety responsibilities 41

m

management
  design *vs.* 68
  plan 100
marketing 9
  discussions 11
  professionals 10
  responsibilities 9
marketing and business development
  beginning 91
  end 91–93
  Go/No-Go decision 93–94
  requests for proposals/qualifications 93
  selection process 94–95
marketing proposals 97
  interview 99–100, 101
  management plan 100
  UVU Fulton Library *98*
Master of Architecture (M. Arch.) 43
Matthiessen, Lisa Fay 25
Mechanical and Electrical Equipment for Buildings
  (MEEB) 26
Meier Partners. *see* Richard Meier & Partners
metal-plate-connected wood trusses 170
Model Rules of Conduct, NCARB's 47, 49

modular buildings   170–171
Morris, Peter   25
multinational conglomerate   80
mutual indemnification   132

n

National Architecture Accrediting Board (NAAB)   41
  NAAB-accredited degree   43
National Conference of State Legislatures (NCSL)   23
*National Council of Architectural Registration Boards
    (NCARB)*   33, 35, 41, 49
  certification   42
  record   42
  rules of conduct   54
National Definition of a Zero Emissions Building   20
net operating revenue accounting   110–111
net-zero building   20
no-effort marketing   7–9
nonrenewable resources and future generations   23

o

Oldest Profession: Why don't architects ever retire?", The
    (Rybczynski)   15
Olympic Speed Skating Oval   25, *26*, 173
organizational culture   72
owner-architect relationship   65
owner-contractor relationship   65
owner-generated contract   146
ownership, building   104–105
ownership transition plan   205
  affordable individual ownership transition costs   206
  architectural firm ownership transition plans,
      characteristics of   205
  culture of   206
  deferred compensation   206
  deferred compensation example   207
  deferred compensation factors   207
  egalitarian firm structure   206
  firm stock ownership assistance program   208
  maximum payout amounts   207
  ownership/leadership positions   206
  stock details   207–208

p

Passive House   31
pay applications   163–164

Pei, I. M.   16
permit submittal   169
personal income   103
personal skillsets   4
potential occupational hazards   130
preconstruction conferences
  for individual trades   159–160
preconstruction meeting   159
pre-engineered metal buildings   170
principal, architecture firm leaders   9
principal/owner accounting responsibilities
    107
pro bono and detective work   148
profession
  American Institute of Architects   50
  architect's responsibility   48–49
  architect's standard of care   50–51
  of architecture   35–38
  continuing education requirements   48
  disciplinary action   48
  incidental practice   47
  licensing board and incidental practice   51
  *National Council of Architectural Registration
      Board*   49
  regulating   47
professionalism   66
professional licensing requirements   54
project approach. *see* management plan
project delivery method   151, 155, 165
project leadership   152
project management   10, 77
  bottom-up level-of-effort budget   83, **85**
  entitlements   79
  facilities program   79–80
  plan   81
  products and tools   85–86
  project   80
  project accounting   **82**
  top-down staffing budget   83, **84**
project management professional (PMP)   87
project manager   8–9, 75, 79, 80–81
  accounting responsibilities   106–107
  architectural   7, 77
  effective   7
  management plan written by   10
project meetings/site visits   160

218 | *Index*

project plan   187–188, *188*
project progress report   209, **210**
project schedule   189–191, *190, 191*
proposal request (PR)   161, 163
public responsibility   41

q

quality   113
quality assurance (QA)   120
   manager of QA training and standards   122
quality control (QC)   125, 128
   design   125–126
   internal document review (end-of-phase review)   128
   internal document review (mid-phase review)   126–127
   production   126

r

Reed, Bill   26
request for proposals (RFP)   5–6, 92, 93, 98
request for qualifications (RFQ)   93
requests for information (RFIs)   161–162
resilience   22
responsibility, delegating   10–11
Richard Meier & Partners   17
risk(s)
   claim   131
   construction management at   166
   contract   131–133
   mitigation   131
   potential occupational hazards   130
   responding to   133, *133*
   reward than   129–130
risk management by striking up conversation   66
Rossi, Aldo   17
Royal Institute of British Architects (RIBA)   15
rule-based exceptions   47
rule of thumb   20
Rules of Civil Procedure   53, 56
rules of conduct for architects   33
Rybczynski, Witold   15

s

Salary. com   36
Salary Dollars   81

Scarpa, Carlo   17
Schematic Design   125
Scouting America   19
Segal, Jonathan   139
senior project manager   10
services, scope of   146
   architect's   147–148
   Pro Bono and detective work   148
   variety of   146–147
severance taxes   23
Siza, Álvaro   17–18
soft skills   87
solicitations   8
specialization   63
standard contracts   175
standard of care architects   50
state licensing board   44–45
stickiness   91
Sticky Marketing Club   91
Sticky Marketing: Why Everything in Marketing Has Changed and What to Do about It (Leboff)   91
stipulated sum design-bid-build project   165
stock ownership assistance program (SOAP)   208
strategic marketing opportunities   8
structural failure, risk of   133
submittals   161
substantial leadership, architecture as   15
succession planning   103–104
superficial knowledge   63
sustainability   31
   architects about   25
   guiding principle of   23
sustainable design   26
Sutton geology and geophysics building   28–30

t

tax planning   103
top-down staffing budget   83, **84**
total enterprise cost—conventional building   *20*
tour de force design   8
traditional design-bid-build delivery   149
training for effective QA program   121
Tunneling through cost barrier   26, *27*

u

U. S. Green Building Council (USGBC) 25
*Utah Department of Natural Resources Office
    Building* 26–27, *27*
  site after value engineering *28*
  site as programmed *28*
Utah Valley University (UVU) 97

v

value engineering (VE) 26

w

women architecture 35
Women's Leadership Summit 35
work, dividing up 197, **198–203**